THE MAKERS OF MODERN ITALY

THE MAKERS OF MODERN ITALY

NAPOLEON—MUSSOLINI

BY

SIR J. A. R. MARRIOTT

Honorary Fellow (formerly Fellow and Lecturer in Modern History) of Worcester College, Oxford; late M.P. for the City of York; Corresponding Member of the 'Comitato Nazionale per la Storia del Risorgimento'

OXFORD UNIVERSITY PRESS
LONDON: HUMPHREY MILFORD

OXFORD UNIVERSITY PRESS
AMEN HOUSE, E.C. 4
London Edinburgh Glasgow New York
Toronto Melbourne Capetown Bombay
Calcutta Madras
HUMPHREY MILFORD
PUBLISHER TO THE UNIVERSITY

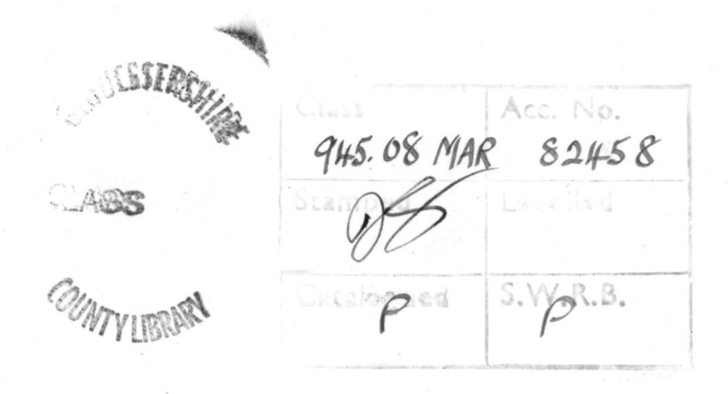

FIRST EDITION 1931

Reprinted photographically in Great Britain in 1937 (with corrections) and 1938 by LOWE & BRYDONE, PRINTERS, LTD., LONDON, from sheets of the first edition

PREFACE

CONTRARY to my intentions this is substantially a new book. About a year ago I set out to revise for republication some lectures originally published under the title of *The Makers of Modern Italy* (Macmillan & Co., 1889). That youthful adventure was rewarded with a measure of success entirely unanticipated by the author. For twenty-five years or more the little book ran a prosperous course, alike in England and in Italy. It has now, however, been for some years out of print, and friends, more flattering perhaps than discreet, urged me to republish it. I assented, imagining that revision of the text with an additional chapter or two would suffice. I soon discovered my mistake. Yet, though it meant not a revision, but re-writing, I found myself for various reasons reluctant to abandon the task.

The original book was the product of youthful fervour evoked by the stirring story of the Italian *Risorgimento*. What Englishman, unless devoid of all political sympathies and historic sense, could fail to be moved by the most romantic political achievement of the nineteenth century? The spell was laid on many besides myself, and much excellent work has since been done, not only in Italy, but in this country and in the United States of America. The works to which, in my revision, I have been consciously indebted are included in the short bibliographical note appended to the text. I must, however, acknowledge a special debt to M. Éduard Driault, Dr. L. Villari, Mr. Bolton King, Dr. G. M. Trevelyan, and Dr. Roscoe Thayer. For any unacknowledged debt I crave pardon.

Why, it may be asked, add yet another book on the Italian *Risorgimento* to a lengthening list? Apart from the kindly importunity of friends I mention only one of several reasons. Most of the works to which I refer—not

all—were written during a period of depression, when the glamour of the Italian movement had faded. If they did not reflect the depression, the fact remains; dates are inexorable.

But Italy has again emerged. At this moment (1931) she is incomparably the most interesting country in continental Europe. (Russia may indeed possess equal or greater interest for some people; but Russia is not wholly European.) The time for estimating the place which Signor Mussolini and the Fascist movement will fill in the history of post-war Europe is not yet. Nor is any attempt made in this little book to anticipate the critical verdict which History must some day deliver. Nevertheless, I have been impelled to extend the narrative which originally ended at 1871 down to the conclusion of the Lateran Treaty in 1929. I have also prefixed to the book an Introductory chapter, and a second on Napoleon's work in Italy. Experience and M. Driault have convinced me that I had not previously attached sufficient importance to that work. Mazzini might have taught me better. I hope I have now learned the lesson. Unquestionably, Napoleon I must be included among the makers of modern Italy.

To this title I have adhered, though it is less appropriate to the present work than to its predecessor, which was biographical in form. But I hope I may be forgiven for preferring sentiment to logic.

Besides the authors already mentioned, I have to thank Professor Holland Rose, the greatest living English authority on Napoleon, for kindly reading the chapter on Napoleon's work in Italy, and for several valuable suggestions. To Dr. Reginald W. Macan, formerly Master of University College, Oxford, I owe a debt for careful revision of the whole book in proof that cannot adequately be discharged in words. For thirty years or more he has been to me the most constant of friends, and at once the sternest and kindliest of critics. What I owe to his fine taste and exact scholarship, and still more to the unfailing encouragement extended to me in many spheres of work, I hesitate to reveal, lest he should be saddled with a responsibility, in no way deserved, for my shortcomings. To him, however, were dedications not *démodés*, this book would in sheer gratitude, and as a small token of unclouded and greatly valued friendship, be dedicated.

J. A. R. MARRIOTT.

September 1931.

TABLE OF CONTENTS

LIST OF MAPS

I

THE PROLOGUE

The Nation-State

ITALY is the creation of the nineteenth century. Rome dominated, for some centuries, the ancient world; on the stage of medieval Europe great parts were played by the Italian cities; but Italy, save as 'a geographical expression', did not exist. 'Since the fall of the Roman Empire (if even before it) there never had been a time when Italy could be called a nation any more than a stack of timber can be called a ship.'[1] Almost brutally spoken, it is true. Modern Italy is the product of ideas evoked, if not generated, by the French Revolution and the Napoleonic wars. For several centuries even the separate Italian States had forgotten what liberty meant; the idea of nationality—of an Italian nation—had scarcely been conceived.[2] The evolution of the Nation-State was, indeed, the characteristic contribution made by the nineteenth century to the science and art of politics. Of this particular political formation the ancient world knew nothing. The City-State it knew, and the World-Empire; but the idea of a State, still more of a Congeries of States, based upon the principle of nationality was a much later conception. England, with unusual precocity, achieved national unity in the thirteenth century; of other European countries Poland, Hungary, and Bohemia were among the earliest to attain similar status. France, with her well-defined frontiers and fortunate in the possession of a strong monarchy, emerged towards the end of the fifteenth century; the Spanish kingdoms were united under Charles I early in the sixteenth century, and before its close the northern Netherlands, shaking off the yoke of Spain, had entered the ranks of state-hood. Portugal regained her independence in 1640, and about the same time the Hapsburgs gave to their conglomerate dominions a species of state-hood though it never developed

[1] Hayward, *Essays*, i. 63.   [2] See note *ad fin.* c. i.

into nationhood. The genius of the Hohenzollern manufactured a Nation-State out of most unpromising materials in North Germany, and the Romanoffs gave to the Russians a semblance of unity—both in the eighteenth century. But not until the close of the nineteenth century was Europe exhaustively parcelled out into a congeries of Nation-States, nominally equal in rank if not in power, all possessed of sovereign authority, and each independent of the others. Belgium and Greece came to birth in the same year (1830), and the rapid disintegration of the Ottoman Empire gave to the peoples of Roumania, Serbia, and Bulgaria the chance, not neglected, of emulating the example of Greece. In northern Europe the dissolution of the Union of Calmar (1523) had long ago brought Sweden into separate national existence alongside Denmark-Norway; but the Cantons of Switzerland, though for centuries united in a loose confederation, cannot be regarded as a Nation-State until the adoption of the federal constitution in 1848. The final stage in the evolution of modern Germany and modern Italy was simultaneously reached in 1871.

The Italian *Risorgimento*

Among all these political creations modern Italy, if not the greatest, was, by general consent, the most interesting, the most romantic.

> 'The mingled associations of a glorious past and of a noble present, the genuine and disinterested enthusiasm that so visibly pervaded the great mass of the Italian people, the genius of Cavour, the romantic character and career of Garibaldi, and the inexpressible charm and loveliness of the land which was now rising into the dignity of nationhood, all contributed to make the Italian movement unlike any other of our time. It was the one moment of nineteenth-century history when politics assumed something of the characters of poetry.'

So Mr. Lecky wrote in 1896. United Italy had then but lately attained its majority; yet Mr. Lecky was constrained to confess that the 'glamour' had already 'faded' —the spell was already broken.

Mr. Lecky wrote at an unfortunate moment, when, as we shall see, Italy was passing through difficult days. His first thought was the better. The Italian movement stands out, even among the remarkable movements of the nineteenth century, as, in many respects, unique. 'The supreme interest of the re-casting of Italy arises', as a gifted Italian writer[1] has truly said, 'from the new spectacle of a nation made one not by conquest but by consent.' Modern Italy inherited great traditions. Though now in possession of Rome as her capital she nevertheless looks back less to the World-Empire of Rome than to the City-State; and not only to the City-State of Rome but to Florence as well, to Genoa, and most of all to Venice. It is, indeed, primarily as the heir to Venice that she has in these last days successfully asserted her claim to *Italia Irredenta*. The Roman Empire was, in fact, grievously obstructive to the national life of Italy, as it was to that of Germany. Yet, paradoxically, its fall did not remove the obstruction.

The Roman Empire

As the curtain rises on the drama of the post-Roman world it discloses a scene of vast and wild confusion. The mighty fabric of the Empire, reeling under repeated shocks from without, undermined by corruption and luxury within, was tottering to its fall. Savage and untutored, but strong in the simplicity to which Roman civilization had long been a stranger, the Barbarian hordes poured into Italy. Twice was Rome itself sacked, first by Alaric the Goth (A.D. 410), and nearly half a century later by the Vandals. The deposition of the boy-Emperor, Romulus Augustulus (476), the investiture of Odovaker as Roman Patrician, the nominal assertion of Byzantine sovereignty in Italy—these things were only the culmination of a prolonged agony.

Their significance for Italy needs no elaborate demonstration. They inaugurated the period, prolonged for thirteen centuries, during which Italy was the prey of foreign invaders and alien rulers. Ostrogoths, Lombards, and Franks in turn made themselves masters of large portions of the soil of Italy. Greeks had preceded Normans; Germans, Spaniards, Austrians followed them.

[1] Countess E. Martinengo Cesaresco, *Liberation of Italy*, p. v.

The Papacy

Meanwhile, another Power, more persistent, more pervasive, not less obstructive to the development of Italian nationality, had emerged from the chaos, had entered upon the heritage of the Roman Empire of the West, and had firmly established itself upon Italian soil. For many centuries central Italy lay in the grip of the Papacy. Territorial unification was thus rendered impossible. More than that. The Pope was not merely a territorial sovereign in Italy; he claimed world-dominion.

The Medieval Empire

That dominion was in one sense substantiated, in another sense imperilled, by the alliance concluded between the Papacy and the 'Barbarians'. The Franks were called in to deliver Italy from the Lombards, as the Lombards had been summoned to expel the Ostrogoths, and in 754 Pepin King of the Franks was rewarded for his assistance with the title of Patriarch of the Romans. Twenty years later the Lombard monarchy was overthrown by his son Charles (Charlemagne), and in 800 there was enacted in Rome one of the most significant scenes in world history.

Charlemagne

In that year Pope Leo III placed upon the brows of Charles the Great, King of the Franks, the Imperial Crown, and thus called into being the Holy Roman Empire.

In one sense the Holy Roman Empire was never more than an unembodied aspiration; in another it was a most remarkable and most persistent political phenomenon. In theory Pope and Emperor were henceforward to occupy a joint throne, acting as the vicegerents of the sole Ruler of the Universe: the one in the spiritual, the other in the secular sphere. 'The theory of the medieval Empire', wrote Freeman, 'is that of an universal Christian monarchy. The Roman Empire and the Catholic Church are two aspects of one society, a society ordained by the Divine will to spread itself over the whole world.'[1] The fact fell lamentably short of the theory, and the results of the lack of correspondence between them are writ large over the whole history of the Middle Ages. For more than five cen-

[1] *Historical Essays*, i. 136.

turies, indeed, the conflict between the occupants of the joint throne supplied one of the main threads of European history.

The Papacy

We are concerned with that conflict only in so far as it reacted upon the national life of Italy. From that angle nothing more fatal could have happened than the 'restoration' of the Western Empire by Pope Leo III. Its effects could not, however, have been foreseen. To contemporaries it seemed to be an event pregnant with brilliant possibilities. 'The coronation of Charles', wrote Bishop Creighton, 'corresponded to the ambition of Latins and Germans alike. To the former it seemed to be the restoration to Rome and to Italy of their former glory....'[1] 'In Charles', wrote Lord Bryce, 'the hero who united under one sceptre so many races, who ruled all as the vicegerent of God, the pontiff might well see, as later ages saw, the new golden head of a second image, erected on the ruins of that whose mingled iron and clay seemed crumbling to nothingness behind the impregnable bulwarks of Constantinople.'[2]

Nevertheless, the melancholy truth persists that until, a thousand years later, Napoleon undid the work of Leo III, Italy, as a Nation-State, could not begin to emerge. For five hundred years the advantages arising from the transaction of A.D. 800 were reaped solely by the Papacy. But from the end of the thirteenth century the Papacy itself fell on evil days. It had reached its zenith in the Pontificates of the great Hildebrand (1073–85) and Innocent III (1198–1216). Boniface VIII (1294–1303) pushed to their uttermost limits the Papal pretensions, but with him its power and prestige began to decline. The arrogant demands which he made upon the temporal Princes of Christendom did not a little to evoke, notably in England and France, the spirit which ultimately proved fatal to oecumenical pretensions—the spirit of nationality.

Only six years after the death of Boniface, the Pope (Clement V) was carried off by Philip the Fair of France as

[1] *History of the Papacy*, i. 11.
[2] *The Holy Roman Empire*, p. 47.

a captive to Avignon.[1] With the 'Babylonish captivity' (1309–78) the definite decline of the Papacy began. To England, just about to embark on the hundred years' contest with France, as to Germany, the Papacy naturally appeared to be little more than an appendage of the French monarchy. Such prestige as survived the Captivity was dissipated by the Great Schism which fills the closing years of the fourteenth century. Christendom was compelled to look upon a mournful spectacle.

'Two Popes,' wrote Macaulay in a characteristic passage, 'each with a doubtful title, made all Europe ring with their mutual invective and anathemas. Rome cried out against the corruptions of Avignon and Avignon with equal justice recriminated on Rome. The plain Christian people brought up in the belief that it was a sacred duty to be in communion with the head of the Church were unable to discover, amidst conflicting testimonies and conflicting arguments, to which of the two worthless priests who were cursing and reviling each other the headship of the Church rightfully belonged.'

Macaulay was a Protestant and a Whig, but no Catholic could fail to acknowledge and deplore the disastrous effects of the schism—disastrous alike to Papal prestige and to the religious life of Christendom. Not, however, until it had lasted forty years was the schism finally ended by the Council of Constance (1414–18); and the Council of Constance, though it restored unity to the Western Church, was hardly less fatal than the 'Captivity' or the schism to the prestige of the Papacy. It definitely asserted the superior authority of General Councils, and this, as Gregorovius has justly said, 'was the first real step towards the deliverance of the world from the Papal hierarchy; it was already the Reformation'.

The Italian Cities

Meanwhile, as regards Italy, the centre of interest and political gravity had long since shifted from the city of the Caesars and the Popes to the City-States of Central and Northern Italy—to the Republic on the lagoons, the fair

[1] Avignon, at that time, was not in France, but in the Kingdom of Arles.

city on the Arno, to Milan, Genoa, Pisa, Siena, and the rest. With the internecine strife of these cities, with their combinations and leagues, with their shifting alliances, with their participation in the long-drawn-out contest between Papacy and Empire, between Guelphs and Ghibellines, with the interesting constitutional experiments which many of them tried, this narrative is not concerned. It is, however, pertinent to recall the great part which, thanks to their geographical situation, Venice and Genoa played in the commercial life of the Middle Ages, nor can we forget that Florence was pre-eminent in the humanistic revival, though most of the Italian cities contributed to that efflorescence of art and literature which has become known as the Renaissance.

The Renaissance

The Renaissance had many aspects, and they are all represented in Italy. But although there was diversity of manifestation, there was throughout the whole movement an underlying unity of spirit. To describe it as the 'new birth of learning' is to concentrate attention upon an important but still partial aspect of a many-sided movement; to regard it as marking the 'new birth' of nationalities is to insist upon another. We may think of it again, quite legitimately, as pre-eminently the 'new birth of art'—of art in its many manifestations, plastic, pictorial, and architectural. The term is properly applied to the re-birth of geographical and astronomical discovery, and to a group of mechanical inventions—notably that of printing. All these things were chronologically coincident, a fact which seems to suggest a common impulse, if not a common origin.

A summary analysis of a movement so many sided must manifestly be inadequate, but we may perhaps venture to say that the Renaissance meant essentially the opening to the gaze of man of a new heaven and a new earth. This is true both literally and metaphorically. The great scientific work of the astronomers, of Copernicus and Tycho Brahe, of Kepler and Galileo, is clearly complementary to the geographical discoveries of Christopher Columbus and Bartholomew Diaz, of Vasco da Gama and the Cabots.

More than this. To the finer minds the Renaissance meant the opening of a new heaven on earth; to the finest minds it meant the opening of a new vision of the Eternal. To all whom it touched it signified the emancipation of the human intellect, the quickening of the human will, the casting off of all external and authoritative restraint upon the activities of man's body and spirit. It meant, in Mr. J. A. Symonds's words, 'the liberation of the reason from a dungeon, the double discovery of the outer and the inner world'.

In most of these activities and manifestations the Italian cities were pre-eminent, though on its religious side the most characteristic fruits of the Renaissance were gathered not in Italy but in England and Germany. But splendid as were Italian achievements during that wonderful epoch, they were the achievements of men who thought of themselves less as Italians than as Florentines or Lombards, Genoese or Venetians. Italy did not yet exist.

Before Italy could come into existence a heavy pall was to descend upon the brilliant activities of her City-States, and Italy as a whole was to pass through the valley of dishonour and desolation.

Eclipse

Towards the end of the fifteenth century the light which had shone so brilliantly in the Italian cities and which thence had illumined the world was suddenly extinguished, and for three hundred years Italy was merely the cockpit of Europe, the arena for the display of Hapsburg and Bourbon rivalry.

To the rapid decadence of the City-States many causes contributed: some operating here, some there; but one cause there was which operated prejudicially on Italy as a whole, though with varying force in different States.

Geography and Trade

During the sixteenth century the Mediterranean, which for long centuries had been the highway of commerce and the centre of world-civilization, was suddenly reduced to the position of a back-water; the cities on her shores were left high and dry; the centre of political and commercial gravity shifted from the inland sea to shores lapped by the tides of the Atlantic. Two causes, not unrelated to each other, contributed to this amazing and momentous revolution. On the one hand the Ottoman Turks made themselves masters of the Balkan peninsula and of the coasts of Asia Minor, Syria, Palestine, Egypt, and North Africa; on the other, Italian navigators sailing westward from Spain and England respectively, sought a new sea-route from Europe to the Indies and stumbled instead upon the West Indian islands and the American Continent; while a Portuguese navigator found a way by the Cape of Good Hope, and established the Portuguese Empire in India. Vasco da Gama thus turned the flank of the historic trade routes by which for thousands of years the spices, fabrics, and precious stones of the East had found their way into the lands bordering on the Mediterranean, and thence into central, western, and northern Europe. By the occupation of Constantinople, Alexandria, and the coasts of Syria and Palestine, the Ottoman Turk obtained control over the great emporia of ancient and medieval trade. If the old trade routes were not actually blocked, traffic was greatly impeded, and the navigators of Europe were consequently impelled to seek and fortunately found new paths. Trade forsook Venice and Genoa and established itself in Lisbon, Bristol, London, and Amsterdam; wealth began to flow into Europe not only from the ancient East but from the new West.

The effect produced by this revolution upon the fortunes of England it were superfluous and, in the present connexion, irrelevant to emphasize; upon the Italian cities it was manifestly disastrous. Columbus and the Cabots had plunged daggers into the commercial hearts of their compatriots.[1]

So the curtain falls upon the Italy of the Renaissance. Before it rises on the Italy of the *Risorgimento*, the land had to pass through much tribulation.

Before we proceed to cast a hurried glance at the inter-

[1] If compatriots they were; doubts are now cast on the Italian origin of Columbus.

vening period, one general observation must be permitted. If Geography has been kind to Italy, Physiography has been cruel. The early efflorescence of the Italian cities was, in large measure, due to the prominence of the Italian peninsula in the Mediterranean. But if a map of the world, as known to the ancients, prefigures the greatness of the Italian Principalities, a physiographic map of Italy reveals the causes which determined for long years its political destinies. Until physical obstacles are overcome by the perseverance of man, Italy will evidently be the home not of a united people but of separate communities and small principalities. The lanky leg cut by the long line of the Apennines; immense length coupled with contracted breadth; enormous distances intervening between Venice and Naples, between Milan and Messina; physical barriers interposed even between adjacent districts; Genoa cut off from Milan, the Ligurian coast from the basin of the Po —these features leap to the eye. Other causes were undoubtedly operative but Physiography alone would suffice to account for the fact that while England and France were welded by enlightened rulers into compact Nation-States, the Italian peninsula continued to be split up into a number of separate and generally antagonistic communities.

Geography and Physiography

Other causes, as was said, contributed to separatism. The Temporal dominions of the Church interposed a barrier between north and south; and racial differences were thus accentuated. A divided Italy suited the book of the Papacy, and enabled it, by playing off city against city, to consolidate its own domain. Similarly the prolonged contest between Papacy and Empire invited the partisanship and rewarded the assistance of rival Principalities.

Rivalry of Bourbon and Hapsburg

Hardly was the contest between Pope and Emperor ended when a fresh element of disintegration entered into Italian politics. The last years of the fifteenth century, and the first years of the sixteenth, witnessed, as we have seen, the national consolidation both of France and Spain under strong and centralized monarchies. One by one the great feudal principalities, whose chiefs had for centuries been the rivals of the king at Paris, were absorbed by the Crown: Burgundy and Aquitaine, Anjou and Poitou, Normandy and Brittany all fell in, either by conquest, forfeiture, or marriage; and France, by the end of the fifteenth century, was for the first time politically one. As medieval France had been a collection of feudal duchies and counties, so medieval Spain had been a congeries of kingdoms; but the marriage of Ferdinand of Aragon with Isabella of Castile, and the expulsion of the Moors from the kingdom of Granada, enabled those sovereigns to bequeath to their grandson a compact and consolidated kingdom. Charles I (1516–56), afterwards elected to the Empire as Charles V, was the first King of Spain.

The ambitious kings of these consolidated kingdoms soon found themselves involved in a contest for supremacy on the Continent. Italy provided the obvious battleground. Tempted in part by its disintegrated condition, partly by the traditional rivalry of its cities; finding excuse in the assertion of hereditary claims on Naples and the Milanese respectively, the Spanish and French kings plunged into a contest destined to last through a great part of three centuries.

The election of Charles V as Emperor (1519) and the union of the kingdom of Spain with the archduchy of Austria gave additional emphasis to the desire of the Emperor for supremacy in Italy. It added also to the anxiety of France to avert 'encirclement' at the hands of the Hapsburgs, who added to the sovereignties of Austria and Spain the lordship of the Netherlands. With the help of England the French kings ultimately dispelled the danger of Hapsburg domination; Richelieu aimed at the achievement of security, at a scientific frontier for France. He had no desire for the acquisition of territory, whether in Germany or Italy, outside the natural boundaries of France, the Rhine, the Alps, and the Pyrenees, but he was determined to have the keys of the doors in his own pocket. Hence his projected league with the Pope, Venice, Savoy, and Mantua, and his persistent endeavours to obtain some fortress at the foot of the Alps which would enable him, should necessity arise, to intervene decisively in Italy.

Louis XIV succeeded to a realm rendered secure by the wise policy of the Cardinal, and having achieved security began to lust after domination. Europe was now threatened by the ascendancy of the Bourbons; but whether the troubler of European peace was Bourbon or Hapsburg, Italy was equally the victim. From the day when Charles VIII led his first expedition into Italy (1494) down to the conclusion of the Treaty of Aix-la-Chapelle (1748) foreign armies were perpetually encamped on Italian soil; her cities were the pawns with which alien monarchs played. Of the historic Principalities some, like Venice and Genoa, lingered on in decadent and unhonoured independence; others were tossed, like Naples and Sicily, from one foreign master to another.

Italy, 1748–89

During the forty years, after the treaty of Aix-la-Chapelle, and preceding the French Revolution, Italy enjoyed, for the first time for centuries, a measure of repose; foreign rulers remained, but they were no longer at war, and in some of the States administration was good and even progressive. Tuscany was especially fortunate in its ruler, the Archduke Leopold of Hapsburg-Lorraine who was conspicuous among the *illuminati*—the reforming sovereigns—of the eighteenth century: nor was Lombardy, though administered directly from Vienna, much behind Tuscany. Tanucci, the enlightened minister of Charles III of Naples, attempted to do for the wretched and ill-governed peasantry of Naples what Pombal was doing in Portugal, D'Aranda in Spain, and Struensee in Denmark. But the material on which Tanucci had to work was more intractable than theirs, and despite his efforts Naples remained a byword for misgovernment. The infection of administrative reform did not reach the Papal States, nor Venice, nor Piedmont. Piedmont alone among Italian States retained something of the old military spirit and still cherished sentiments capable, when a happier day dawned, of translation into Italian patriotism. But socially Piedmont was among the least progressive of Italian States. It was, as an Italian writer has observed, 'merely a passive, neutral, stationary, nook of a province; a half-priestly, half-soldierly fraternity, a drumming, bell-ringing community. It had little of the pleasures and less of the sins of Florence or Paris, of Rome, Milan, or Venice.'[1]

So Italy, after long turmoil, slumbered. When the adorable dreamer was suddenly awakened, it was not by the kiss of a fairy Prince, but by the raucous call of the French Revolution, and the loud tramp of the armies of the French Republic.

The advent of Napoleon announced the opening of a new period in Italian history; the real beginning of the history of Italy, as opposed to that of her divided States. For Italy Napoleon did an immense and enduring work. The diplomatists of Vienna attempted to pluck up the seed he had sown; but it was good seed and sown deep; they could not eradicate it. A period of reaction, broken only by sporadic insurrections, followed on the restoration of 1815. For a whole generation Italian politics were dominated by Metternich; but Austrian oppression called forth a great prophet. With genuine reluctance Mazzini forsook the life of the student for that of the agitator; but having made the great sacrifice he never faltered in the pursuit of his supreme end, the liberation of his country. The achievement of Italian liberty was largely his work; but the work of unification called for a diplomatist rather than a prophet. Italian unity was the work of Cavour, sustained throughout by the sound and steady judgement of King Victor Emmanuel, and seconded by the splendid if embarrassing enthusiasm of a brilliant adventurer. If Mazzini was the prophet and Cavour the statesman, Garibaldi was the knight-errant of the *Risorgimento*. Widely as the three men differed in temper and in tradition and

[1] Gallenga, *History of Piedmont*.

in method, their life-work was inspired by a common purpose. Nor was one behind the others in purity and loftiness of aim. Mazzini would have liked to see Italy unified under a republic; Cavour believed in monarchy, but might have preferred federalism to unity; Garibaldi's overmastering ambition was to make Rome the capital of a united Italy, whether under King or Republic he cared little. The goal has been attained. Italy is one; Rome is its capital. But the attainment of unity and the occupation of Rome, though marking the triumph and culmination of the *Risorgimento,* did not solve all the problems of the young Nation-State.

Far otherwise. For more than half a century the soul of Italy was tortured by the impossibility of reconciling patriotism with religion. The persistent refusal of the Papacy to accept the olive branch held out by the Italian kingdom imposed an intolerable strain upon the conscience of all who wished to be at once good Italians and good Catholics. And if the soul of Italy suffered, so did the body. Italy was made too fast. The process would doubtless have been slower and surer had Cavour lived. Yet it was Cavour who, in his zeal for the English Constitution, imposed upon Italy a type of Parliamentary Democracy, for which, if not manifestly unfitted by tradition, temperament and training, she was certainly unready. Consequently, Italy incurred the nemesis which invariably waits upon premature constitutional development. Just as in England the weakness of the Lancastrian Executive proved that socially and economically the nation was not yet ready for parliamentary government, so in Italy, the disorder, distress, and the political ineptitude of successive ministries proved that a nation, so recently and imperfectly unified, needed a period of discipline before it could safely assume the exacting responsibilities of self-government. In England a century of strong government, of apprenticeship in local government, of economic recuperation and social discipline, preceded the renewal of the parliamentary experiment. Only the dictatorship of the

Tudors rendered possible the success of the Puritan Revolution under the Stuarts. Italy, too, has found salvation in the acceptance of a popular dictatorship. Whether the rule of Signor Mussolini will prove as educative and ultimately beneficent as that of the Tudors in England time alone can show.

Note to p. 1.—Some may hold that Dante and Machiavelli should be excepted from this generalization. Both passionately desired that Italy should be *free*; but did either conceive of Italian *nationality*? Cf. *Il Principe*, c. xxvi, and for Dante's influence see Holland Rose, *Nationality as a Factor in Modern History*, pp. 6–10.

II

NAPOLEON I AND ITALY

NAPOLEON came to Italy as a conqueror, as the general of the army of the French Republic. An Italian might well have regarded him as merely the latest in a long series of foreign soldiers, French, Spanish, and German, coming, like his predecessors, to dye the patient soil of Italy with blood. The premonition would have been only partially correct. Napoleon was enough of an Italian to cherish a genuine sentiment for Italy. Moreover, he discerned, as no Italian had previously discerned, the destiny which awaited her.

'Italy is surrounded by the Alps and the sea. Her natural frontiers are defined with as much precision as if she were an island. . . . Isolated within these frontiers Italy is surely destined to become one sole nation: unity of customs, language, and literature must some day, sooner or later, unite her inhabitants under one sole government. Rome is undoubtedly the city which the Italians will select as their capital. It is, indeed, essential to the well-being of Europe that Italy should form a single united State which shall maintain the equilibrium on the continent between France and Austria, and on the sea between France and England.'

These words were actually indited at St. Helena, but it cannot be doubted that they reflect ideas which had long been germinating in Napoleon's mind.

It was a remarkable prediction. How far did Napoleon himself contribute to its fulfilment?

Condition of Italy in 1796

To answer that question it is necessary to examine the condition of Italy when in March 1796 the young general set out for Nice to take up the command entrusted to him by the French Directory.

Needless to say that there was no idea at that time of an Italy united from 'Alp to Etna'. Even into the minds of the prophets and the poets such a conception never

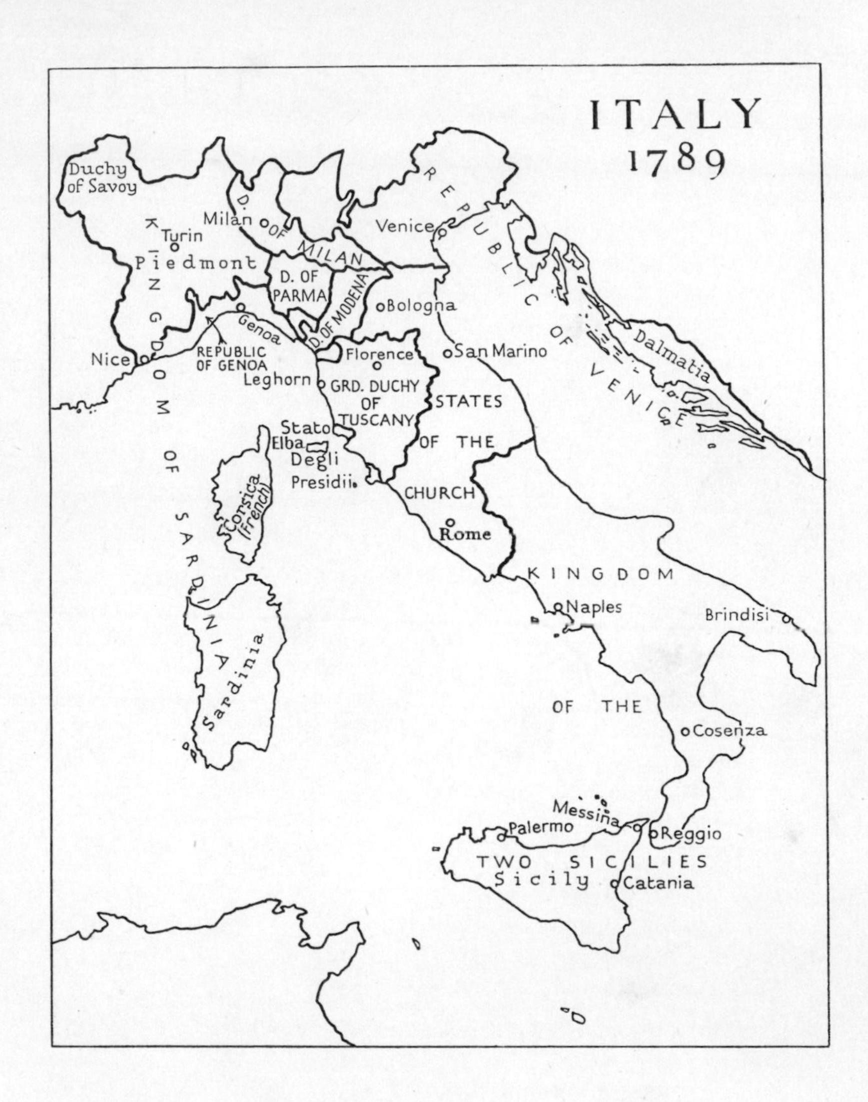
ITALY
1789
Duchy of Savoy
Milan
D. OF MILAN
Turin
Piedmont
KINGDOM OF SARDINIA
D. OF PARMA
D. OF MODENA
Venice
REPUBLIC OF VENICE
Bologna
Genoa
REPUBLIC OF GENOA
Nice
Florence
San Marino
Leghorn
GRD. DUCHY OF TUSCANY
STATES OF THE CHURCH
Dalmatia
Stato Degli Presidii
Elba
Corsica (French)
Rome
KINGDOM OF THE TWO SICILIES
Naples
Brindisi
Sardinia
Cosenza
Messina
Palermo
Reggio
Sicily
Catania

entered. Italy was at that time divided into a number of separate States, variously enumerated according to the classification adopted. We can count a round dozen. In the extreme north-west was the sub-alpine Duchy of Piedmont, united with the Duchy of Savoy and ruled by a scion of the House of Savoy as King of Sardinia. The Hapsburgs were in possession of the Milanese (Lombardy) as well as the Duchies of Mantua and Modena, while the Duchy of Tuscany had been held as an apanage of the same house since the Treaty of Vienna (1738). The kingdom of the Two Sicilies was still ruled by the Spanish Bourbons, as was the Duchy of Parma; Venice, Genoa, Lucca, and San Marino still recalled the Italy of the Republics; the Pope gripped the centre of Italy and divided the north from the south by his continued possession of the States of the Church.

Between these different States there was, speaking generally, little or nothing in common. Austrian influence was evidently predominant, but how could the Hapsburgs, as Dr. Rose pertinently asks, masters of eleven distinct peoples north of the Alps, 'hope permanently to dominate a wholly alien people south of that great mountain barrier?'[1] It was, doubtless, his perception of the weakness inherent in this position that decided Napoleon to deliver his attack on the Austrians in Italy. From the rest of the Italian States there was little to fear. In most of them there was, indeed, a party not ill disposed towards the French Republic. Since the outbreak of the Revolution in France propagandists had been busy in the chief Italian cities, but the response to their preaching had been limited. Yet if there was little enthusiasm for the principles proclaimed at Paris there was less for the existing régime in most of the Italian States. Enthusiasm was not, indeed, a plant likely to flourish on soil saturated with foreign blood. The flag of Liberty was raised in half-hearted fashion at Bologna in 1794, and in the same year the Sicilians tried to establish a republic at Palermo. The

[1] *Life of Napoleon*, i. 78.

Grand Duke of Tuscany was the first sovereign of the Old Régime to recognize the French Republic (1795). Napoleon entered Italy in 1796 with the old republican catchwords on his lips, but his avowed object was to replenish, by the spoliation of the Lombard cities, the exhausted treasury at Paris, to attach his soldiers to his own person by good living and high rewards at the expense of an enemy, and to improve the strategical position of France in the conflict with Austria. To troops marching barefooted, half-starved, ill-armed, he held out glittering hopes:

'Soldiers, you are starving and in rags. Government is in arrears with your pay and has nothing to give you. Your patience and your courage amidst these rocks are admirable, but they bring you no fame: no ray of glory lights upon you. I am about to lead you into the most fertile plains in the world; fruitful provinces and large cities will soon lie at your mercy; there you will find honour, profit, and wealth. Soldiers of Italy, have you the needful courage and perseverance?'

Campaign of 1796

Such was the prospect held out by the young general to his troops.

The details of his campaign must not detain us. Bonaparte's first task, as he advanced into the Maritime Alps from the coast-road between Nice and Genoa, was to drive in a wedge between the Austrians and their Piedmontese allies. This was accomplished in a fortnight; the King of Sardinia sued for an armistice, and on 15 May concluded a Treaty by which he renounced his alliance with Austria, handed over his strongest fortresses to Bonaparte, and ceded Nice and Savoy to France.

Having put the Piedmontese army out of action Bonaparte turned upon the Austrians, forced a passage over the bridge of Lodi (10 May), and entered Milan on the 16th. Alarmed by his rapid advance, other Italian princelings hastened to come to terms with the victorious general. Hercules D'Este, Duke of Modena, and the Bourbon Duke of Parma made their peace with him in May, Ferdinand of Naples and Pope Pius VI in June. In February 1797 the Pope concluded the definitive Treaty of Tolentino, by the terms of which he agreed to surrender all claim to Avignon and the Venaissin (already annexed to France), and also to Bologna, Ferrara, Romagna, and the valuable port of Ancona; disband his army; hand over to Bonaparte a number of art treasures and manuscripts; pay a large money indemnity (30,000,000 francs), and close his ports against the ships of the allies and in particular of England.

The Client Republics

The Pope also agreed to recognize the 'Cisalpine Republic', for Bonaparte had already begun the reorganization of Italy. As early as October 1796 Austrian Lombardy had been converted into the Lombard or Transpadane Republic, and a Cispadane Republic had also been set up to include Modena, Bologna, Ferrara, and Reggio.

The new Republic quickly adapted itself to the French model. The feudal laws were abolished, all citizens were declared equal in the sight of the law, and an assembly, to be elected on a popular franchise, was summoned to meet in Bologna at Christmas. These events are held by one of the most distinguished of Napoleon's biographers to mark the real beginning of the Italian *Risorgimento*.[1]

But the military situation demanded attention. The great fortress of Mantua, the key to the Austrian position in Italy, still resisted all the attacks of General Bonaparte. The Austrians made heroic efforts to succour it, but in vain; and after prolonged fighting at Arcole (15 to 19 November), and a fierce battle at Rivoli (14 January), Mantua at last surrendered (2 February); preliminaries of peace were signed at Leoben in April, and after six months of negotiation Bonaparte concluded his first treaty with Austria at Campoformio (17 October 1797).

Peace negotiations with Austria by no means absorbed all his activities. In May he picked a quarrel with the Venetian Republic, and having, in the sacred name of 'Liberty', deposed the ruling oligarchy, he occupied the city itself and the Venetian islands in the Greek archipelago. Then came the reorganization of northern and central Italy. In June Genoa was converted into the Ligurian

[1] Rose, *Napoleon*, i. 120.

Republic, in close dependence upon France; in July the Transpadane and Cispadane Republics were consolidated into the Cisalpine Republic, to which were subsequently added the Valtellina, all Venetia west of the Adige, and other strips of territory. It thus extended from the Lake of Como and Verona in the north to Rimini in the south.

Meanwhile Bonaparte kept an eye on the development of events in Paris, and though he was too prudent and patient to pluck the pear before it was ripe, he sent Augereau, a trusted lieutenant, to save the tottering Directory from a royalist attack. The so-called *coup d'état* of 18e Fructidor (4 September 1797), though it saved the Republic for the moment, marked in reality an important stage in General Bonaparte's journey towards the Consulate and the Empire. His language had already begun to indicate an increasing independence of the politicians in Paris, whom he still acknowledged as his nominal masters.

'Do you suppose', he wrote in May 1797, 'that I win victories in Italy merely to enhance the authority of the lawyers of the Directory, a Carnot or a Barras? Do you suppose that I mean to establish the Republic? What an idea? A Republic of thirty millions of people! With our morals, our vices! How is such a thing possible? What the French people want is glory, the satisfaction of their vanity. As for liberty they know nothing about it. . . . The nation wants a chief, a chief covered with glory, not theories of government, fine phrases, ideological essays—these things the French do not understand. They want some playthings; that will be enough; they will play with them and let themselves be led, always supposing they are cleverly prevented from seeing the goal towards which they are moving.'

Peace of Campo-Formio

His tone in the peace negotiations with Austria matched these words. He was less the servant of the Republic than the independent conqueror, and as such he granted to the Emperor the terms finally embodied in the Peace of Campoformio (17 October 1797). By this exceedingly important treaty the Austrian Netherlands were definitely ceded to France; the Republic of Venice was annihilated and its territories partitioned; continental Venetia east of the Adige, Istria, and Dalmatia were annexed to Austria; Venetia west of the Adige to the Cisalpine Republic and the Ionian islands to France; finally, Austria recognized the Cisalpine Republic and agreed to indemnify the Duke of Modena with Breisgau. Such was the public treaty; the secret terms were even more significant, but they do not concern this narrative.

Of all the articles the most full of portent, perhaps, was that which gave France the Ionian islands. With all northern and central Italy his for the asking, why did Bonaparte content himself with this insignificant addition to the immediate dominions of France?[1] The answer contains the key to Bonaparte's policy and indicates the trend of his personal ambition. England, not Austria, was the enemy. 'Really to conquer England' (so he wrote in August 1797) 'we must make ourselves masters of Egypt.' To Egypt the Ionian isles were stepping-stones.

The Peace of Campoformio proved to be little more than a truce. To Austria it brought only a brief cessation of arms. Between England and France the war was continued without interruption, Egypt providing the main battle-field. During Bonaparte's absence in Egypt events moved rapidly in Europe. In the winter of 1798–9 a fresh coalition against France was formed between Great Britain, Austria, and Russia. Naples also adhered to it, and it was in southern Italy that the continental war was resumed.

The Roman Republic

Before sailing for Egypt, Bonaparte struck another blow at the Papacy. The young general had already begun to establish a 'dynasty', and the embassy at Rome had been accordingly bestowed on his brother Joseph. The Palazzo Corsini, where Joseph Bonaparte resided, became the centre of a republican agitation, mainly fomented by outsiders from other Italian cities. There were collisions between these republicans and the Papal troops, and a member of the French embassy,

[1] The Secret Treaty gave her the Rhine frontier and Belgium.

General Duphot, was killed (28 December 1797). This gave Napoleon the excuse he wanted, Joseph was promptly withdrawn from the city, which was occupied by a French force under General Berthier, Napoleon's brilliant chief of the staff. A tumultuous assembly met in the Forum, renounced the authority of the Pope, and declared Rome to be an independent Republic (15 February 1798). The aged Pontiff refused to abdicate and took refuge in the Vatican, whence he was carried off as a prisoner, first to Siena and from there to Valence in Dauphiné, where at the age of eighty-two he died (29 August 1799).

The Republic was, meanwhile, constituted in Rome on the Directorial model, with five Directors and a Legislature of two Houses, styled the Senate and the Tribunate respectively. A Praetor and a Quaestor gave to the administration of French justice an appropriately Roman flavour. But consuls, senators, and praetors did not save the city from spoliation. Masséna, who temporarily superseded Berthier, proved himself another Alaric: French soldiers and brokers, who descended on the city like a swarm of locusts, carried off statuary and pictures, manuscripts and furniture; nothing at once valuable and portable was left behind.

'In sending me to Rome', wrote Berthier to Bonaparte, 'you appoint me treasurer to the expedition against England. I will try to fill the exchequer.' His efforts did not fail of success. Nor must we ignore the object which the spoils of Rome were intended to achieve. Bonaparte, as we have seen, was looking to the conquest of England as the supreme object of his ambition, and his most trusted generals shared it.

The next act of the drama has a special interest for the English spectator, connected as it is with one of the most brilliant victories ever won by the English navy, and also with the one discreditable episode in the career of the greatest of English sailors.

For eighteen months the Mediterranean had been a 'French lake', but in April 1798 Pitt entrusted to the youngest flag-officer in the service the task of 'reconquering the Mediterranean'! Sir Horatio Nelson was but thirty-eight when he hoisted his flag on the *Vanguard* and was told off to keep watch on the suspected movements of Bonaparte at Toulon. The latter came out on 18 May, managed to evade the British fleet, captured Malta in June, and reached Egypt on 1 July. Yet his great victories in Egypt availed him little; Nelson and the British fleet were on his track and on 1 August they annihilated the French fleet in Aboukir Bay. The formation of the Second Coalition was the immediate result of Nelson's great victory at the Battle of the Nile. Before the end of September Nelson himself was back at Naples.

The Two Sicilies

The royal family of Naples belonged to the inner circle of the ruling hierarchy of Europe. The King, Ferdinand IV (Ferdinand I of the Two Sicilies), was a Bourbon, brother of the reigning King Charles IV of Spain. The Queen, Marie Caroline, the ablest of the daughters of the Empress Maria Theresa, was an aunt of Francis II, the last of the Holy Roman Emperors, the first to assume the new title of Emperor of Austria, and was sister of his two predecessors Joseph and Leopold, and of the unfortunate Marie Antoinette, Queen of France. Marie Caroline's detestation of revolution and republicanism was profound, but not, in view of her sister's cruel fate, unnatural. Her husband was a good-natured indolent buffoon; but the Queen, hardly less than the King, was under the influence of the British Minister Sir William Hamilton and his beautiful and fascinating wife. Nelson, sad to relate, fell a victim to the same lady's charms. The Government of Naples, though popular with priests and peasants, was perhaps the most inefficient and corrupt in Italy. Nelson himself described the country, in a sailor's blunt language, as made up of 'fiddlers, poets, harlots, and scoundrels'. The description was not inaccurate.

Encouraged by Nelson and the Hamiltons, Marie Caroline and her consort declared war on France (22 November), and a large Neapolitan army commanded by Mack, one of the most incompetent and pusillanimous of Austrian generals, advanced on Rome. The French retired from the city, and on the 29th King Ferdinand entered it and 'proclaimed to Europe from the summit of the Capitol that the hour of the Kings had come'.

The Parthenopean Republic

The hour of the King of Naples was a fleeting one. The French under Championnet scattered Mack and his Neapolitan army, re-entered Rome, and in turn invaded Naples. Nelson carried the Royal Family and the Hamiltons off into safety at Palermo (21 December), and there, under the protection of the British fleet, the Neapolitan Sovereign continued his inglorious reign. Early in January the greater part of Naples surrendered to the French, who proclaimed the Parthenopean Republic (January 1799). But the indignities inflicted by the French upon the Pope and the Holy City inflamed a peasantry devoted to their Church, and the 'army of the Faith', mobilized and commanded by the intrepid Cardinal Ruffo, harassed the French in the country districts, and, supported by English and Russian ships in the harbour, attacked Naples itself. For some days the city was given over to massacre and outrage, but on 23 June Ruffo accepted the surrender of the forts held by the French and their republican allies under a flag of truce. A general amnesty was to be proclaimed and the French were to be allowed to return unmolested to Toulon. Captain Foote, who commanded the English forces, assented to the terms, and a flag of truce was flown from his ship *Seahorse*.

Within two days Nelson, accompanied by King Ferdinand and the Hamiltons, returned to Naples. The King denounced the terms accepted by Cardinal Ruffo and a terrible retribution was inflicted on the republicans of the city; Prince Francesco Caracciolo, the aged Commodore of the Neapolitan fleet, was hanged at the yard-arm for treason. Nelson assented to the execution of the sentence; Lady Hamilton witnessed it. Controversy still rages as to the degree of Nelson's responsibility for these deplorable events. Admiral Mahan[1] and Sir J. K. Laughton,[2] both high authorities, exonerate Nelson, but Southey,[3] with all his hero-worship, was constrained to admit that the transactions have left 'a stain upon the memory of Nelson and the honour of England', and many of the best modern authorities concur in his judgement. More detailed discussion would be irrelevant to the present narrative; the whole episode is important mainly for the light it throws on the character of Bourbon rule in Naples, and the condition of the kingdom—matters which will demand a good deal of attention in later chapters.

Suvaroff's campaign in North Italy

We have anticipated the sequence of events. The war in the south was an episode. Far more resounding, and more important in their reaction alike upon the general European situation and upon the fortunes of Italy, were the victories of the Austro-Russian armies in the north. Kray's victory on the Adige (Magnano, 5 April) drove the French back on Milan, and Suvaroff's brilliant campaign (April–June) completed their discomfiture. After the great battle of Trebbia (17–19 June) the French power in Italy seemed to be annihilated. The Roman, Parthenopean, and Cisalpine Republics were overthrown; only in Genoa was the French tricolour still flown. But despite reverses in the field France held the key of the strategical position, and both in a military and a political sense the coalition was a rope of sand. Suvaroff, owing to his own insolence and Austrian jealousy, had to retire over the St. Gothard. While he was still in the Pass Masséna inflicted a crushing defeat on the Russians under Korsakoff at Zürich (26 September), the fruits of Suvaroff's great campaign were lost, and Russia withdrew in dudgeon from the war. Nevertheless, it was Suvaroff's victories that had stimulated the enemies of the Republic to the efforts already recorded in south Italy.

The campaign of 1800 opened under very different conditions. The *coup d'état* of 18 Brumaire (9 November 1799)

[1] *English Historical Review*, July 1899 and October 1900.
[2] *Life of Nelson*, p. 139.
[3] *Life of Nelson*, p. 163.

had overthrown the Directory; Napoleon was First Consul; all the resources of France, political and military, were concentrated under the control of a single dominating will. Napoleon again attacked Austria in North Italy, and a brilliant campaign was crowned by the great victory of Marengo (14 June). General Moreau had penetrated into the heart of South Germany and inflicted on Austria a crushing defeat at Hohenlinden (3 December). The Emperor was consequently constrained to accept the terms offered by Napoleon at Lunéville (February 1801). They were remarkably lenient. The concessions already made at Campoformio were confirmed: the Emperor Francis definitely accepted the Adige as his boundary in North Italy; provided compensation in the district of Breisgau for the Grand Duke of Tuscany, who was to surrender Tuscany to the son of the Bourbon Duke of Parma, an arrangement preliminary to the latter's elevation to the kingdom of Etruria: and recognized the Cisalpine, the Ligurian, the Helvetic, and the Batavian Republics, though with the stipulation that those Republics were to remain permanently independent and choose their own form of government.

Two months later Napoleon concluded peace with Naples. King Ferdinand agreed to abandon the British alliance and to exclude British and Turkish vessels from his harbours, to surrender to Napoleon the Stato dei Presidi (i.e. the maritime districts of Tuscany) for the augmentation of the future kingdom of Etruria, and to allow the French to garrison Otranto, Brindisi, and Taranto. On the possession of Taranto, Napoleon laid particular stress as a stepping-stone to the East, and as a counterpoise to Malta, which Great Britain held and refused to surrender —except to its original owners, the Knights of St. John. 'Taranto', he wrote to Murat, 'is the point destined to play the greatest part some day.'

Treaty of Amiens, 1802

A year later, Great Britain, for the first and only time, concluded peace with Napoleon. The latter agreed to restore Egypt to the Porte, to evacuate Naples and the

Papal States, and to acknowledge the independence of the Ionian isles. Great Britain, apart from restorations not here relevant, tacitly accepted the continental settlement as defined at Lunéville.

The reorganization of Italy

The interval of peace, though brief, gave Napoleon the opportunity of reorganizing the administration of Italy. In September 1802 Piedmont, despite Napoleon's express promise, was formally incorporated in the French Republic. Its young ruler, Charles Emmanuel IV, had been compelled to abdicate and retire to Sardinia in 1798. Since then it had been governed by French generals; it was now organized in six departments, after the French model, while the more antique Roman model was imitated by the establishment of a military colony, composed of French veterans, and planted near Alessandria. Elba was also annexed to France, while a bargain struck with Spain gave Napoleon Louisiana (presently to be sold to the United States) and the Duchy of Parma. The former Duke of Parma, a Spanish Bourbon, received in compensation the Grand Duchy of Tuscany with the title of King of Etruria —a title ominous of the approaching end of the republican régime.

The Italian Republic

A most important change following on, but in defiance of, the Treaty of Lunéville was the transformation of the Cisalpine into the *Italian* Republic.

This was effected in January 1803, when four hundred and fifty representatives of the Cisalpine Republic were summoned to meet the First Consul at Lyons, there to confer with him as to the future Constitution of their State. The consultation, though dramatic in its circumstances, and dazzling in the splendour of the fêtes and entertainments with which the deputies were amused, was in fact purely formal. Talleyrand had already prepared the draft of a Constitution, which the delegates had no choice but to accept. Napoleon himself was elected President of the new Italian Republic, with Count Melzi, a Lombard noble, as Vice-President. Executive and legislative functions were practically vested entirely in the President, but there was to be an Executive (*Consulta*); a legislative body of 150 members, and a High Court of Justice charged to secure the observance of the fundamental laws of the Constitution. Executive, Legislature, and Judicature were to be elected by three electoral colleges which were to meet for the purpose biennially at Milan, Bologna, and Brescia.

More significant, however, than any article of the paper constitution was the change in the name of the State and the style of its President. On this change a brilliant French commentator lays great stress:

'Le titre et le nom révèlent les aspirations au gouvernement de toute la péninsule . . . Car l'évocation de l'Italie dans cette proclamation de la République a soulevé dans toute la péninsule une émotion profonde. Car C'EST LA NAISSANCE DE L'ITALIE; à l'appel de Bonaparte, elle se lève, elle veut être, elle veut vivre parmi les nations, parmi les grandes nations. Il n'y a rien de plus beau dans toute l'histoire de Napoléon: à lui la gloire unique d'avoir créé des nations.'[1]

Though expressed with an exaggeration pardonable in a French writer, M. Driault's enthusiasm is essentially justified. None the less, however, is it necessary to observe that to all intents and purposes the Cisalpine, not to add the Ligurian Republic as well, was incorporated, despite the specific provisions of the Treaty of Lunéville, in the French Republic.

The Kingdom of Italy

That Republic was itself doomed to speedy extinction. The Empire was proclaimed in May 1804, and the new Emperor offered the client Kingdom of Italy to his brother Joseph. Joseph declined the Crown. Thereupon Napoleon declared the Crown of Italy to be hereditary in the Napoleonic House (March 1805), and on 26 May, in the stately Duomo of Milan, he assumed the iron crown of the Kings of Lombardy. The King of Italy appointed his stepson, Eugène Beauharnais, as Viceroy, annexed the Ligurian Republic (Genoa) to the French Empire, and handed over Lucca and Piombino to the administration of his sister Elisa and her husband Felice Bacciocchi.

[1] E. Driault, *Napoléon en Italie*, p. 101.

This profitable period of peace was now coming to an end. War with England had been renewed in May 1803, and in 1805 Pitt was able to form a third coalition against Napoleonic France. But it did not endure. A crushing defeat inflicted upon Russia and Austria at Austerlitz (2 December 1805) in some measure compensated for the blow sustained at Trafalgar, broke up the Third Coalition, and enabled Napoleon to dictate to the Emperor Francis the terms embodied in the Treaty of Pressburg. Austria, hitherto treated with remarkable leniency, was spared no longer. She lost 3,000,000 subjects and was cut off from Switzerland, from the Rhine, and from Italy. Worst of all, she was deprived of Venetia, with the Adriatic Provinces in Istria and Dalmatia, which were added to Napoleon's Kingdom of Italy.

The Illyrian Province

Illyria played an important, if not an essential, part in Napoleon's scheme of Empire, and Napoleon played an important part in shaping the destinies of the modern triune kingdom which we know conveniently as Yugoslavia. 'In Croatia', writes a high authority, 'the real awakening of national sentiment dates from the Napoleonic era.'[1] To suppose that Napoleon was inspired in his policy towards Illyria by any motive of nationalism would be fantastic: that he nevertheless planted seeds which produced a nationalist harvest there, as in Italy, is undeniable. As to his own motive in annexing them, there is no obscurity.

The Illyrian provinces [writes Dr. H. A. L. Fisher] 'provided a strong bulwark against Austria, a military base against Turkey, and distant endowments for the French marshals. It was worth while to acquire a string of harbours, in which a fleet might be built and whence an expedition might start for the recovery of Egypt; worth while to win a new strip of coast for the Continental blockade and to direct the overland consignments of Eastern cotton from the German route to Imperial territory.'[2]

[1] Dr. Seton Watson, *The Southern Slav Question*, p. 26.

[2] *Cambridge Modern History*, ix. 419.

The historian is, however, concerned less with motives than with results: the French Codes were introduced into the provinces of Croatia, Carniola, Carinthia, Istria, Dalmatia, and Ragusa; lycées were set up at Ragusa and Leybach; primary, secondary, and technical schools were established throughout the country, justice was administered on a uniform system and with impartiality; means of communication were improved; and the people tasted the blessings—not always appreciated by the recipients—of a really efficient administration. How efficient French administration was may be gauged by a Dalmatian saying about the great coast road constructed by Marshal Marmont from Zara to Spalato: 'The Austrians discussed plans for eight years; Marmont mounted his horse, and when he got off the road was made.'

Union with France

Marmont was created Duke of Ragusa in 1808, but in the following year Istria and Dalmatia were detached from the kingdom of Italy and united with Trieste, Croatia, Carniola, and the greater part of Carinthia to form the Province of Illyria in the Empire of France. Marmont was retained as Governor-General under the Emperor, and gave to his Province an admirable civil, as well as military, administration.

From the first days of his independent command Napoleon had, as we have seen, looked towards the East. Illyria was not only, as M. Driault insists, an essential item in the scheme of a *Roman* Empire;[1] it was another stepping-stone towards the East. 'Napoléon', says Driault, 'était dès lors mieux placé que les Russes sur le chemin de Byzance.'[2]

The Kingdom of Naples

The day after he had dictated the Treaty of Pressburg, Napoleon announced that the Bourbon dynasty had ceased to reign in Naples. A French army marched into Naples to enforce the Decree. The King and his Austrian

[1] Op. cit., p. 230.

[2] 'La restauration de ce vieux nom Romain de l'Illyrie avait un grand sens historique; elle fit une vive impression sur les populations, leur sentiment national en est encore profondément pénétré.' Op. cit., p. 229.

Queen once more fled to Sicily to find safety under the protection of the British Navy, but the Crown of the Two Sicilies was bestowed on Joseph Bonaparte, who took possession of the continental portion of his kingdom in February 1806. Sir Sidney Smith, with a British squadron, captured Capri in the same month, and in July a British force under Sir John Stuart crossed from Sicily to the mainland, and encouraged the efforts of the fanatical peasantry of Calabria by inflicting a defeat on the French troops at Maida—a barren victory commemorated in the name of a London suburb. A fortnight later Gaeta surrendered to Masséna, who crushed the resistance of the Calabrian peasants with a ferocity matching his treatment of the citizens of Rome.

King Joachim 'Napoleon'

If good administration can justify the rule of an alien, Joseph's government in Naples did not lack justification. Naples had never been so well governed before, and has never been better governed since. But Joseph's reign was a short one. In 1808 he was promoted to the kingdom of Spain and his place in Naples was taken by Marshal Joachim Murat, the vainglorious and ambitious husband of Napoleon's youngest sister, Caroline. Murat would have preferred the throne of Spain, and between him and his imperial brother-in-law there was friction when he was put off with Naples. His administration was strong and efficient, but his head was evidently turned by his promotion. He kept up magnificent state; created a new nobility; aped in every way the part of an independent sovereign, and actually went so far as to demand the withdrawal of French troops from Naples and to insist on the 'naturalization' of the French inhabitants of his kingdom. Napoleon curtly refused these demands and told Murat to play his 'monkey tricks' no longer. No independent sovereignty was to be allowed in Europe.

Napoleon and the Pope

In Italy there remained in 1808 only one sovereign who could pretend to independence. Napoleon had from his first advent to power appreciated the value of friendship with the Pope; but his preference oscillated between the parts of Constantine and of Diocletian. As First Consul he had, however, concluded a concordat with Pope Pius VII (1801), reversing the policy of the Revolution and recognizing the Pope as head of the Catholic Church, while maintaining the supremacy of the State over the Gallican Church. But Pius had a will as stubborn as Napoleon's. He had indeed journeyed to Paris to be present at the coronation of Napoleon and his Empress, but he refused to compromise his position as a temporal sovereign in Italy. The Papal States bordering on two seas were essential to the completion of the Continental system, the boycott of English trade on the Continent. Pope Pius VII would neither enter the Italian Federation nor enforce the Continental system.

'Why will this overmighty Pope not render unto Caesar the things that are Caesar's?' asked Napoleon (22 July 1807). 'If a stop is not put to this disturbing of my States, the time is not perhaps far distant when I shall recognize the Pope only as Bishop of Rome and as on the same footing with the other Bishops of my States.'

It was no empty threat. On the 17 May 1809 the new Charlemagne issued from Vienna a decree which declared the States of the Church to be annexed to the French Empire. The Pope, in turn, issued a Bull of Excommunication; but was arrested in the Quirinal and carried off as a State prisoner, first to Savona and thence to Fontainebleau. Ten months later Rome was by a *Senatus Consultum* formally incorporated in the French Empire, and officially declared to be the 'Second city of the Empire'.

Italy in 1810

Caesar was at last master in Rome; Italy was French. Thanks to the unbroken supremacy of Great Britain at sea, the House of Savoy still reigned in Sardinia, and the Bourbons in Sicily; but the whole of continental Italy lay under the heel of the Emperor. As King of Italy Napoleon ruled over Lombardy, Modena, the Papal Legations, Venetia, and the Italian Tyrol; Savoy and Piedmont, Genoa, Tuscany and Parma, the Illyrian Provinces and Rome, with the circumjacent territories, were incorporated

ITALY
1810
KINGDOM OF ITALY
EMPIRE OF FRANCE
Turin
Milan
Venice
Genoa
Bologna
Nice
Princ. of Lucca
Florence
San Marino
Leghorn
Elba
Princ. of Piombino
Corsica
Rome
Illyrian Provinces
Dalmatia
KINGDOM OF NAPLES
Naples
Brindisi
Taranto
KINGDOM OF SARDINIA
Messina
Palermo
Reggio
KINGDOM OF SICILY
Catania

in the French Empire; the Kingdom of Naples was ruled by Murat as a dependency of France.

Results of Napoleonic occupation

From the Alps to the Gulf of Messina the administrative system of France was reproduced in all its centralized efficiency; good roads were constructed—notably two great roads over the Simplon and Mont Cenis; canals were cut; bridges were built; education was improved and ancient universities were reopened; justice was administered with heavy but equal hand; taxation though not light was regularized; many redundant bishoprics were suppressed—in the Papal States alone their number was reduced from thirty to eleven; convents were closed, monasteries suppressed, and the Jesuits fled; brigandage was extinguished; feudal customs abolished, and the ownership of land widely extended; not least, the Italians were roused from their lounging and frivolous habits and taught to fight, and to fight, if under an alien flag, not as Lombards and Tuscans, Neapolitans and Romans, but as Italians. M. Sorel attributes to Napoleon the definite intention of uniting the whole of Italy into a single and independent kingdom for a second son. Other commentators, not less competent, are doubtful whether he harboured any such plan; but as to the effect of the Napoleonic occupation there can be no doubt whatever. Even Mazzini, no friend to France, bore testimony to the influence of Napoleon's rule upon the national self-consciousness of Italy:

'The intellectual rise, the rapid increase of national prosperity, the outburst of fraternization . . . are facts, especially in the period 1805–13, ineradicably registered in history. Notwithstanding our dependence upon the French Empire, under the heel of a political despotism, and despite war, the sense of nationality, specially embodied in our brave soldiers, elevated our souls, picturing in the distance the unity of Italy, the supreme goal of all our efforts.'

Mazzini was right. Among the makers of modern Italy, Napoleon holds a foremost place.

'L'Italie voulut aussitôt revivre ou plutôt vivre; car il n'y avait encore jamais eu une nation italienne . . . C'est par Napoléon que l'Italie a commencé d'être autre chose qu'une expression géographique; nulle nation en Europe ne lui doit autant.'[1]

M. Driault does not exaggerate Italy's debt to Napoleon.

Napoleon's ambition, it is true, extended far beyond the boundaries of Italy. But to his final conception of empire Italy, or rather Rome, was not less essential than Gaul itself. From the moment of his marriage to the Princess Marie Louise he reserved for the hoped-for son the title of King of Rome. Following Roman precedent he had adopted his stepson Eugène Beauharnais, and until the birth of the King of Rome (1811) allowed him to expect the succession. From that moment he had to content himself with the hope of the Grand Duchy of Frankfort. Similarly, Murat might have the Kingdom of Poland, but from the day on which the heir was born Murat became aware of the fact that his tenure at Naples was precarious, and began to intrigue with Metternich. Of these intrigues more will be heard in the next chapter.

Napoleon, then, was looking beyond Italy: the Roman Empire should in his person be revived; nor would he share his throne with the Pope. To be a new Charlemagne no longer satisfied his ambition; he would be a second Diocletian.

But the base on which his power rested was already crumbling, and the process though slow was certain. The first effective blow was struck by Nelson at Trafalgar; Trafalgar convinced Napoleon that if he would conquer England he must have recourse to an economic weapon. Hence the continental blockade. To enforce it he must be master of the whole Continent. He must control the ports of the Iberian peninsula, as well as the Italian and the Balkan. The attack on Spain evoked a new spirit in Europe—the hitherto dormant spirit of nationality—and gave England her first real chance of an effective land campaign, sustained from the sea. She eagerly embraced it. From Spain, as Southey sang, 'the living spark went

[1] Driault, op. cit., p. 668.

forth'. It fired the German nationalists, and when Napoleon returned from his disastrous adventure in Russia—an adventure forced upon him be it said by the imminent breakdown of the continental blockade—he found himself confronted by a Germany inspired by a new spirit. After the disaster of Jena, Stein and Hardenberg, Fichte and Humboldt had created a new Prussia and the new Prussia led a new Germany to victory over Napoleon. Like Frankenstein, Napoleon had in truth called forth a monster; he was beaten by the new spirit he had himself evoked.

Elba

But though vanquished he still retained a fragment of sovereignty, if it was only the tiny rock of Elba. Elba was contiguous to the coast of Italy, and had Napoleon been content for a while with the constricted sovereignty of the island he might have played some part in the subsequent story. From Elba Napoleon kept up an active correspondence with his friends on the mainland—among them with his brother-in-law Murat, and in May 1814 a small group of Italians, including Pellegrino Rossi, destined to play a tragic part in the history of the reforming Papacy, met at Turin and decided to offer Napoleon the Crown of Italy. The new Kingdom of Italy was to be divided into four vice-royalties; Rome was to be the capital and the Pope was to receive a large financial indemnity; Napoleon was to renounce all ideas of conquest and to accept a constitution drafted by Rossi and his friends. The story of these negotiations is wrapped in considerable obscurity. Fournier only commits himself to the statement that 'it is possible that Napoleon did not altogether discourage the idea'.[1] M. Villari categorically says that Napoleon accepted the proffered Crown and the conditions attached to the offer, and in October 1814 issued the following statement:

'I shall make of the peoples of Italy a single nation; I shall impress on them unity of manners and customs, at present lacking, and this will be the most difficult enterprise which I

[1] *Napoleon*, ii. 379.

have ever undertaken . . . I shall give the Italians laws suitable for them . . . Within twenty years Italy will have 30,000,000 inhabitants: then she will be the most powerful nation in the world, and as inaccessible to invasion as Russia. We shall abstain from wars of conquest, but I shall have a brave and powerful army. I shall write on the standards my motto of the Iron Crown, "Woe to him who touches it", and no one will dare to do so. After having been Scipio and Caesar in France, I shall be Camillus in Rome; the foreigners shall cease to tread on the Capitol and shall never reappear there again.'[1]

This speech, though it accords with the known sentiments of Napoleon, is of doubtful authenticity. But even if it lacks historical substantiation, it can claim to be philosophically true. It represented the dream of the prisoner of Longwood, if it was not actually delivered by the Sovereign of Elba. The prisoner, disconsolately reflecting on the past, did not fail to predict with singular accuracy the future. With the realization of Napoleon's dream the remaining chapters of this book will be concerned.

[1] Villari, *Italy*, p. 36. The statement appears to be derived from an anonymous pamphlet *La vérité sur les cent jours*, p. 218, but Fournier (op. cit., ii. 379) throws doubts on its authenticity. To me it sounds like an echo of the passage already quoted from the *Reflections in Exile*.

III

RESTORATION, REACTION, AND REVOLUTION

The fall of Napoleon

THE Napoleonic structure in Italy collapsed like a house of cards. To that collapse Italy contributed little, save indirectly through the treachery of King Joachim towards the man who had made him. After the abdication of Napoleon the fate of Italy, like that of the rest of Europe, lay mainly in the hands of three men: the Czar Alexander, Lord Castlereagh, and, pre-eminently, Prince Metternich—with Talleyrand closely watching events and decisions in the interests of 'Legitimacy' in general and in particular of the legitimist claims of the several branches of the House of Bourbon. The Czar was suspected by Metternich and by the Italian Conservatives of intriguing with the revolutionary societies in Italy, and until his complete adherence to the policy of Metternich the suspicion was not wholly unwarranted. Metternich's supreme object was to restore the *status quo ante* Revolution, and above all to eradicate from the minds of the Italian peoples all traces of the 'poison' of nationalism and liberalism. 'Austria', wrote Stewart to Castlereagh, 'trembles at the very name of a Constitution founded on a national representation in Italy.' Lord Castlereagh supported in general outline the policy of Metternich, though, as this chapter will show, from different motives and with large reservations in detail. As Castlereagh wrote to A'Court, the British envoy to Naples, the British Government 'desire to see the Austrian influence predominate in Italy, liberalized, however, in some of its views, and better adapted to the prejudices of the country, because they wish to see Italy tranquil and strong and not divided against itself'. The unity, the tranquillity, and the strength of Italy have ever been the objects of English policy—not least in the period after the Napoleonic wars.

The territorial settlement effected in 1814–15 was en-

The Settlement of 1815

tirely in accord with the wishes of Metternich. Except for the extinction of the ancient republics, Venice and Genoa, the map of Italy in 1815 did not differ materially from that of 1789. The Emperor of Austria found more than adequate compensation for the loss of Belgium in the acquisition of Venetia, which, with the Venetian dependencies on the eastern shore of the Adriatic, was added to Lombardy. The Kingdom of Lombardy-Venetia not only gave Austria a dominating position in north Italy, but made her mistress of the Adriatic. Metternich would have liked to add the Romagna, if not the whole of the States of the Church to the Lombardo-Venetian Kingdom, but the adroit diplomacy of Cardinal Consalvi, the Papal Minister, secured the restoration of the Temporal Power of the Papacy in its integrity, though Austria retained garrisons in Bologna, Ferrara, and Ravenna. The Ionian isles were placed under the protection of Great Britain. The King of Sardinia recovered his ancestral dominions of Savoy, Nice, and Piedmont, and received in addition the territory of the Genoese republic.

Genoa

Genoa presented a difficult problem to the diplomatists; and their decision was severely criticized by contemporaries, especially by lovers of liberty in England, who were naturally concerned at what the Genoese regarded as a distinct breach of faith. In April 1814 Lord William Bentinck had gone to Genoa as a liberator, and restored the Republic. That he was tempted by his personal sentiments to exceed his instructions was doubtless the case, but the Genoese accepted him as the representative of England, and relied implicitly on English sympathy and protection. Bitter, therefore, was their chagrin when they heard the sentence pronounced from Vienna, under which, in order to provide a barrier against French incursions into Italy, they were to be handed over to a neighbour whom they heartily disliked. Nor has the solution of the Genoese problem escaped censure at the hands of historians. The problem, in truth, supplies a conspicuous illustration of the danger threatened to diplomacy by the facile accept-

ITALY
1815
AUSTRIA
KINGDOM OF LOMBARDY-VENETIA
Duchy of Savoy
Magenta
Novara
Milan
Custoza
Verona
Solferino
Peschiera
Venice
Turin
Mantua
Legnano
Piedmont
DUCHY OF PARMA
D. OF MODENA
Bologna
Duchy of Genoa
Genoa
KINGDOM OF SARDINIA
Nice
D. of Lucca
Florence
San Marino
Leghorn
DUCHY OF TUSCANY
STATES OF THE CHURCH
Elba
Corsica (French)
Abruzzi
Rome
Molise
KINGDOM OF THE TWO SICILIES
Naples
Brindisi
Basilicata
Sardinia
Cosenza
Messina
Palermo
Reggio
Sicily
Catania

ance of popular catchwords. The Genoese were proud of their nationality and anxious to exercise the rights of 'self-determination'. To concede the right of 'self-determination' to Genoa was to deny it prospectively to Italy. Nationalists who applauded the achievements of Cavour and Garibaldi could not logically lament the annihilation of the independence of Genoa. In the application of the principle of 'self-determination' everything, in fact, depends on the selection of the unit.

The Central Duchies

Tuscany was restored to the Grand Duke Ferdinand III of Hapsburg-Lorraine, who was also to obtain the reversion of the ex-Republic of Lucca. Lucca was, in the meantime, assigned to Marie Louise, a Spanish Bourbon; but, on the death of the Empress Marie Louise, the consort of Napoleon, the Spanish Bourbons were to be replaced in Parma, which, with Piacenza was to be the portion, for her life, of the ex-Empress of France. Not, however, until (in 1817) the reversionary claims to Parma were secured to the Spanish Bourbons would Spain give her assent to the Treaty of Vienna. Francis IV, son of the Archduke Ferdinand of Austria, and through his mother Maria Beatrice heir to the ancient House of Este, was reinstated in the Duchy of Modena. The tiny Republic of San Marino looking sadly forth over the waters of the Adriatic alone recalled the Italy of the Middle Ages, an Italy divided but independent.

Murat and Naples

Naples might have proved a grave embarrassment to the diplomatists at Vienna had Metternich been less clever or more scrupulous, or King Joachim less inconstant in treachery. Murat, as we have seen, had long since tired of the position of a vassal-king, and, after Napoleon's defeat at Leipzig, he decided to make his terms with Austria. Metternich agreed (11 January 1814) to guarantee him the Crown of Naples as the price of his desertion, and even Castlereagh condescended to conclude an armistice with 'the person exercising the Government of Naples' (22 January), but refrained pointedly from recognizing his title to the throne. Murat, however, was as faithless to his new friends as to his old master. Talleyrand was feverishly anxious to send a French army to restore the Bourbon King to the throne of Naples. Metternich declined to allow it, but equally refused to allow Murat to march northward to resist the threatened invasion of the French. Murat, accordingly, broke with Metternich and attempted to place himself at the head of a national movement in Italy. The attempt was a complete fiasco; he could not even persuade his Neapolitans to face the Austrians, at whose hands he suffered complete defeat at Tolentino (2 May). The Austrian force then advanced on Naples, and restored Ferdinand IV; Murat fled to France and offered his sword and services to Napoleon, by whom they were contemptuously declined. After the final overthrow of Napoleon at Waterloo, Murat took refuge in Corsica, and, refusing Metternich's offer of an asylum and a pension for himself and his family, he made a desperate descent on the coast of Calabria, was captured, tried by court-martial and shot (13 October 1815).

Murat's widow assumed the title of Countess of Lipona and resided near Trieste until her death in 1839. Her two sons went to the United States. The elder settled in Florida and married a niece of George Washington; the younger, after many vicissitudes, returned to France in 1848, attached himself closely to his cousin Louis Napoleon, and was ultimately nominated by him to the Senate.

Austrian domination in Italy

Meanwhile, neither the treachery nor the bravado of Joachim Murat seriously interrupted the completion of Metternich's programme. The final settlement of Vienna made him completely master of Italy's fate. The House of Savoy maintained its independence in the subalpine kingdom, but, for the rest, it mattered little whether Austria was in immediate possession (as in the Lombardo-Venetian Kingdom) or (as in most of the Central Duchies) through friendly kinsmen, or (as in Naples) by diplomatic agreement with a vassal-king. Ferdinand of Naples, for example, had engaged, as the price of restoration to his continental possessions, not to introduce any system of government incompatible with that adopted by Austria in her Italian possessions.

Thus for a full generation Italy was to all intents and purposes governed from Vienna. Yet, despite the completeness of Metternich's triumph, despite the restoration of Hapsburg and Bourbon princelings to the petty courts of central Italy, despite the collapse of Napoleonic institutions and the eradication of revolutionary ideas, the Italy of 1815 was not the Italy of ante-Napoleonic days. Strive as they might the diplomatists of Vienna could not set back the hands of time, nor 'make things seem as though they had not been'. They might it is true replace an Austrian here, a Bourbon there; they might annihilate ancient republics and carve out modern dukedoms; they might mark out with jealous care dividing lines which had been erased, and again set up boundaries which had been broken down; but they could not erase from the minds of the Italian people the new-born recollection of their ancient fame; nor stifle their newly conceived longing for the realization of their national identity.

Piedmont

In no Italian State had the effects of the Napoleonic occupation been more bracing and beneficent than in Piedmont. Devoted as the Piedmontese were to the House of Savoy, they could not but recognize the contrast between the vigorous efficiency of French administration and the sleepy acquiescence in time-honoured abuses pre-eminently characteristic of pre-revolutionary Piedmont. After the restorations of 1815 Turin was the only capital, except Rome, where Metternich's authority was not unquestioned. He ruefully confessed that he looked upon the Piedmontese as 'the Prussians of the south', and expressed his conviction that 'their design of erecting themselves into a much greater power than they had any right to assume would some day cause a convulsion'. With a view to neutralizing the anticipated danger he conceived the idea of obtaining control over the Simplon road, but Castlereagh refused to abet his design and it was regretfully abandoned. In 1819 Metternich carried his imperial master off for a triumphal progress through Italy. They were accompanied by Sir George Gordon, whose reports to Castlereagh throw a lurid light both upon the condition of Italy and upon the hopes and fears of Metternich. The Austrian minister could not conceal his disappointment at the reception accorded to him and his master in the cities they visited. French influence was evidently predominant in the Papal States, and on every side Metternich detected or imagined traces of Russian intrigue. Gordon clearly thought that 'the perfect Paul Pry found out more than ever happened'. 'Phantoms', he wrote, 'are conjured up and magnified in the dark, which probably, if exposed to light, would sink into insignificance.'[1] Metternich's idea of a federation of all the Italian States under the presidency of Austria seemed to the same careful reporter entirely chimerical.

'If there existed', he wrote, 'anywhere in Italy a regard for Austria of this nature it would perhaps be due to the idea that she marches with the British colours: but it is on the contrary to be feared that the strongest discontent may be traced in the very parts of Italy which are subjected to her.'[1]

As to the accuracy of the last observation, there may be some doubt. Anyway, it was not in Lombardy but in Naples that impatience with the policy of the restoration first manifested itself in open insurrection.

The Two Sicilies

Not that Ferdinand IV was unpopular among the mass of his Neapolitan subjects. On the contrary, cowardly and indolent as the King was, the Neapolitans were well content with a régime which, if 'unenlightened', was mild and tolerant of the abuses cherished by the people. 'Quiet and prosperous' was the description given by A'Court, the British minister at Naples on the eve of the 'Revolution', the outbreak of which astonished him. 'A kingdom in the highest degree flourishing and happy under the mildest of governments, and by no means oppressed by the weight of taxation, crumbles before a handful of insurgents that half a battalion of good soldiers would have crushed in an

[1] Webster, *Foreign Policy of Castlereagh*, p. 184.

instant.' Such was A'Court's observation at the time, and its accuracy was confirmed by the event.

There were, however, centres of disaffection of which A'Court was ignorant or perhaps made too light. There were some who genuinely regretted the order and efficiency characteristic of the Napoleonic régime. There were Muratist officers who resented the idea of being placed under the command of an Austrian General (Nugent),[1] there were more who, from one motive or another, joined the *Carbonari* (charcoal-burners) or other secret societies which had lately sprung up in different parts of Italy, and particularly in Naples.

The Carbonari

The origin and character of the *Carbonari* have been hotly disputed. The society was denounced by the Papacy as allied to freemasonry, with the ritual and objects of which it had something in common. As organized or re-organized in the Italy of the early nineteenth century it set before its members two supreme objects: the independence of Italy, and constitutional liberties in the several states.

Insurrection in Naples

It was, however, the success of the revolution in Madrid, and the restoration of the Spanish Constitution of 1812, which gave unity to the several elements of disaffection in Naples, and encouraged the hope that what one Bourbon had conceded in Madrid might be extorted from another Bourbon in Naples. Besides, had not Lord William Bentinck secured for the Sicilians in 1813 the blessing of Parliamentary Government on the English model? How far an 'English' Constitution was calculated to heal the wounds of Sicilians in 1813, or of Neapolitans in 1820, were not questions which troubled the leaders of the Neapolitan insurrection any more than they troubled a typical English Whig. Lord William, as he subsequently proved in India,[2] was a sentimental soldier, with a touching but undiscriminating belief in the virtues of English 'liberty' as a

[1] Count Nugent, though an Irishman, was a General (later Field-Marshal) in the Austrian army.

[2] First Governor-General of India, 1833–5.

panacea, under all conditions of time and place, for every political disease. 'Liberty', however, is not a drug to be prescribed, but a plant of slow growth demanding careful cultivation.

Ferdinand of the Two Sicilies promptly conceded the demands of the insurgents, fervently protesting his gratitude to the Almighty, who had granted him, in his old age, the opportunity of conferring so great a benefit upon his people. A few days later the concession was ratified in the most solemn manner. The King, having heard Mass, approached the altar and, in presence of his Court and ministers, took an oath of fidelity to the Constitution. Then, fixing his eyes upon the Cross, he cried: 'Omnipotent God, who lookest into the heart of man and can discern the future, if I lie, or if one day I should prove faithless to my oath, do Thou at this moment strike me dead.' The King then kissed the Bible, the oath was taken by his sons, and the new Constitution was publicly proclaimed.

But it was soon made manifest that the seat of authority was not at Naples but in Vienna. Metternich, greatly alarmed by the revolutionary outbreaks in southern Europe, and especially in Naples, summoned a conference of the allies to meet at Troppau, for the purpose of considering the situation and determining the policy to be adopted by the Allied Powers. At Troppau the Czar Alexander made the final and complete renunciation of all the 'liberal' principles he had formerly professed. 'To-day', he said, 'I deplore all that I have said and done between the years 1814 and 1818.' There was to be no more dallying with revolution, no coquetting with *Carbonari* or other secret societies. Henceforward the Czar was the sworn ally, or rather the abject slave, of Metternich.

Castlereagh's attitude

Lord Castlereagh declined to attend the conference or to send a British plenipotentiary, though he allowed his brother, Lord Stewart, British Ambassador at Vienna, to go to Troppau, as an 'observer'. Castlereagh, like Metternich, took a serious view of the Neapolitan insurrection, which, unlike the Spanish revolution, seemed to him to be devoid of any reasonable excuse. He recognized, moreover, that by the terms of the Treaties, Austria had the right, if she was not under an obligation, to suppress it. But if Austria intervened to protect her own interests, 'her plans must be limited to objects of self-defence'. Even so, she must act alone and on her sole responsibility; not as the mandatory of the Allied Powers. The Czar Alexander, on the contrary, insisted that if there was intervention it must be the act of the European Concert, not of Austria alone. But Castlereagh stood firm. He adhered to the principles and policy laid down by his master, Pitt. Great Britain would fight the Revolution if, like the French Revolution in 1792, it became aggressive, and attempted to impose revolutionary doctrines on other nations. A revolution in a particular State was a different matter. Great Britain could not, consistently with her own traditions, deny the right of any individual nation to change the form of its government by a revolution; but such a revolution must not be allowed to threaten the independence or security of a neighbour.

The Protocol of Troppau

The firm refusal of Great Britain to assent to concerted intervention whether in Naples or elsewhere, virtually broke up the 'Moral Pentarchy' which had been established at Aix-la-Chapelle. But the original members of the 'Holy Alliance', nothing daunted, promulgated on 19 November 1820 the Protocol of Troppau.

This document contained a startling revelation of the fundamental doctrines of the Holy Alliance, according to the revised version.

'States [it declared] which have undergone a change of government due to revolution, the result of which threatens other States, *ipso facto* cease to be members of the European Alliance, and remain excluded from it until their situation gives guarantee for legal order and stability. . . . If, owing to such alterations, immediate danger threatens other States, the Powers bind themselves by peaceful means, or, if need be, by arms, to bring back the guilty State into the bosom of the Great Alliance.'

Castlereagh's Reply

Despite a further explanation of their motives issued by the Holy Allies on 8 December, the Government of Great Britain declined to make itself a party to measures not only inadmissible in themselves, but 'in direct repugnance to the fundamental laws of this country'. As to the Neapolitan Revolution, the British Government had already 'expressed their strong disapprobation of the mode and circumstances under which that Revolution was understood to have been effected', but they did not consider themselves as justified in interfering. 'No Government', the Circular proceeded, 'can be more prepared than the British Government is, to uphold the right of any State to interfere where their own immediate security or essential interests, are seriously endangered'; they admitted the *individual* right of Austria to interfere in Naples, but denounced the principles enunciated at Troppau on the ground that they 'would inevitably sanction . . . a much more frequent and extensive interference in the internal transactions of States than . . . can be reconcilable either with the general interest or with the efficient authority and dignity of independent Sovereigns'.[1]

The effect produced by Castlereagh's masterly memorandum, alike on the Holy Allies, on other Powers, and in particular on the small States of Germany and Italy, was immense. Nevertheless, Metternich went on his way. The Conference adjourned from Troppau to Leybach, a small town in Austrian Carniola; to Leybach Ferdinand was summoned to give an account, at the judgement-seat of the Holy Allies, of his dealings with his turbulent subjects. The wretched king repudiated his solemn oath, protesting that all his concessions had been wrung from him by force, and were consequently of no effect. Sentence was duly delivered, and Austria, as the executive of the European police, was entrusted with the congenial task of restoring order in southern Italy. Fifty thousand white-coats were marched into Naples; the Neapolitan troops ran away; the King was restored; the Constitution torn up; stern

[1] *British and Foreign State Papers, 1820–1821*, iv. 1160–2.

vengeance was executed upon all who had taken part in the Revolution. The victims are said to have numbered eight hundred. Four years later (3 January 1828), King Ferdinand's long reign of sixty-five years was brought to an end by his death.

Insurrection in Piedmont

The insurrectionary movement of Naples was re-echoed, though confusedly, in the north. Piedmont was, as we have seen, less dependent than any other of the Italian States on the whims of Metternich. But nowhere was the reaction against the Napoleonic régime more complete. The Queen, Maria Theresa, was an Austrian princess; the King, Victor Emmanuel I, a strong clericalist. The Jesuits were recalled, their privileges restored, and education replaced wholly in their hands; the administrative system of Napoleon was abolished; all his functionaries were dismissed; and the old régime with all its abuses and corruptions was resuscitated.

It is not therefore remarkable that in this most reactionary of Italian States the Carbonari should have been exceptionally powerful. The members of that society were, however, recruited chiefly from the ranks of the nobles, the educated *bourgeoisie*, and the younger officers of the army. The Piedmontese movement was primarily directed against Austrian domination in Italy; though liberal, it was not democratic, least of all was there in it anything of hostility towards the Sardinian Monarchy, to which all classes in the triune kingdom were sincerely devoted. 'Our hearts are faithful to the King, but we wish to deliver him from perfidious counsels. War against Austria; a Constitution on the model of that granted to Spain—these are the wishes of the people.' The profession was perfectly sincere; but the old King Victor Emmanuel, though not personally opposed to liberal reform was too deeply committed to Metternich; his Queen was not merely an Austrian in blood but also in convictions; and, accordingly, on the first sign of revolution, Victor Emmanuel resigned the throne to his brother Charles Felix.

The revolution broke out on 10 March 1821, in the garrison at Alessandria, whence it spread to Turin. When the King abdicated Charles Felix was absent. A regency was accordingly set up in favour of his cousin and heir-presumptive, Charles Albert, Prince of Savoy-Carignano, a young man of twenty-three. As Charles Felix, though married, was childless, and as the old King Victor Emmanuel had no male issue, Charles Albert had been designated as heir and married to a daughter of the Archduke of Tuscany. Brought up among Jacobins and Bonapartists, the young prince had already given evidence of liberal, not to say democratic, convictions, and Metternich had consequently endeavoured to exclude him from the throne and to bring the sub-alpine kingdom under Austrian influence. Both objects were to be accomplished by marrying the eldest daughter of Victor Emmanuel to her uncle Francis, Duke of Modena, and getting the Salic law, then in force in Piedmont, set aside in their favour. The marriage took place, but Metternich's project was revealed by the indiscretion of Duke Francis, and the rights of Charles Albert were maintained.

Naturally, therefore, he shared with his prospective subjects their impatience of Austrian hegemony; but he had no mind to be involved in conspiracy, and revealed to the King such of the plans of the conspirators as had been communicated to him. Nevertheless, as Regent, he proclaimed the Constitution which they demanded.

From the first, however, the insurrection hopelessly miscarried: the Lombard Liberals were unready and failed to co-operate; the Piedmontese leaders were divided; Charles Felix on his return from Modena repudiated the action of the Regent and sent him into exile in Tuscany; an Austrian army, with the assent of Charles Felix, crossed the Ticino, and an almost bloodless skirmish at Novara sufficed to crush the conspiracy. Some of the leaders were condemned to death, but all managed to escape, and Piedmont settled down into a political apathy, hardly disturbed by the events of 1830–1, and not dispelled until the much more serious movement of 1848.

Milan

Upon Lombardy, despite the fact that the liberal movement led by Count F. Confalonieri had failed to materialize, Metternich poured out the vials of his wrath. The Carbonari of Milan had been in correspondence with their fellows in Turin. That was enough for Metternich. He had already immured the poet Silvio Pellico in the fortress-prison of the Spielberg. After the failure of the Piedmontese insurrection Pellico was joined in captivity by several of the noblest sons of Lombardy, including Confalonieri, whose life was spared only on the intercession of his courageous and beautiful wife.

The sporadic insurrections of 1820–1 had served to reveal on the one hand the persistence of the ideas generated by the Revolutionary and Napoleonic era, and, on the other, the weakness of isolated conspiracies. They proved also that revolutionary ideas, though deeply embedded in the minds of an enlightened minority, had got no real hold on the mass of the people, who had little interest in the assertion of liberty, and had not the faintest conception of national unity. Most of all they testified to the vigilance and power of Metternich. The insurrections were suppressed with ease; the Austrian yoke was again riveted on the Italian States; every symptom of independence, much more of revolt, was promptly crushed, and individuals who ventured to give expression to the idea of Italian independence or Italian unity were mercilessly punished. What wonder that in those dark days a dull despair fell on many of the bravest of Italian patriots! But not on all.

> Italia! when thy name was but a name,
> When to desire thee was a vain desire,
> When to achieve thee was impossible,
> When to love thee was madness, when to live
> For thee was the extravagance of fools,
> When to die for thee was to fling away
> Life for a shadow—in those darkest days
> Were some who never swerved, who lived and strove
> And suffered for thee, and attained their end! [1]

[1] Mrs. Hamilton King, 'The Disciples'.

Mazzini

Among those who 'lived and strove and suffered' was a young student at Genoa, destined to play a great part as the prophet of the Italian *Risorgimento*, Giuseppe Mazzini. Born at Genoa in 1805, Mazzini, like Cavour and Garibaldi, was a Sardinian subject. Even in childhood he was impressed by the misery and degradation of his country. In his early schooldays, as throughout his life, it was his morbid fancy to wear nothing but black. 'In the midst of the noisy tumultuous life of the scholars around me I was', he writes, 'sombre and absorbed, and appeared like one suddenly grown old. I childishly determined to dress always in black, fancying myself in mourning for my country.' It was after the failure of 1821 that Mazzini first became conscious of the mission of his life. While walking one sunny day with his mother and a friend in the streets of Genoa they were addressed, so he tells us, by 'a tall black-bearded man with a severe and energetic countenance and a fiery glance that I have never since forgotten. He held out a handkerchief towards us merely saying "for the Refugees of Italy".' The incident—simple as it was—made a profound impression on Mazzini's sympathetic spirit.

'The idea of an existing wrong in my own country against which it was a duty to struggle and the thought that I too must bear my part in that struggle, flashed before my mind on that day for the first time, never again to leave me. The remembrance of those refugees, many of whom became my friends in after-life, pursued me wherever I went by day and mingled with my dreams by night. I would have given I know not what to follow them. I began collecting names and facts and studied as best I might the records of that heroic struggle, seeking to fathom the causes of its failure.'

Shortly after the completion of his university career, Mazzini joined the ranks of the Carbonari, and thus embarked on a career of political agitation. To him, as to many men of similar temperament, such a step was a great sacrifice. He had looked forward from childhood to a literary career.

A thousand visions of historical dramas and romances floated before my mental eye—artistic images that caressed my spirit as visions of gentle maidens soothe the soul of the lonely hearted. The natural bias of my mind was very different from that which has been forced upon me by the times in which I have lived and the shame of our degradation.'

But Mazzini saw, clearly enough, that the literary issues then at stake, as between Classicists and Romanticists, important as to him they seemed, must be postponed to the solution of the vital political problem.

'Without a country and without liberty we might perhaps produce some prophets of art but no *vital* art. Therefore it was better for us to consecrate our lives to the solution of the problem—Are we to have a country? and turn at once to the political question. If we were successful the art of Italy would bloom and flourish over our graves.'

Were the Italians to have a country? That was the problem which confronted Mazzini and his contemporaries, and to the solution of which many of them sacrificed career, liberty, and even life. It is impossible to defend the means which they were compelled to adopt for the attainment of their end. Mazzini himself heartily disliked the methods of many of his associates, and in particular, the whole machinery of secret societies. But if Mazzini and his associates are to be fairly judged it is essential to realize the conditions under which, in the years between 1815 and 1848, all patriotic Italians had to work.

It is death
To speak the very name of Italy
To this Italian people.

After the abortive insurrections of 1821–2, the surface of Italian politics remained for nearly a decade unbroken. Nor did political reaction, however galling to the ardent spirits of Italian patriots, obstruct material progress. The Duke of Argyll, a man of strong liberal sympathies, was among those who bore testimony to the prosperity enjoyed by the Austrian provinces in Italy at that period. 'If ever', he wrote, 'the dominion of one race over another seemed justified by at least material prosperity it was the dominion of the Austrian Empire over its Italian provinces . . . the whole face of the people and the country was the face of pleasantness and peace.'[1]

The 'pleasantness and peace' observed by the British statesman had, however, to be purchased at a price: the complete abandonment, if not of patriotic aspirations, at least of political activity. The name of Italy might not even be whispered.

The Revolutions of 1831

The 'July Revolution' which finally disposed of 'Legitimacy' in France reacted powerfully upon Italy. But only in Central Italy did discontent reach the point of open insurrection. In the Papal States and Modena revolution broke out at the beginning of February 1831. From Bologna the movement spread rapidly to Forlì, Ravenna, and other towns in the Romagna. At Ferrara, despite the presence of an Austrian garrison, the functionaries of the Pope were expelled and a provisional government was set up. Within a fortnight the whole of Umbria and the Marches had followed suit. Only in the Patrimony of St. Peter did Papal authority withstand the shock. The new Pope Gregory XVI, only elected to the Papal chair on 1 February, made some trifling concessions to popular feeling, but at the same time applied to Austria for assistance.

In Modena an insurrection occurred on 5 February, and Duke Francis fled for safety into Austrian territory, carrying off with him Ciro Menotti, the leader of the Modenese liberals. After the Duke's flight one of the citizens, Biagio Nardi was appointed Dictator and proclaimed the unity of Italy. But the rest of Italy did not heed him. The Austrians marched troops into the disaffected districts, and before the end of March had restored the authority of the Duke in his Duchy and that of the Pope throughout his Temporal dominions. Menotti was brought home to Modena and hanged. Parma had followed the example of

[1] *Autobiography*, i. 211.

its neighbour, and the ex-Empress Marie Louise, despite her personal popularity, had thought it prudent to withdraw to Piacenza. She also was in due course restored under the protection of Austrian troops, and peace once more reigned in her not unhappy Principality. Pope Gregory XVI made large promises of reform to his subjects, but nothing was done, and as soon as the Austrian troops evacuated the Papal States (July 1831) insurrections broke out afresh. Again the Austrians returned, with the intention of occupying Ancona; but at this point a further complication entered into the Italian problem.

France and the Papacy

Louis Philippe, on his accession, had ostentatiously proclaimed to Europe the doctrine of non-intervention. But the repeated intrusions of Austrian troops into the Papal States aroused the susceptibilities of the French, and before the Austrians reached Ancona it had been occupied by a French force (February 1832). Metternich declined to abandon his role of protector of the Pope. Louis Philippe preferred that the Austrians should go first, and so for six years (1832–8) the two armies confronted each other in the Papal States. A collision between the rival protectors was avoided, but neither the Papal States nor Italy as a whole derived any advantage from the occupation, nor from the jealous patronage of the two Great Powers.

Mazzini

Nevertheless, the patriotic movement made considerable progress throughout Italy. This was primarily due to the new spirit infused into Italian politics by the organization founded at this time by Mazzini.

Shortly after the July Revolution of 1830 Mazzini, having been entrapped by a government spy into the performance of some trifling commission for the Carbonari, was arrested and imprisoned in the fortress of Savona on the western Riviera. 'The Government were not fond', so his father was informed, 'of young men of talent the subject of whose musings were unknown to them.' After six months' imprisonment Mazzini was acquitted of conspiracy, but nevertheless was exiled from Italy.

Early in the year 1831 Charles Felix, King of Sardinia, died at Turin and was succeeded by Charles Albert. The accession of a king who, in earlier days, had coquetted with the Carbonari, naturally aroused the hopes of Italian Liberals, and from Marseilles, where he had found refuge, Mazzini promptly addressed to him his memorable 'Letter to the King'.

'The people', it declared, 'are no longer to be quieted by a few concessions. They seek the recognition of those rights of humanity which have been withheld from them for ages. They demand laws and liberty, independence and union. Divided, dismembered, and oppressed, they have neither name nor country. They have heard themselves stigmatized by the foreigner as a helot nation. They have seen free men visit their country and declare it the land of the dead. They have drained the cup of slavery to the dregs, but they have sworn never to fill it again.'

Let the King champion the cause not merely of Piedmont but of Italy.

'All Italy waits for one word—one only—to make herself yours. Proffer this word to her. Place yourself at the head of the nation and write on your banner: "Union, Liberty, Independence." Proclaim the liberty of thought. Declare yourself the vindicator, the interpreter of popular rights, the regenerator of all Italy. Liberate her from the Barbarians. Build up the future; give your name to a century: begin a new era from your day. . . . Select the way that accords with the desire of the nation; maintain it unalterably; be firm and await your time; you have the victory in your hands. Sire, on this condition we bind ourselves round you, we proffer you our lives, we will lead to your banner the little states of Italy. We will paint to our brothers the advantages that are born of union; we will prosecute national subscription, patriotic gifts; we will preach the word that creates armies. . . . Unite us, Sire, and we shall conquer.'

Whether Mazzini's appeal was wholly sincere is doubtful. Sincere or not the King was deaf to it; his only answer was an order that if Mazzini attempted to cross the frontier into Italy he should be instantly arrested.

The attitude of Charles Albert was a bitter disappointment to Mazzini and his associates, and a plot was formed for his assassination, to which Mazzini was unhappily a party. In August 1832 Mazzini was ordered to quit French territory, but for a whole year he continued to live in Marseilles, eluding the vigilance of the French police. In 1833 he took refuge in Switzerland, and in 1834 joined in the ill-starred and abortive raid into Savoy—an enterprise which contributed to damage still further Mazzini's reputation among moderate Liberals. In 1836 even the Swiss Government felt compelled to deny him further hospitality, and in the following year he found, like most political refugees, a home in England. England became to him, as he himself wrote, 'almost a second country where I found the lasting consolation of affection in a life embittered by delusions and destitute of all joy'.

From England he continued to direct the affairs of his *Young Italy* Association.

IV

YOUNG ITALY

The Neo-Guelphs and Pope Pius IX

Mazzini IN the history of every great movement there arrives a moment when the supreme need is for a man inspired with lofty enthusiasm and possessed of the gift of inspiring others. After the failures of 1821, followed by the still more pitiable fiascoes of 1831, such a moment had evidently arrived in the history of the Italian *Risorgimento*.

And with the moment there had come the man. Mazzini's repute has suffered from the extravagant—almost hysterical—eulogies of contemporary disciples. He was not impeccable; he had on the contrary his full share of human frailties: he was vain and self-conscious, even something of a *poseur*. What man with the histrionic sense is wholly devoid of these weaknesses? He may have lacked physical courage: his enemies averred that he sought safe shelter in London while he sent brave youths like the Bandieras to their death in Italy. The same accusation has been made against others who have not lacked prophetic fire. Obviously Mazzini did not possess the physical equipment of a Garibaldi. Still less was he a Cavour. No sane critic has claimed for him the gift of constructive statesmanship. Few prophets possess it. Thomas Carlyle, a friend of Mazzini, could never have carried a Reform Bill through Parliament. It is doubtful whether Cobden could have carried the repeal of the Corn Laws. Certainly, Bright could not. But what Italy supremely needed in the early days of the *Risorgimento* was a prophet. Literary men of high gifts she possessed, as we shall see presently, in abundance. Cesare Balbo and Massimo d'Azeglio, even Gioberti, made more practical contributions to the achievement of Italian unity than did Mazzini. But Mazzini had a gift denied to them, though common to all the greatest among the sons of men—the gift of a magnetic personality. It is this which differentiates the greatest from the great: it is this which differentiated Chatham from Walpole; Nelson from Abercromby; Napoleon from Carnot; Disraeli from Peel. The greatest have often more frailties than the great. Chatham was a self-conscious rhetorician, but in Macaulay's glowing words, 'The ardour of his soul had set the whole kingdom on fire. It inflamed every soldier who dragged the cannon up the heights of Quebec, and every sailor who boarded the French ships among the rocks of Brittany.' Nelson and Napoleon had grave faults of character, but they won their resounding victories less because they were superb strategists or skilled above others in the technique of tactics, than because they could make men follow them to the death. Peel might persuade; Disraeli could inspire.

Mazzini, then, was a great prophet, gifted with that personal magnetism which he could communicate by voice and even more effectively by pen. Consequently the foundation of his *Young Italy* Association, despite all the blunders and maybe the crimes of the associates, marks the turning-point in the history of the Italian *Risorgimento*.

His Programme

Ever since his first imprisonment at Savona Mazzini had been pondering over a scheme for establishing a society which should supplant the secret societies with which in these latter years Italy was honeycombed. Mazzini mistrusted their aims and disliked their methods. Their creed was purely negative; they were the sworn foes of tyranny, the courageous and determined opponents of the existing régime in Italy. That régime they were resolved to overthrow, but they looked no further. In a word they had no constructive policy.

Young Italy

This lack of an inspiring creed, a vivifying faith, Mazzini sought to supply in his Association of Young Italy. The Carbonari movement had failed, as it deserved to fail, though not perhaps for the particular reasons to which Mazzini attributed its failure. To Mazzini's thinking it had leaned too much on the support of the educated, influential classes. 'Revolutions', he says, 'must be made by the people and for the people. This is our word, it sums up our whole doctrine; it is our science, our religion; our heart's affection.' But the Carbonari were not only too aristocratic: they lacked the machinery for simultaneous and concerted action. Worst of all: they had no programme, no faith, no lofty ideal. The first duty of the new association was to declare war on the existing idolatry of material interests; to convince the Italian people that 'the sole path to victory was through sacrifice, constancy in sacrifice'. They must begin with the education of the people. Italy was materialist, Machiavellian, believing in the initiative of France and seeking rather to emancipate and ameliorate the condition of her separate States than to constitute herself a nation. The country was regardless of high principles and ready to accept any form of government, any mode of assistance, or any man brought forward with a promise of relieving her immediate sufferings. 'On my side I believed . . . that the great problem of the day was a religious problem.' This sentence reveals the strength of the man and gives the clue to his character,—his passionate ardour; his unswerving faith, his lofty idealism—an idealism which revolted from the use of means other than those which he himself selected. And it was in this spirit that Mazzini himself drew up the statutes of the new Association.

'Young Italy is a brotherhood of Italians who believe in a law of Progress and Duty and are convinced that Italy is destined to become one nation. . . . They join this Association in the firm intent of consecrating both thought and action to the great aim of reconstructing Italy as one independent sovereign nation of free men and equals.'

The means by which the end was to be attained were—'education and insurrection to be adopted simultaneously'. The expulsion of the hated Austrians was the first prerequisite. Since to avoid a war, bloody and inexorable, was impossible, the sooner it was declared the better. Such a war must be waged by Italians and for Italy. No reliance must be placed on foreign governments, or on the efforts of diplomacy. All thoughts of Federalism, of Independence without Unity must be laid aside. 'Federalism would cancel the great mission of Italy in the world.' *Young Italy*, therefore, is Unitarian. 'Never', said Mazzini to his followers, 'never rise in any other name than of Italy and of all Italy.' Mazzini himself was by conviction a stern Republican, and the members of *Young Italy* were sworn to educate the Italian people in that doctrine. But there was to be no forcing of the deliberate conviction of the people. The ultimate form of government, when once unity had been achieved, was to be left to the people's deliberate choice. The Republicanism of Mazzini was of a truly liberal sort. 'We shall bow the head', say the statutes, 'and accept any form of government chosen by universal suffrage, because it is the duty of individual opinion to give way before the voice of the nation.' Such in rough outline was the political programme of Mazzini carefully elaborated in the statutes of *Young Italy*. Those statutes will be found in the collected edition of his works.

The effect produced by this propaganda was immediate and profound. Men flocked in their thousands to join the new Association, which quickly became dominant from end to end of Italy.

'It was', says Mazzini, 'the triumph of *principles*; the bare fact that in so short a space of time a handful of young men, themselves sprung from the people, unknown, without means . . . found themselves thus rapidly at the head of an association sufficiently powerful to concentrate against it the alarmed persecution of seven Governments is, I think, in itself enough to show that the banner they had raised was the banner of truth.'

Amazing, however, as was the progress made by the *Young Italy* Associations, and great as was the influence which Mazzini, though an exile, began to exercise, the liberals, in the several States of Italy were far from unanimity in acceptance of Mazzini's programme.

The Neo-Guelphs

As we approach the fateful year of revolution it is, indeed, possible to discern the gradual formation of at least two other powerful parties which, while sharing Mazzini's enthusiasm for Italian independence, for personal and political liberty, and for closer union among the Italian States, if not for their complete fusion, sought to attain these objects by methods widely different from those recommended by Mazzini.

One of these parties looked for leadership to a reformed and reforming Papacy; the other looked to the House of Savoy and the hegemony of Piedmont.

The Neo-Guelphs, as the former party came to be called, hoped to see the Pope put himself at the head of a patriotic movement, encourage, by precept and example, liberal reform in the component States, and bring them together in an Italian federation under his own presidency. The leaders of both parties were, it is significant to observe, subjects of the King of Sardinia, as indeed were Mazzini, Cavour, and Garibaldi.

Gioberti, 1801–52

Of these pioneers in the work of Italian independence perhaps the most important was Vincenzo Gioberti. Born at Turin in 1801, Gioberti was educated for the priesthood, to which he was ordained in 1825. He was appointed chaplain to King Albert, but became deeply interested in the political movement, and in 1833 was arrested on a charge of conspiracy. He was never brought to trial, but, like Mazzini, was nevertheless expelled from Italy. He spent the next fifteen years in Paris and Brussels. At Brussels he published (1843) his famous and immensely influential book *Il Primato Morale e Civile degli Italiani*. No better contemporary estimate of the significance of this work is to be found than that in the *Recollections* of Marco Minghetti.

'The book', writes Minghetti, 'seemed to some an extravagance, to others a revelation. The truth is that while many of its ideas were peculiar to the author and partook of his character, his studies, and his profession, the substance of it responded to a sentiment which had been slowly developing in the minds of Italians. The idea of nationality had spread far and wide through many channels, open and secret, and the desire of a great and free country had taken possession of the majority of the younger men; but the methods hitherto employed had proved so inefficient that weariness and disgust had followed . . . the mystic declamations of Mazzini . . . his inciting of others to insurrection and murder while he remained safely in London . . . all these things showed that the time had come to try another method more serious, more practical and surer. . . . The purpose of the book was to prove that Italy, though entirely without repute among foreign nations, contained in itself all the conditions of moral and political revival; that there was no need, in order to effect this, of revolutions or foreign models or intervention; *unity* and *independence* might be attained by a Confederation of the various States under the presidency of the Pope; while *liberty* could be achieved by internal reforms effected by their respective Princes in the several States.'

Thus might Italy once more assume the moral and political leadership of the world.

To peoples who had not for long centuries heard the name Italian, or thought of Italy as one, this was indeed a trumpet-call. But although, as we shall see, the election of Pope Pius IX in 1846 seemed to give substance to the dream of Gioberti, events were to prove that Metternich judged the situation more accurately than did Gioberti.

'A liberal Pope', said Metternich, 'is a contradiction in terms.' Moreover, Gioberti overrated both the willingness and the ability of the petty princes to effect internal reforms. The naked truth was that as long as Metternich ruled Italy from Vienna neither independence nor liberty could be achieved in the peninsula. Mazzini was right: the expulsion of the Austrians was the first essential step. Nevertheless, the appeal of Gioberti to the idea of an *Italian* patriotism fell on attentive ears. By close argument, by appeals to history and geography, he claimed to show that 'Italy alone has the qualities required to become the chief of nations, and that though to-day she has almost completely lost that chiefship, it is in her power to recover it'.

The first years of Pius IX's Papacy seemed to enthusiastic Neo-Guelphs to justify up to the hilt Gioberti's faith; but his dreams were cruelly dissipated by the events of

1848–9. Gioberti himself, having received an amnesty from Charles Albert in 1846, was enthusiastically welcomed back to Turin in 1848, and became for a few months Prime Minister under the new Parliamentary Constitution. But with the new King Victor Emmanuel II (succeeded March 1849) he had grave differences, and though serving in the Cabinet for a time without portfolio, he accepted a mission to Paris and died there in 1852. Like many other philosophers Gioberti failed when put to the practical test of administrative responsibility.

Count Césare Balbo, 1789–1853

More practical, more clear-sighted, and not less enthusiastic than Gioberti was Count Césare Balbo. His father belonged to the stiff Piedmontese nobility, his mother was a d'Azeglio. From 1808 to 1814 Césare served the Napoleonic Empire in Florence, Rome, Paris, and also in Illyria. On the restoration of the House of Savoy in Piedmont he joined the Piedmontese army, but was employed chiefly on diplomatic missions to London and Paris. Though he disapproved of the insurrection of 1821 he was suspected of complicity and was for a short time sent into exile; nor, on his return, could he obtain political employment. He determined, therefore, to serve his country with the pen, and in 1843 he published at Paris his famous work *Delle Speranze d'Italia*.

Like Gioberti, Balbo rejected the idea of an Italian Kingdom; like him, he wanted a federation of the Italian States; like Mazzini (with whom he had little else in common), but unlike Gioberti, he perceived that neither internal reform nor political federation was feasible until the Austrians had been expelled from Italy. With rare foresight he proposed that the Hapsburg Empire should seek and find compensation in the Balkans. The Ottoman Empire, he believed, was on the point of dissolution: partition, therefore, was inevitable. Let the death of the Turkish Empire provide the means for the rebirth of Italy. Whether Balbo looked to Rome or Turin to provide the president of his Federation is still a disputed point, so cautious and veiled is his appeal. There can be no dispute, however, as to the means by which independence was to be obtained. Italy must win its independence by strenuous effort and purity of aim. 'A nation of twenty millions is invincible if it has union and character. But there must be no more lounging indifference; Italy must cease to be "the land of the olive and the orange": each man must do his duty at his post.'

Like Gioberti, Balbo held that a Federation was the only possible form of government for Italy; but Federation could not be achieved so long as Italy was ruled from Vienna. 'Without national independence other good things are as naught.' The first step, then, must be the expulsion of the Austrians.

d'Azeglio, 1798–1866

Was it possible that the Papacy would co-operate in that essential work? No one was better qualified to answer that question than Massimo d'Azeglio. D'Azeglio was born at Turin in 1798 of a noble Piedmontese family. After the restoration of Pius VII in 1814 his father was sent on a special mission to Rome, and Massimo went with him. Rome inspired the impressionable youth with a love of art, and for some years he made his home in the Papal city. After his father's death (1834) he betook himself to Milan and there got first-hand knowledge of Austrian methods of administration. In Milan he lived for nearly twelve years, and having married the daughter of Manzoni, the novelist, he abandoned painting for literature. In the autumn of 1845 he undertook an unofficial mission to the Romagna, and was consequently able to describe at first hand the brutalities which followed on the suppression of the insurrection at Rimini (September 1845). The Papal Provinces had indeed for some years been in a condition of chronic insurrection. Nowhere in Italy was the government more incompetent or more corrupt.

Even Metternich recognized the fact. 'Among the numerous difficulties', he wrote, 'to which the condition of the countries under Papal rule daily give rise, undoubtedly the most insuperable arises from the fact that the government has not the faintest notion how to govern.'

That was the brutal truth, and it was revealed to the world in the book published by d'Azeglio at Florence in 1846. *Gli Ultimi Casi di Romagna* (*Recent Events in the Romagna*) is hardly more than a pamphlet, but its publication by a man in d'Azeglio's position produced a profound impression. He was no revolutionary fanatic: his mission to the Romagna had been undertaken with the hope of inducing his liberal friends to conduct their agitation within the limits of legality. Pietro Renzi's rising at Rimini proved the vanity of d'Azeglio's hopes and proclaimed the failure of his mission. But it provided a text for his pamphlet.

'I Casi di Romagna', says Minghetti, 'was the first practical exposition of the programme then first adopted—the substitution of public, peaceful, serious, courageous discussion of our affairs, for secret societies and plots. The book . . . condemned the insurrection of Rimini as imprudent, ineffective, disastrous, but at the same time it clearly revealed the evils of ecclesiastical rule.'

The Tuscan Government, not less than other Italian governments, recognized the force of d'Azeglio's reasoning, but they nevertheless expelled the author from Tuscany.

His expulsion did not diminish the influence of his book. It was read from end to end of Italy and far beyond its borders. It even penetrated to the Vatican. Towards the Papacy d'Azeglio was entirely respectful: he believed that Italian unity could not be achieved without its co-operation; but for the leadership of the Italian *Risorgimento* he looked not to Rome, but to Piedmont. Thus d'Azeglio more than any other man prepared the way for the Piedmontese hegemony. Before the leadership was definitely assumed by the House of Savoy, an event of resounding significance had happened in Rome.

Pope Pius IX

In 1846 the old Pope Gregory XVI died and in his place was elected Cardinal Mastai Ferretti, best known to history as Pius IX. The new Pope, destined to wear the Papal diadem for thirty-two years, was born at Senigaglia in 1792 and was therefore only fifty-four at the time of his election. Though subject from childhood to attacks of epilepsy he lived to the age of eighty-six, and if he was not the greatest of modern Popes his reign is certainly the most memorable in the recent annals of the Papacy. His administration of the See of Imola had earned him the reputation of a liberal reformer, and as such, greatly to the chagrin of Metternich, he was elected to the Papal chair. A liberal in the modern sense he was not; perhaps no Pope could be; but he was a reformer of the eighteenth-century type. He desired to see his dominions honestly and efficiently administered. Moreover, he was an Italian patriot: he would gladly have seen Italy rid of the foreigners—could the Papacy have been defended without their help. Rome and the Papal States were, on his accession, governed wholly by ecclesiastics; and no government in Italy—not even that of Naples—was worse. The administration was egregiously extravagant and grossly corrupt; the courts of law were wholly medieval in methods and procedure; justice was a byword; there was no curb on immorality, but the strictest censorship on printing and the press. Rome surpassed even Naples in profligacy and mendicancy, and when the Czar Nicholas visited the city in 1845 he is said to have been greeted by an army of 17,000 beggars.

The election of Pius IX was hailed with the greatest enthusiasm by Italian liberals. They saw in him, as Mr. Thayer has well said, 'the Messiah whose coming had been foretold by the prophet Gioberti'.[1] Even Mazzini shared these hopes and wrote to Pius IX, as he had written to Charles Albert, pointing out the great opportunity which opened before him, and urging him to redeem it. Garibaldi wrote from Montevideo offering the new Pope his services and his sword.

Reforms

Nor did the first acts of the reign disappoint expectations. An amnesty was offered (with few exceptions) to political prisoners, and refugees were permitted to return; the disabilities of the Jews were removed, and Cardinal Gizzi, the idol of the Roman populace, was appointed

[1] *Dawn of Italian Independence.*

Secretary of State: unofficial newspapers were for the first time permitted to be published in Rome (March 1847), and a month later a *Consulta*, formed of persons selected by the Pope from panels nominated by each of the Legations, was appointed. In June of the same year a Council of Ministers, all of them, it is true, ecclesiastics, was appointed, and in July the Pope yielded to the demand of the citizens for the creation of a Civic Guard.

The reactionary ecclesiastics were scandalized by these reforms, and in the hope of warning the Pope against such dangerous innovations invented, if they did not actually organize, a plot for the extermination of the liberals and the imprisonment of the Pope (14 July). About the same time Metternich reinforced the Austrian garrison in Ferrara by a large body of Croatian troops. The Papal Legate protested, but Metternich referred him to the Treaty of Vienna, and declared that if the Papal police could not keep order it was his duty to do so. An Italian historian does not hesitate to assert that Metternich's move was arranged between himself and Pius IX, but the assertion is unsupported by evidence, and the overt insult to the Pope served only to alienate Roman sympathies from Austria and increase the enthusiasm of the liberals for the victim of Austria's insolence.[1] Metternich, however, took the opportunity to point the moral of recent events. He warned his vassal princes that there was no essential difference between the Moderates and the Mazzinians; that the triumph of the national principle in Italy must mean the downfall of 'Legitimacy, and the setting up of republics in the several States, and that any concession to liberalism would be certain to start an avalanche of revolution'.[2] England is wont to avert revolution by timely reform; but it is not certain that under the peculiar circumstances of the Italy of that day, Metternich's advice was unsound. The Pope, however, ignored it; in October he took the important step of conferring municipal self-government upon

[1] Bianchi, v. 24, but cf. Thayer, ibid., ii. 53.
[2] *Memoirs*, vii. 401–6.

Rome; summoned his *Consulta*, which consisted almost exclusively of laymen, promptly published a comprehensive scheme of reform, and announced the formation of a Customs Union between the Papal States, Tuscany, Piedmont and other States, to take effect as soon as Naples and Modena had signified their adherence.

Meanwhile Metternich kept a tight hold on Ferrara, threatened Tuscany, Piedmont, and Rome itself with Austrian intervention, and doubled the strength of the Austrian 'army in occupation' of Lombardo-Venetia. That he did not actually march an army into Rome itself to arrest the liberalizing tendencies of Pius IX is attributed, by a distinguished American writer, solely to the fact that Lord Palmerston presided over the English Foreign Office.[1] In the matter of the Swiss *Sonderbund*, and in other connexions, Palmerston had already shown his teeth; and though an English whig was more likely to bark than to bite, Metternich had no mind to run the risk of seeing England installed as the protectress of Italian liberties.

From the Alps to the Straits of Messina Italians of all classes, and in particular the nobles, were intent on asserting those liberties for themselves. On the eve of the revolutionary year the ferment of ideas was well-nigh universal. But the position was nevertheless curious, and in some sort paradoxical. A liberal Pope was leading Italy on the path of reform; Austria was offering insults to the head of the Church of which she was a foremost champion; and Charles Albert of Piedmont—*Re Tentenna*[2]—having vacillated for seventeen years, was seemingly determined to throw in his lot at last with the liberators and patriots. The prevailing temper was manifested in a variety of ways. An Agricultural Congress at Casale (7 September) and the Scientific Congress which met at Genoa a week later, if not political gatherings under a thin disguise, did not confine themselves to the discussion of technical subjects but gave vent to the emotions uppermost in the minds of all Italian patriots. At the Congress at Casale, meeting on the anni-

[1] Thayer, *Dawn*, ii. 56.

[2] 'The wobbling King.'

versary of the Pope's amnesty, a letter was read from Charles Albert.

'Austria', wrote the King, 'has declared her intention to retain Ferrara. . . . Should Providence call us to a war for the independence of Italy I will mount my horse and with my sons put myself at the head of my army . . . glorious will be the day on which we can raise the cry of a war of Italian independence.'

Never before had Charles Albert alluded in public to the possibility of war with Austria. His words aroused the wildest enthusiasm among delegates from all parts of Italy, and the Congress besought the King to place himself at the head of the Italian movement and to unsheath the sword at once, and pledged itself to his support.

Promises of co-operation poured in from all parts and from all classes. But though the minutes were speeding on, the hour had not yet struck.

By a curious irony it was the death (17 October) of Napoleon's widow, the Archduchess Marie Louise of Hapsburg-Lorraine, that nearly set alight the inflammable materials. On her death the Duchy of Parma passed, under the arrangement already described, to Charles Lewis, Duke of Lucca, whose little Duchy of Lucca went to Tuscany, while the outlying Tuscan districts of the Lunigiana were to be divided between Parma and Modena. This game of general post, played over the heads of the inhabitants, was little to the liking of the Tuscans, especially those who were to exchange the mild rule of the Duke of Tuscany for that of the contemptible despot who made legitimacy stink in the nostrils of the Modenese. Tuscany was almost driven into war, but an arrangement was patched up, and persisted until the rights and wrongs of these local squabbles were lost in the larger issues so soon to be raised.

Before the year closed Metternich so far yielded to pressure (applied in particular by Palmerston) as to withdraw the Austrian troops from Ferrara (16 December). Less than a month later (12 January 1848) a match was dropped at Palermo which set all Italy ablaze.

V

THE YEAR OF REVOLUTION (1848–9)

Venice and Rome

JANUARY 1848 was a bad moment to choose for dropping matches; there was much inflammable material lying about not only in the Two Sicilies, not only in every part of Italy, but throughout a great part of continental Europe. So widespread, indeed, was the resulting conflagration that the year 1848 is known pre-eminently as 'the year of Revolution'.

Metternich

Particularly was this true of the many countries subject directly or indirectly to the rule of the Hapsburgs. No statesman of the nineteenth century has been the object of more bitter criticism than Prince Metternich. That he showed scant sympathy with the increasingly fashionable doctrine of 'Nationality' is true. Is he, therefore, to be blamed for 'lack of foresight', for failure to discern the forces destined to re-draw the map of Europe? May it not be that he appreciated the strength of those forces more clearly than most of his contemporaries; that he realized that the existence of the Hapsburg Empire was a negation of these forces, and that unless their operation could be neutralized, if not defeated, the doom of the House he served was certain? The triumph of the principle of 'self-determination' in 1918 involved the disintegration of the conglomerate Empire which it was Metternich's care to maintain. 'The Emperor does not intend to lose his Italian possessions.' Such was the emphatic assertion of Metternich when, at the beginning of 1848, the hour of fate seemed to have struck. Metternich himself fell; but the Empire which for more than thirty years he had served so well emerged intact from the troubles of the year of Revolution. To the events of that year in Italy we now turn.

Sicily and Naples

At the close of the year 1847 Italy was on the tiptoe of

expectation. It had not long to wait. On the 5th of January a demonstration occurred in the streets of Messina, and the windows of the royal palace were broken; on the 12th, the birthday of King Ferdinand, a serious insurrection broke out in Palermo, under the veteran patriot Ruggiero Settimo, Prince of Fitalia. The insurrectionists demanded the 'English Constitution of 1812'. The King's reply was the dispatch of 5,000 troops; but in face of tumults in Naples itself, and the refusal of the Pope to allow Austrian troops a passage through his dominions, the King deemed it prudent to promise concessions. A new ministry of a liberal complexion was appointed, and on 10 February a Constitution, closely modelled on the French Constitution of 1830, was promulgated.

Piedmont

The North did not lag behind the South. The relaxation of the Press censorship in Piedmont in 1847 had given a great stimulus to journalistic activity, and in the *Risorgimento*, men like d'Azeglio, Balbo, and Cavour vehemently urged Charles Albert to establish parliamentary government in the sub-alpine kingdom. The King hung back; but Cavour in particular insisted that nothing less than a Constitution could save the Crown. On 4 March the King gave way and a Constitution was promulgated which formed, later on, the basis of responsible government in the Kingdom of Italy. Elsewhere thrones were tottering. In France the July monarchy had collapsed in February, and the Republic had once more been proclaimed. By 17 March news began to reach Italy of the still more significant revolution in Vienna. Metternich had been forced to resign on the 13th, and on the 14th was already on his way as a refugee to England.

Rome and Florence

Before the end of March, Pope Pius IX in Rome and Duke Leopold in Tuscany had followed the lead of Piedmont, and conceded parliamentary Constitutions to their respective subjects. The Roman Constitution was predominantly clerical: the College of Cardinals was to form the Senate, and even in the Lower House nominees of the Pope were to be associated with the elect of the people.

Still, a Parliament, however constituted, meant an immense advance upon a pure Theocracy.

Lombardy and Venice

Earlier in the year there had been renewed symptoms of unrest in Milan and Venice. The 'Tobacco Riots' in Milan (January), though half-burlesque in character, were indicative of the rising temper in Lombardy.[1] Daniele Manin, a Venetian jurist of Jewish origin, was arrested by the Austrian authorities in Venice (18 January), and on 22 February martial law was proclaimed throughout Lombardy. But with the fall of Metternich Austrian government in Italy collapsed. Count O'Donnell, the Austrian Vice-Governor of Lombardy, announced large concessions on 18 March; his proclamations were pasted over with the words 'Too late'; revolution had already broken out, and for five days (the *Cinque Giornate* of Milan) a fierce conflict raged in the streets of the city. The casualties were variously estimated at from 500 to 5,000; but the fighting ceased only when the Austrians evacuated the city. Marshal Radetsky, the veteran Commander-in-Chief of the Austrian forces in Italy, was compelled to retreat on the Quadrilateral. The whole of Lombardy was lost to Austria.

On 17 March the citizens of Venice rose and released all the political prisoners, among whom were their heroes Daniele Manin and Niccolò Tommaseo. Manin at once took control of the situation, on the 23rd he proclaimed the Republic and was himself elected President. Not a drop of blood was shed in Venice; the Austrians bowed to the inevitable, evacuated the city, and by the end of March their flag flew only over the great fortresses of Mantua, Verona, Legnago, and Peschiera. Radetsky had made the Quadrilateral virtually impregnable, and the value of that

[1] In order to deal a blow at the Austrian revenue and to demonstrate their own willingness to make sacrifices on the altar of patriotism the Milanese agreed to boycott the use of tobacco, and for the first two days of January 1848 none but Austrian soldiers and unpatriotic citizens were seen smoking in the streets of Milan. Collisions occurred between smokers and non-smokers, and Radetsky used the opportunity to repress disorder by violence.

great strategical position, guarding the route from Vienna and Innsbruck by the Brenner Pass into north Italy, was amply demonstrated in the days immediately ahead.

Charles Albert

On the day when the Republic was proclaimed in Venice Charles Albert of Piedmont declared war on Austria. His subjects, notably in Genoa, had for weeks past been clamouring to be led against the white-coats. Cavour in the *Risorgimento* had been urging his sovereign to take the plunge. 'The supreme hour of the dynasty has struck; there are circumstances where audacity is prudence; where temerity is wiser than calculation.' A similar crisis arose in the history of Italy in 1853, and Cavour, as we shall see, gave identical advice. But we anticipate.

Tuscany

Duke Leopold of Tuscany promptly followed the lead of Piedmont and published a stirring proclamation to his troops as they left Florence for the north:

> 'Soldiers! the holy cause of Italy's independence is now to be decided on the Lombard plain. The citizens of Milan have already bought with their blood their liberty. Already the Sardinian army, led by its great-hearted king, moves into the field. Sons of Italy, heirs of Tuscan glory, shall not remain in slothful ease at such a moment. Fly then to the succour of our Lombard brothers.'

The Tuscans needed no bidding; they flew to join the troops of Piedmont.

Naples and Rome

Even King Ferdinand and Pope Pius IX were forced to simulate sympathy with the general enthusiasm, and Neapolitan and Roman troops were dispatched to the north. As far as the sovereigns were concerned, it was, however, a mere empty demonstration. The Pope subsequently declared that he had never any intention of fighting Austria and that the troops were not to cross the frontiers of the Papal States. King Ferdinand, despite his fervid protestations of adherence to the cause of Italian liberty and nationality, recalled his troops as soon as the domestic situation made it safe for him to do so.

For the moment, however, the tide of Italian enthusiasm seemed likely to carry everything before it.

The spirit of those days was exactly captured by a gifted English poetess:

> Italia Una! Now the war-cry rang
> From Alp to Etna: and her dreams were done,
> And she herself had wakened into life,
> And stood full armed and free; and all her sons
> Knew they were happy to have looked on her,
> And felt it beautiful to die for her.

Those were great moments in the history of the Italian *Risorgimento*; but the brutal fact remained, the Austrian power was essentially unbroken. Not even the enthusiasm of Garibaldi, not the ardour of Mazzini who hurried back from exile to enrol himself as a volunteer in the Garibaldian legion, could avail against the military skill of Radetsky.

The Papacy and the Revolution

Moreover, the unity of Italy was as yet entirely superficial. Military cohesion in the war zone was loose; political unity was hardly skin-deep. The Pope, Pius IX, was the first of the rulers to draw back. On 29 April he addressed to his Cardinals an allocation in which he disavowed all participation in the war against Austria, declared that the Papal troops had been sent north only to defend the frontiers of the States of the Church, and definitely repudiated the Neo-Guelph idea of an Italian federation under his presidency.

This declaration was a shattering blow to the hopes of Italian Catholics; for the moment it gravely discouraged the movement towards Italian unity, and even towards Italian independence. In the long run, as we shall see, it served both causes well by compelling concentration upon the hegemony of the House of Savoy. Encouraged by the attitude of the Papacy, King Ferdinand, who at the end of March had been deposed by his Sicilian subjects, effected a *Coup d'état* in Naples (15 May), and recalled the army which, under the command of General Pepe, was on the march for Lombardy. Pepe refused to obey, but his army melted away, and when he joined Charles Albert in Venetia he brought him less than fifteen hundred men.

North Italy

Nor were things going too well in the north. The Piedmontese army had crossed the Ticino on 24 March, but their reception in Milan was by no means cordial. In Milan and other Lombard cities separatist and republican feeling was still strong. Venice had definitely proclaimed the Republic. To drive out the Austrians was one thing; to accept the Piedmontese monarchy was another. 'You drive out an Emperor only to make submission to a King.' Such was the taunt of the Milanese republicans to their pro-Piedmontese compatriots. In April proposals for peace reached Charles Albert from Vienna: the Emperor was prepared to give up Lombardy, but not Venetia. Lord Palmerston advised Piedmont to accept the compromise. Charles Albert, however, refused to desert Venice and on 26 April crossed the Mincio. Yet in Venice, as in Milan, the spirit of civic independence was still strong, and when at last (3 July) the Venetian Parliament decided upon fusion with Piedmont, Manin resigned. Milan, Parma, Piacenza, and Modena had, by plebiscite, decided on fusion in the early summer. The union of north Italy under the hegemony of Sardinia seemed to be assured.

Yet the position of Charles Albert was, alike in a military and a diplomatic sense, precarious. Prussia and Russia had withdrawn their ministers from Turin; the French Republic had mobilized an army of observation on the frontiers of Savoy, and had hinted that if Piedmont annexed northern and central Italy, France ought to receive compensation in Savoy. Palmerston, however, though urging moderation on Charles Albert, would not have permitted spoliation at the hands of France. But the Austrian power in Italy, based on the impregnable Quadrilateral, was unbroken.

Recovery of Austria

Charles Albert had won a few skirmishes, but he proved himself as undecided in the field as in the council chamber; Radetsky was allowed to retake Vicenza (10 June); other Venetian towns soon shared the fate of Vicenza, and on 25 July Charles Albert suffered a serious defeat at Custoza. That battle decided the campaign; Charles Albert retreated on Milan, but found it impossible to hold the city, which Radetsky entered on 6 August. Three days later an armistice, providing for the evacuation of Lombardo-Venetia by the Italian troops, was signed at Vigevano.

The Milanese, goaded to frenzy by the surrender of their city, turned upon Charles Albert. The unhappy king barely escaped from Milan with his life; even in Turin and Genoa his position was gravely imperilled; in fine, the Sardinian leadership of the hegemony was, for the time being, at an end.

The extreme republicans did not conceal their satisfaction. 'The war of the Princes is over,' said Mazzini; 'now for the war of the peoples.' 'Good news! The Piedmontese have been beaten. Now we shall be our own masters; we will fight a people's war; we will chase the Austrians out of Italy, and set up a federal republic.' Such was the comment of Cattaneo, the leader of the Milanese republicans, and it reflected the views of not a few republicans in other cities. Few were those who could think in terms of Italy. Most Italians still cherished the old ideal of the City-State, independent and preferably republican.

Radetsky

But could the isolated cities achieve or maintain independence? The brilliant generalship of Radetsky, still vigorous in his eightieth year, had not only saved Lombardo-Venetia for Austria; it had gone far to re-establish the Hapsburg Empire. Throughout that Empire the reactions of the Italian victories were felt far and wide; but the story of Hapsburg recovery is outside the scope of this narrative.[1]

The Roman Republic

In Italy itself the failure of the Sardinian leadership encouraged the Mazzinians and republicans; notably in Venice and Rome. In Rome the relations between the Pope and his subjects became increasingly strained during the summer of 1848, until in mid-September Pius IX called to his councils Pellegrino Rossi, who, though Italian by birth, had been French ambassador in Rome, and was

[1] I have told the story elsewhere. Cf. Marriott, *A History of Europe, 1815–1923* (Methuen, 1931), c. ix.

known as a man of strong character and enlightened views. Rossi, though mistrusted alike by clericals and republicans, laboured assiduously to bring order into the chaotic administration of Rome, till on 15 November he was foully assassinated. His murder dispelled all hope of a reformed or reforming Papacy. The Pope fled in terror to Gaeta, where he placed himself under the protection of King Ferdinand of Naples. Rome, left without government of any kind, was for the moment a prey to anarchy.

The Triumvirate

Presently, however, a Constituent Assembly met and on 9 February proclaimed the overthrow of the Temporal Power and the establishment of the Republic, not only for Rome but for the whole of Italy. The immediate government of the city was at the same time entrusted to three triumvirs, of whom Mazzini was one. Mazzini, assured that the day of his dreams had dawned, hurried south to do his part in organizing the government. But in the desperate plight of the Papacy the new President of the French Republic saw his chance. Louis Philippe had alienated the army and the Church. By one stroke Louis Napoleon hoped to win the affection of both those important interests. A French expedition was accordingly dispatched to Rome, with orders to effect the restoration of the Pope. On 25 April, General Oudinot landed with 8,000 men at Civitavecchia, and on the 30th attempted to capture Rome by surprise. But on their side the defenders had been reinforced by the arrival of Garibaldi, who, on the outbreak of the Revolution, had hurried back from exile in South America to place his person and his sword at the service of his country. His offer was coldly received by Charles Albert (June 1848), and accordingly Garibaldi went on to Milan, where he was enthusiastically welcomed. From all parts of Italy volunteers flocked to the standard of the now famous chieftain, and in a very short time he found himself at the head of 30,000 men. With this band, notwithstanding the armistice of Vigevano, Garibaldi carried on a desultory but harassing campaign.

Garibaldi

This guerrilla warfare, though it did not materially improve the political or even the military situation, succeeded in doing two things: it stimulated the enthusiasm of the populations from which the volunteers were drawn, and it concentrated that enthusiasm upon the gallant adventurer who commanded them. Before the opening of the campaign of 1849 Charles Albert offered Garibaldi a regular command; but almost simultaneously news came from Rome which caused Garibaldi—to whom, as to Mazzini, Rome represented the embodiment of patriotic aspiration —to fly with a band of 1,500 followers to her aid. He was immediately entrusted with the defence of the frontier which was menaced by Ferdinand of Naples.

Garibaldi and his legion covered themselves with glory in two battles at Palestrina and Velletri (May 1849), where they inflicted crushing defeats on Bomba's Neapolitans. But the heroic struggle was drawing to a close. 'The situation', wrote Garibaldi, 'grows more difficult every day.' An Austrian army was advancing through the Legations and General Oudinot, largely reinforced from France, was preparing to assault the city. After a heavy bombardment his troops stormed the breaches, and on 3 July the French entered the Holy City.

Just before the entry of the French, Garibaldi, accompanied by his heroic wife and some 4,000 followers, escaped from the city and took to the country, resolved, as he said, 'to try our fate again rather than submit to the degradation of laying down our arms before the priest-ridden soldiers of Bonaparte'. Dogged first by the French and then by the Austrians, Garibaldi and his band crossed the Apennines, and then, after a month of hairbreadth escapes (which the wise reader will follow in Mr. Trevelyan's brilliant narrative),[1] embarked at Cesenatico (1 August), meaning to make their way to Venice, which was still maintaining its superb struggle against the Austrians. But in the Adriatic they were confronted by an Austrian squadron which compelled them to put back and land near Ravenna. 'I leave it to be imagined', wrote Garibaldi, 'what was my

[1] *Garibaldi and the Defence of the Roman Republic*, by G. M. Trevelyan.

position at that unhappy moment: my poor wife dying, the enemy pursuing us inshore, and the prospect of landing on a coast where more enemies probably awaited us.' Many of the boats were taken, but Garibaldi with Anita and a few followers managed to reach the shore. Still the pursuers came on; many of his friends, including Ugo Bassi, were captured and shot; Garibaldi himself escaped, but not until he had seen his beloved Anita expire in his arms. For four years he was a wanderer; but in 1854 he settled down in his island home in Caprera, until he was again called forth from retirement by the events of 1859.

Campaign of 1849 in North Italy

Meanwhile, the Roman Republic collapsed and the Pope was restored to his temporal power; but Venice still held out. On 12 March, Charles Albert of Piedmont had denounced the armistice, and had again taken the field with a mixed force of 80,000 men, though the command was entrusted to a Polish general, Chrzanowski. Within a fortnight, however, the Piedmontese suffered a crushing defeat at the hands of Radetsky at Novara (23 March). On the evening of that fatal day the old King resigned his sceptre to his son, famous to all time as the creator of Italian unity —Victor Emmanuel. Charles Albert went immediately into exile and in July died at Oporto. The young King's first task, no easy one, was to negotiate a truce with the Austrian conqueror. He showed his characteristic courage in his negotiations with Radetsky. The latter offered generous terms, but on condition that the Parliamentary Constitution of Piedmont were abolished. Victor Emmanuel was adamant in his refusal.

'Marshal,' he said, 'sooner than subscribe to such conditions I would lose a hundred Crowns. What my father has sworn I will maintain. If you want war to the death, be it so. I will call my people once more to arms. If I fail, it shall be without shame. My house knows the road of exile but not of dishonour.'

Radetsky insisted on an indemnity, on the evacuation of all districts occupied by the Italian army outside Piedmont, on the occupation of certain places in Piedmont until the peace was concluded, and on the withdrawal of the Italian fleet from the Adriatic. These harsh terms were perforce accepted; but the Piedmontese Constitution was intact; the son had kept his father's pledge inviolate, and all Italy could look, and came to look, to *il re galantuomo*, to the man who kept his word, as the destined liberator of his country, the champion of Italian unification.

Reaction in Italy

Novara was followed by restorations; restorations by reaction. Bomba re-established autocracy in Naples, and Sicily was compelled again to submit to his rule; Leopold was reinstated in Tuscany. Venice still held out. By the end of May, however, the devoted city was blockaded by land and sea; in July the bombardment began and continued for three weeks; within the city cholera was raging, the horrors of famine were added to those of plague, and at last on 23 August the capitulation was signed, and the siege, which had lasted 146 days, was at an end. Radetsky made a triumphal entry into the city on the 30th, and the Patriarch celebrated the restoration of Austrian rule by a *Te Deum* in St. Mark's.

Radetsky had promised an indemnity to all who had taken part in the defence of the city, but had excepted Manin, and thirty-nine others. The 'forty' left Venice on board a French steamer, and Manin settled in Paris, where he earned bread for himself, his son, and a sick daughter, by giving lessons in Italian. His wife had died at Marseilles, and in 1854 his daughter, after years of suffering, passed away. Three years later death brought release to Manin himself (22 September 1857). But the years of his exile had not been spent in vain. He made many friendships among the best Frenchmen of the day. 'He helped to keep alive in France the flame of her Italian sympathies. He helped to lay the foundations for Plombières.'[1] For he had come to believe with Cavour that French help was indispensable to the liberation of Italy; he had renounced

[1] Trevelyan, *Manin*, p. 243.

his republican creed, and was content to merge the City-States, even the city he had saved, in a united Italy under the House of Savoy. Shortly before his death he published the following manifesto:

'Faithful to my flag—independence and unification—I reject everything opposed to it. If regenerated Italy must have a King, there must be only one, and that one the King of Piedmont. The Republican party, so bitterly calumniated, now performs another act of abrogation, and makes a sacrifice to the national cause. . . . It says to the House of Savoy: *Make Italy and I am with you. If not—no.*'

Meanwhile, in the Italy Manin had left for ever, the triumph of Austria and the absolutism for which Austria stood was to all outward seeming complete. The year of Revolution, at one time bright with hope for Italy, had come and gone and had left Italy, to all appearance, as helpless and hopeless as ever. 'The Pope', wrote Mazzini, 'clutches the soul of the Italian nation; Austria the body whenever it shows signs of life; and on every member of that body is enthroned an absolute prince, viceroy in turn under one or other of those powers.'

Well might Mazzini and the republican zealots despair of the situation. Yet the Italy of 1850 was not the Italy of 1815, nor even of 1847. She had awakened from the death-sleep of centuries. The insurrections of 1820, 1831, and 1848, abortive as they appeared, had at least proved that the Italians were conscious of their degradation, that they had begun to dare to hope. Most of them had begun to hope for freedom; some of them to dream of unity; and gradually they had begun to realize, however provincial their patriotism, that the one was impracticable without the other, that liberty could only be achieved through unity. But neither of liberty nor of unity could there be any hope until the army which encouraged disunion and maintained autocracy was driven from Italian soil. More than one lesson had been taught by the events of the last few years. It was vain to look for political salvation to a reformed and reforming Papacy. The Neo-Guelph ideal was shattered. Republicanism nurtured on civic patriotism was unequal to the task of national emancipation. A unitary Republic was as impracticable as Papal Federalism. Mazzini's ideal, like Gioberti's, was shattered. Mazzini had done a great work for Italy; but it was as teacher of Ethics rather than of Politics. To him Democracy meant not the rule of an uneducated proletariate, still less of a lawless mob; but as he himself defined it, 'the progress of all through all under the leading of the best and wisest'. To him the sole origin of every right lay in a duty fulfilled.

'If', he says in the preface to his *Duties of Man*, 'you would emancipate yourselves from the arbitrary rule and tyranny of man you must begin by rightly adoring God. And in the world's great battle between the two great principles of Good and Evil you must openly enrol yourselves beneath the banner of the first and ceaselessly combat the second. . . . It was because I saw these two lies—Machiavellism and Materialism—too often clothe themselves before your eyes with the seductive fascinations of hopes which only the worship of God and Truth can realize that I thought to warn you by this book. I love you too well either to flatter your passions or to caress the golden dreams by which others seek to win your favour. My voice may sound too harsh and I may too severely insist on proclaiming the necessity of virtue and sacrifice; but I know, and you too, untainted by false doctrines and unspoiled by wealth, will soon know also, that the sole origin of every right is in a duty fulfilled.'

'Life', he said elsewhere, 'is a mission; duty, therefore, its highest law. . . . Each of us is bound to purify his own soul as a temple; to free it from egotism; to set before himself, with a religious sense of the importance of the study, the problem of his own life; to search out what is the most striking need of the men by whom he is surrounded, and then to interrogate his own faculties and capacity and resolutely and unceasingly apply them to the satisfaction of the need. . . . Young brothers, when once you have conceived and determined your mission within your soul let naught arrest your steps. Fulfil it with all your strength; fulfil it whether blessed by love or visited by hate; whether strengthened by association with others or in the sad solitude that almost always surrounds the martyrs of thought. The path is clear before you: you are cowards, unfaithful to your own future, if in spite of sorrows and delusions you do not pursue it to the end.'

Not a few of the younger men of Italy had learnt the lesson taught by Mazzini; they had studied the problem of their lives; their choice was taken; their mission was determined; their path was clear, they had vowed to pursue it to the end. But to pursue it, paradoxical as it may sound, they had to renounce the ideal of the master who had first inspired them with the fire of patriotism. In politics, as in ethics, it is often so: life is made possible only by death. For modern Italy to live it was necessary that Mazzini's immediate ideal should die.

Thus in the general disillusionment of federalists and republicans, by the exhaustion of alternatives, the hopes of all patriotic Italians began to be concentrated on the House of Savoy. Yet they, too, had suffered disillusionment in 1848–9. *L'Italia farà da sè.* Such was the hope and expectation of Charles Albert. It proved vain. Italy, unaided, could not work out her own salvation. Diplomacy must come to the assistance of idealism. The prophet must yield place to the statesman. Where Mazzini had failed, Cavour shall succeed. But he will not succeed without the steadfast support of his own king, nor without the mercenary assistance of Napoleon III.

VI

THE HOUSE OF SAVOY

Victor Emmanuel II—Cavour

AN Italian of 1849, contemplating the condition of his country, might well have been filled with despair. He would have recalled the bright dawn of the year 1848, when Italy seemed suddenly to have awakened after the sleep of centuries. He would have seen the sovereigns of the Italian States hastening, each more eagerly than the other, to concede the demands of their subjects, and to bestow upon them the doubtful blessing of a ready-made Parliamentary Constitution. He would have heard Neapolitans, Romans, and Tuscans, no less than Genoese and Piedmontese, clamouring to be led against the Austrians who had so long held Italy in thrall. He would have noted with delight the revival of the old spirit in Milan and Venice inspiring their citizens to declare their independence, and he might well have thought that with the fall and flight of Metternich, with the outbreak of revolution in Prague, in Budapest, in Vienna itself, the conglomerate Empire of the Hapsburg was at last tottering to its fall.

Such were the portents in the spring of 1848. Very different was the aspect of affairs in the autumn of 1849. On every side the revolution had collapsed. The young Emperor Francis Joseph was master in his own house: in Austria, in Hungary, and in Bohemia the power of the Hapsburgs had been completely re-established; the attempt on the part of the German liberals to give to Germany a Parliamentary Constitution and to transfer the headship of Germany from Vienna to Berlin had ended in a fiasco, and under the strong rule of Felix Schwarzenberg, Austria was about to renew her strength and re-establish her hegemony in Germany.

Not least complete was the triumph of the Hapsburgs in Italy. It was, indeed, with the assistance not of Austria but of France that Pius IX was restored to his Papal throne; but for the rest the power of the Hapsburgs seemed to be unshaken, their prestige undimmed by the year of Revolution. On Venetia and Lombardy the Austrian yoke was riveted more firmly than ever; under Austrian protection the vassal princes crept back to their thrones in Tuscany, Parma, and Piacenza; Brescia, alone among the Lombard cities, supporting Piedmont in the renewal of war in 1849, was, after a gallant struggle, reduced to obedience, by the ferocious energy of the Austrian General Haynau, the 'Hyena of Brescia'. Even Piedmont, the hope of liberal Italy, lay prostrate for the moment under the crushing defeat of Novara—a defeat, not the less complete because it might so easily have been a victory.

To all outward seeming, then, the triumph of Austria was complete; yet the work of the last thirty years had not gone for nothing. Some ideals had, as we have seen, been shattered; some illusions had been dissipated; but painful though that process be, it is not necessarily to the ultimate disadvantage of the patient. The disillusionment of the Neo-Guelphs, the disappointment of the republicans, had the wholesome effect of concentrating the hopes of all Italian patriots on the House of Savoy.

Gioberti

A significant symptom of this concentration is found in the work, published in 1851, of Vincenzo Gioberti, *Rinnovamento civile degli Italiani*. In this work the prophet of the Neo-Guelphs renounced his earlier views and frankly accepted a Sardinian hegemony as the only possible hope for Italian independence, the inevitable basis on which to build the edifice of Italian unity. 'Italy', he wrote, 'has in herself, especially through her religion, all the conditions necessary for her national and political *Risorgimento*, and has no need, in order to effect it, of internal revolutions or foreign invasions or imitations.'

The Northern Campaign, as J. A. Symonds truly said, had 'baptized the cause of Italian independence with the best blood of Piedmont; it gave it a royal martyr, and it pledged the dynasty of Savoy to a progressive policy from which it never afterwards deviated.' This truth was gradually recognized by all parties.

'Except the young sovereign who rules Piedmont I see no one', wrote Gioberti, 'who could undertake our emancipation. Instead of imitating Pius, Ferdinand (of Naples) and Leopold (of Tuscany) who violated their sworn compacts, he maintains his with religious observance—vulgar praise in other times, but to-day not small, being contrary to example.'

A reign of thirty years, the most illustrious in Italian history, was to demonstrate the accuracy of Gioberti's estimate of the young King's character.

Victor Emmanuel II succeeded to the throne of his fathers at a moment of profound depression. Yet the motto of his House, *J'attends mon astre*, was justified by the good fortune which, in the main, its members had for centuries enjoyed. Nor did the proverbial luck of his House forsake its latest representative.

The House of Savoy

A combination of shrewd calculation and romantic adventure had for many centuries distinguished the House of Savoy. In view of the part which that House was to play in the making of Italy it is worth while to take a brief retrospective glance.

Half a century before William the Bastard landed at Pevensey, Humbert of the White Hands, the cadet of a House of Teutonic origin, was endowed by a grateful Emperor—Conrad II—with the County of Savoy. Humbert's son Otto acquired the Val d'Aosta and Turin as part of the dowry of an Italian wife, and thus, for the first time, the House of Savoy 'straddled the Alps'. Geography determined their destiny. Planted at Geneva and at Turin, the Counts of Savoy commanded the passes of the Western Alps. The Alps have never, indeed, despite the historic claim of a long succession of French rulers, formed a 'natural frontier' like the Pyrenees. They can be turned by the Corniche road, and they are pierced by a series of passes. But the Corniche road only gives access to the Italian riviera, not to the heart of Italy, Lombardy and the basin of the Po. Otto's marriage was, consequently, of primary importance to the fortunes of his House, and when his grandson took the title of Prince of Piedmont he started a train upon one of the great trunk lines of modern history.

All through the ensuing centuries the House of Savoy consistently followed the path indicated to them by the geographical distribution of their lands. 'Geography', as the Prince de Ligne cynically observed, 'hardly permitted the House of Savoy to behave like honest men.' A less caustic commentator might prefer to say that they wisely took full advantage of a unique position in the European polity. Anticipations of their later policy may perhaps be discerned in the part they play in the medieval contests between Emperors and Popes, and between the Emperors and the Lombard cities. In these contests the Dukes of Savoy are generally found on the side of the Emperors, but with exceptions sufficient to enhance the value of their adhesion, and to excite in Imperial breasts a lively sense of favours to come, or to be withheld, according as circumstances might dictate. Thus, bit by bit, these astute princes accumulated territories at the hands of gratified patrons and allies, and in course of time built up a noble patrimony. By the end of the fourteenth century their dominions extended on the north to the Lake of Geneva, while on the south (by the acquisition of Nice) they touched the Mediterranean.

From the end of the fifteenth until the middle of the eighteenth century the contest between France and the Austro-Spanish Hapsburgs gave further opportunities to the Dukes of Savoy-Piedmont. The plains of Lombardy provided, as we have seen, one of the main campaigning grounds for Frenchmen, Germans, Spaniards; but owing to the persistent neutrality maintained by the Swiss Cantons, the French could reach the battle-field (save by the circuitous route of the Col de l'Argentière) only through the passes held by the Dukes of Savoy. The French were, consequently willing to pay a high price for the accommodation. The Hapsburgs were likewise ready to pay highly for such a valuable alliance.

But the situation of the frontier-State, though potentially profitable, was also perilous. This was clearly demonstrated in the sixteenth century. In the duel between the Emperor Charles V and Francis I, Duke Charles III (1504–53) espoused the cause of the Emperor, and suffered for it. Francis overran the whole of Savoy-Piedmont, save Nice, and for nearly a quarter of a century the frontier-State was virtually incorporated in the Kingdom of France. By the Treaty of Câteau-Cambrésis it was restored to Duke Emmanuel Philibert, though France retained several of the most important fortresses, while Philip II insisted, as a set-off, on keeping Spanish garrisons in Nice and Villafranca.

Fortune was somewhat inconstant during the seventeenth century. Charles Emmanuel I (1580–1630) married a daughter of Philip II of Spain and thus committed himself to the party of the Counter-Reformation. With the help of the Catholic party he seized the vacant Marquisate of Saluzzo, and on the failure of heirs male to the Duchy of Mantua (1627) he also laid claim to the Marquisate of Montferrat, which for a century past had been incorporated in Mantua. Montferrat was in fact purchased by his son Victor Amadeus I under the terms of the Treaty of Cherasco, which in 1631 brought to an end the long-drawn-out quarrel about the Mantuan succession. At the same time Richelieu, whose ambition it was to restore to modern France the frontiers of ancient Gaul, retained possession of Pinerolo, a fortress which commanded the chief pass from Dauphiné, and Casale the key fortress of Montferrat. These transactions were facilitated by the fact that Victor Amadeus had married a daughter of Henry IV of France. His grandson Victor Amadeus II also married a French princess, the daughter of Philip of Orleans, with the result that Louis XIV began to treat Savoy as a mere dependency of France. But in 1690 the Duke Victor Amadeus II, tiring of French tutelage, joined the great European coalition—known as the League of Augsburg—against Louis XIV. Fortune once more favoured the House of Savoy, for by the Treaty of Ryswick (1697) they obtained the coveted fortresses of Pinerolo and Casale. So long as they were held by France, Savoy could be neither independent nor secure. On the outbreak of the war of the Spanish Succession Victor Amadeus sided with Louis XIV, but the fact that his daughters were married to the two elder grandsons of Louis XIV—the Dukes of Burgundy and Anjou (afterwards Philip V of Spain)—did not prevent his defection as soon as the Imperialists bid high enough for his support. His calculations were rewarded at the Peace of Utrecht (1713) by the acquisition of Sicily and a royal crown. In the following year, however, his daughter the Queen of Spain died, and Philip V promptly married, *en secondes noces*, an ambitious Italian princess, the famous Elizabeth Farnese. With the help of Cardinal Alberoni—a native of Piacenza—the new Queen of Spain quickly developed her ambitious schemes in Italy, and Victor Amadeus found himself compelled to accept Sardinia in exchange for Sicily.

Thus the House of Savoy bore the title of King of Sardinia until the Crown of the island was merged in that of the Peninsula. It is interesting to speculate what the effect on the history of the *Risorgimento* might have been had the Duke of Savoy-Piedmont retained the throne of Sicily. But amid the political permutations of the eighteenth century that was out of the question, and the exchange to Sardinia, though marking a temporary setback to the ambitions of Savoy, was probably advantageous to the dynasty if not to the Italian peoples as a whole.

During the wars of the eighteenth century the Dukes of Savoy-Piedmont changed sides no fewer than five times; but if they were more shifty than some of their neighbours they were not lacking in courage or in straight-dealing. Thus in a treaty of alliance concluded by Charles Emmanuel III with Maria Theresa in 1742 one of the articles specifically stipulated that the Duke should be free to change sides as circumstances might dictate. Nor was the article a dead letter. Like the Hohenzollern (whose story presented many parallels with their own) the Dukes of Savoy have always been frankly realist in politics. They have regularly worshipped in the Temple of Ambition, and have never gone after strange gods. Nor was the reward of persistence withheld. Rarely was a war fought, or a peace concluded, however remote the primary issues at stake and however detached the principal combatants might be, but the House of Savoy was able to acquire several of the towns of Lombardy, stripping it, as the common saying went, 'like an artichoke leaf by leaf.'

After a prolonged parenthesis we return to Victor Emmanuel and the situation with which he was confronted.

On his accession to the throne in 1849 Victor Emmanuel was a young man of twenty-nine. The prospect alike for Piedmont and for Italy was gloomy, yet there was nothing of undignified despair in the King's attitude.

> 'All our efforts', he declared in his first proclamation to his people, 'must be directed to maintain our honour untarnished, to heal the wounds of our country, to consolidate our liberal institutions. To this undertaking I conjure all my people, to it I will pledge myself by a solemn oath, and I await from the nation a response of help, affection and confidence.'

From the purpose indicated in this proclamation Victor Emmanuel never swerved.

Massimo d'Azeglio

Early in May 1849 he appointed as Prime Minister Cavalier Massimo d'Azeglio. Artist, novelist, man of fashion, politician—d'Azeglio played many parts but none of them with complete success. He was, however, scrupulously honest, and his personal popularity and known moderation were of great value to his sovereign during the early and more turbulent period of the reign.

His first business, on taking office, was to conclude peace with Austria. That disagreeable duty done, he turned to the urgent task of domestic reform. He had first, however, to deal with a rising organized in Genoa by the republican irreconcilables who still followed Mazzini's lead. Mazzini and his friends did not scruple to impute to the Sardinian

Government the basest treachery in connexion with the events of the recent war and the still more recent peace. 'Better Italy enslaved than handed over to the son of the traitor Carlo Alberto.' Mazzini was utterly intractable.

Ecclesiastical reforms

Interrupted though not deterred by sporadic disaffection, d'Azeglio and Victor Emmanuel pressed steadily forward on the path of reform. The first problem to be tackled was that of the relations between State and Church. In the little kingdom of Sardinia there were at that time forty-one Bishoprics, over 1,400 Canonries, and 18,000 persons who had assumed the monastic habit. Taking the whole population through, one person in every 214 was an ecclesiastic.

These figures are the more significant when it is remembered that the Church still claimed exclusive jurisdiction over all 'ecclesiastics', the right to afford asylum to malefactors, and the rest of the anomalous privileges which in progressive and Protestant countries had long since been abolished. Victor Emmanuel, like our own Plantagenets, was anxious to reduce all men to an equality before the civil law. The continued existence of the clerical courts in the plenitude of power, the vast pretensions of the Jesuits to the exclusive control of education, and the censorship of domestic morality were, however, utterly inconsistent with this reasonable ambition.

The Siccardian Laws

Victor Emmanuel, profoundly anxious to avoid friction between the Civil and Ecclesiastical authorities, dispatched in the autumn of 1849 an envoy to the Pope—Count Siccardi. Pius IX firmly declined to sanction any change in the relations between Church and State in Sardinia. 'The Holy Father', said the papal representative, 'was willing to please the King of Sardinia as far as going into the antechamber of the devil, but into his very chamber he would not go.'

Despite this check the King, with the assistance of Count Siccardi, determined to push on the work of reform; the *Foro Ecclesiastico* (or chief clerical tribunal) was finally abolished, and the privileges and immunities of the vast army of ecclesiastics were drastically curtailed. The clerical organs thundered denunciations against the infidel King and his heretic ministers, but the work of reform went steadily on. That work unfortunately involved a breach with the Papacy, which, widened by the events of 1870, was not healed until the statesmanship of Signor Mussolini found a solution in the Vatican Treaty of 1929.

Apart from their intrinsic importance the debates on the Siccardian laws are memorable for having brought for the first time into prominence the statesman with whose name the controversy between Church and State, not to add the consummation of Italian unity, is imperishably associated.

VII

CAVOUR

Sardinia and the Crimean War

Cavour COUNT Camillo Benso di Cavour was born at Turin on 10 August 1810. His father was Michele Benso, Marquis of Cavour, and in his veins was the blood of 'twenty generations of Piedmontese ancestors'. But Cavour owed more to his mother, a Genevan Calvinist, than to his Piedmontese father. 'The old-fashioned political Calvinism of Geneva which moulded the character of Guizot, exercised from a very early age,' as Lord Acton has shrewdly and justly remarked, 'a profound influence upon Cavour.' Adèle de Sellon, Cavour's mother, was the daughter of a remarkable Huguenot family which had long been settled in Geneva. Her brother, Jean Jacques, was 'the friend and associate of reformers in France and England', and was himself known as 'the Swiss Wilberforce'. Of such stock did Cavour come. As a younger son he was destined for the army, and at the age of ten was sent to the Military Academy at Turin. But a soldier's life was not congenial to him, while at home he found himself entirely out of sympathy with the reactionary views which rendered his father a *persona grata* at the sub-alpine Court of Carlo Alberto. Before he was twenty he learnt English and read deeply in Adam Smith and Bentham, then nearing the zenith of their influence and popularity. Intellectually, 'his one safety-valve was his intercourse with his Genevan relatives.' In 1830 he was sent to Genoa, where he frequented the salons of the advanced Liberals, much elated, just then, by the success of the July revolution in Paris. But, though confessing himself as a 'Liberal, very Liberal, desiring a complete change of system', Cavour then as always, 'recoiled with equal loathing from absolutists and Jacobins.' In 1831 he got his discharge from the army, and was sent off by his father to manage one of the family farms in a remote country district, forty miles from Turin.

For the next seventeen years Cavour devoted himself, mind and body, to agriculture, a pursuit which gripped his eminently practical mind. Yet he did not neglect intellectual interests. His study of the social, economic, and political problems of the day was stimulated by frequent visits to Geneva, and twice he visited England. To him England appeared to be 'the vanguard of civilization', and he became deeply interested in the questions which were then (1830–46) agitating English politics. Already in 1834 he had prepared as a member of the Piedmontese Statistical Commission a Report on the English Poor Law, and the fruits of a second visit (1843), which extended to Ireland, were seen in his *Considérations sur l'état actuel de l'Irlande* (1844), and *De la question relative à la législation anglaise sur le commerce des céréales* (1845). In the former he revealed himself as a strong opponent of Repeal and a penetrating critic of statesmen living and dead. 'O'Connell's conduct', he wrote, 'proves clearly that he is audacious only in proportion to the patience of his adversaries.' In the article on the Corn Laws Cavour confessed himself to be an ardent advocate of free trade, and a whole-hearted disciple of Adam Smith and the younger Pitt. His debt to England was fully acknowledged. 'From England', he wrote in 1859, 'I have learned the greater part of the political ideas which have guided me.' He was not content, however, with the study of blue books and economic treatises.

Night after night, the young Piedmontese, destined to be the real founder of parliamentary government in Italy, was to be seen in the strangers' gallery of the House of Commons, following with rapt attention the debates, and closely observing the methods of conducting public business and the tactics of party leaders. No experience could have been of greater value to Cavour.

Meanwhile, he did not neglect his immediate job. But although he contrived to make a large fortune out of farming he never lost sight of the wider issues. In 1842 he helped to found the *Associazione Agraria*, a society which afterwards became, as Acton says, 'an important channel and instrument of political influence'; and in 1847 he started, in conjunction with Cesare Balbo and others, *Il Risorgimento*, a journal devoted to the advocacy of constitutional reform. Besides constitutional reform for Piedmont Cavour and his colleagues stood for the independence of Italy, with a federal league between its several States.

Not, however, until the outbreak of the Revolution of 1848 had they any opportunity of putting their principles to a practical test. In February of that year Charles Albert, as we have seen, granted a parliamentary Constitution to his people. The Constitution, like that of Naples, was modelled upon the French Constitution of 1830. It contained provision for a legislature of two Chambers—a Senate nominated by the King, and a Chamber of Deputies elected on a restricted franchise, with an Executive responsible to Parliament.

The first Parliament met on the 8th of May. Cavour offered himself for election in three constituencies, but mistrusted by the Conservatives as a progressive, and denounced by the democrats as the son of a reactionary police official, and on his own account as a lukewarm moderate, he failed in all three. In June, however, he was elected at a by-election for Turin, and took his seat as one of the members for the capital. For the second Parliament, elected in January 1849, he did not secure reelection, and d'Azeglio offered him the London Embassy. The temptation to accept it was strong, for he loved England and had many friends there. But, as he wrote to a friend, 'to leave Piedmont in these difficult days seems to me an act of egoism that is repugnant to me.'

To the third Parliament, elected in the midst of the peace negotiations, Cavour was again returned as member for Turin, and gave strong and consistent support to the ministry of his friend d'Azeglio. The reforms which d'Azeglio was impelled to initiate evoked strong opposition, but it was only, as Cavour insisted, by timely reform that revolution could be averted.

'Do not think', he said, 'that the constitutional throne will be weakened; it will on the contrary be strengthened, and it will plant roots so profound in our soil that when Revolution again threatens us not only will the constitutional throne direct it but that throne will group around itself all the living forces of Italy and conduct the nation to the destiny which awaits it.'

In the splendour and in the certainty of that destiny Cavour had a profound belief. The value of his support was recognized in 1850 by his appointment as Minister of Commerce and Agriculture. His commanding intellect, his soaring but strictly honourable ambition, his unbending will and slightly domineering temper were already recognized—not least clearly by Victor Emmanuel. 'Look out what you are doing,' said the King to d'Azeglio; 'Cavour will soon be master of you all; he will dismiss you; he will never be content till he is Prime Minister himself.'

Cavour's Ministry

It was a shrewd forecast. In 1851 Cavour took over, in addition to the supervision of commerce and agriculture, the administration of the navy, and the charge of the finance department. Everywhere his driving power was felt. To industry and trade he gave a notable impulse; he cut down expenditure, and yet was able to meet La Marmora's requirements for the army and for national defence. But he was not popular either with king or people, the general view being that, though able, he was crafty and unscrupulous. Detesting the extremes of revolution and reaction, he was mistrusted, like most moderates, by men of all parties; yet, despite all opposition, he pushed on the work of administrative, commercial, and fiscal reform, and in 1852 he attained the goal of his immediate ambition and succeeded d'Azeglio as Prime Minister.

His programme on taking office is thus succinctly stated by himself:

'Piedmont must begin by raising herself, by re-establishing in Europe, as well as in Italy, a position and a credit equal to her ambition. Hence there must be a policy unswerving in its aims but flexible and various as to the means employed, embracing the exchequer, military reorganization, diplomacy, and religious affairs.'

'Re-establish her credit in Europe.' How was it to be done? The chance presented itself in 1854; but it needed a man of extraordinary courage and astuteness to seize it. If there is one quality more essential to a statesman than caution, it is rashness. Cavour possessed the two qualities in combination in exceptional degree. He knew that in the affairs of States, as of men, there comes a moment when rashness is the height of prudence.

> He either fears his fate too much,
> Or his deserts are small,
> That dares not put it to the touch
> To gain or lose it all.

Such a crisis had arrived in the history of Sardinia when in 1854 the Western Powers embarked on the Crimean War. To appreciate the courage demanded of Cavour at this crisis it is necessary to realize the position occupied at the time by Piedmont. One of many States in Italy, not the oldest, nor the largest, nor the richest; loaded with debt; prostrate beneath the recent recollection of a crushing military disaster; by no means on the best of terms with its immediate neighbours, and very lightly regarded by the Powers of Europe. This was the State which proposed in 1854 to join England and France in the defence of the dominions of the Porte. The negotiations were protracted for months. Among his colleagues Cavour stood absolutely alone in advocating this seemingly desperate enterprise. To them the whole scheme was sheer insanity. But the King stood firm. One after another ministers were permitted to resign, and in January 1855 the memorable treaty was signed by which Sardinia pledged herself to go to the assistance of the Western Powers with 15,000 (afterwards increased to 25,000) men.

'It was', says Massari, 'a solemn moment for the king and decided the fate of his country: that treaty was the fortune of

Italy. To overcome so many difficulties the genius of Cavour was not enough; there was needed also the firmness of Victor Emmanuel, for without him the treaty would not have been concluded.'

Massari insists on an important truth, realized to the full by Italians, but imperfectly appreciated in England, the immensely important part played at every great crisis in the drama of Italian unification by the King. Victor Emmanuel was in many respects neither an admirable nor an attractive figure. Almost repulsively plain, he had, like many ugly men, an inordinate passion for women; his tastes were coarse; his temper was indolent, and his prejudices were strong; but time after time his clarity of judgement, his sound common sense, his stubborn will, his courage, moral and physical, and, above all, his passionate belief in the mission of his House and the future of his country, proved of incalculable service to Italy. Here in the Crimean Treaty; again after the Armistice of Villafranca; again in regard to the critical situation arising from Garibaldi's conquest of Naples; and, finally, in the extremely delicate and difficult negotiations of 1870—in all these crises it was the courage and firmness and tact of the King himself which ensured success.

In none of these crises was the path of statesmanship more difficult to discern than in that of 1854. What possible interest could Sardinia have in the Crimean war? Cavour himself anticipated the question. In a great speech on the Treaty he showed that, in possession of the Bosphorus and Dardanelles, Russia would be irresistible in the Mediterranean.

'But I may be asked', he said, 'what matters it to us if Russia has the mastery in the Mediterranean? It may be said that that mastery does not belong to Italy nor to Sardinia: it is now the possession of England and of France; instead of two masters the Mediterranean will have three. I cannot believe that such sentiments can have an echo in this assembly. *They would amount to a giving up of our hopes of the future!* . . . How will this treaty avail Italy?' he concluded; 'I will tell you;

in the only way in which we or perhaps anyone can help Italy in the present condition of Europe. The experience of past years and of past centuries has proved how little conspiracies, plots, revolutions, and ill-directed movements have profited Italy. So far from doing so they have proved the greatest calamity which has afflicted this fair part of Europe; not only from the vast amount of human misery they have entailed, not only because they have been the cause and the excuse for acts of increasing severity, but especially because these continual conspiracies, these repeated revolutions, these ineffectual risings have had the effect of lessening the esteem, and even to a certain extent the sympathy, which the other nations of Europe once felt for Italy. Now I believe that the first condition of any improvement in the fate of Italy is that we should restore to her her good name, and so act that all nations, governments, and peoples should render justice to her great qualities, and to this end two things are necessary—first, that we should prove to Europe that Italy has sufficient civil virtue to govern herself with order and form herself for liberty, and that she is capable of receiving the most perfect system of government known to us; and secondly, that we should show that in military virtue we are not inferior to our ancestors. You have already rendered one service to Italy by the conduct you have pursued for seven years, proving in the clearest way to Europe that the Italians are able to govern themselves with wisdom, prudence, and loyalty. It remains for you to render her no less a service, if not even a greater, it remains for you to show that the sons of Italy can fight like brave men on the fields of glory. And I am persuaded that the laurels which our soldiers will gather in the plains of the East will do more for the future of Italy than all that has been done by those who have thought by declamation and writing to effect her regeneration.'

Cavour was conscious that in sending a contingent to the Crimea he was playing for high stakes, but he was confident of victory. By the end of April 1855 the expedition, commanded by General Alfonso La Marmora, had left Italy. 'You have the future of Italy in your haversacks.' Such was Cavour's farewell message to the troops. The response came presently from a private soldier in the trenches before Sebastopol: 'Out of this mud Italy will, we hope, be made.' It was.

The Battle of the Tchernaia

The story of the operations in the Crimea belongs to general European history; one incident, however, belongs especially if not exclusively to that of Italy. In June the Russians had repulsed with heavy loss the attacks of the English and French upon the Redan and the Malakoff—two formidable outworks on the east of Sebastopol. Yet slowly but surely, during the summer months of 1855, the allied armies pushed forward their lines towards the Russian fortifications. Once more, however, the covering Russian army, under the command of Prince Michael Gortschakoff, made a gallant though desperate effort to raise the siege. On the night of the 15th–16th August the Russians descended from the Mackenzie Heights upon the Tchernaia river. The brunt of the attack fell upon the Italians, and, after many hours of desperate fighting, the Russians, 50,000 strong, were driven back with the loss of 3,000 killed, 5,000 wounded, and 400 prisoners. This was the first real chance of showing their mettle given to the Italians, and splendidly did they redeem it. Fighting with the utmost gallantry they were mainly responsible for the decisive repulse of the Russian army. Thus were Cavour's calculations precisely fulfilled. In the waters of the Tchernaia the stain of Custoza and Novara was wiped out for ever; out of the mud of the trenches before Sebastopol was modern Italy built. Henceforward Cavour could speak confidently with his enemies—and with his friends—in the gate.

The Congress of Paris

The Crimean episode was the turning-point in the fortunes of Cavour, of Sardinia, and of Italy. Hitherto Sardinia had been lightly regarded by the European Powers. Cavour himself had hardly been distinguished from the crowd of Italian 'patriots' or revolutionaries who were anathema to the respectable European courts and chancelleries. After 1856 things were different. Sardinia was a 'Power'; Cavour was recognized as among the ablest of European diplomatists.

To the Peace Conference at Paris Cavour was, thanks to the insistence of Great Britain, and despite the insolent protest of Austria, admitted, on equal terms with the other delegates. He sat there as the representative not merely of Sardinia, but, in a real though not formal sense, of Italy. At the end of 1855 Cavour had accompanied his sovereign on a visit to the courts of France and Great Britain—a journey which, according to his own account, was 'the equivalent of ten years of life'. Consequently he found at the Congress of Paris many personal friends, but of political enemies not a few. Walewski, who as the chief representative of France presided, was an opponent, even more persistent perhaps than Count Buol the Austrian delegate. Benedetti, however, the secretary to the Congress was a Corsican, and in him Cavour found a cordial and valuable ally. Lord Clarendon, too, was consistently kind and cordial, while both the Russian and Prussian representatives were greatly impressed by Cavour's personality, even if they were not prepared to support him in Council. Oldofredi, indeed, did not exaggerate when he wrote to Massari: 'Cavour was and is the most eminent man here [in Paris]; he is the lion of the Conference.' Thiers also spoke with astonishment of the prestige which Cavour—'the Benjamin of the Plenipotentiaries'—had acquired.[1]

During the earlier sessions of the Conference Cavour, acting on a hint from Clarendon, observed much but said little. He strongly supported the idea of a union between the Danubian Principalities, partly because he saw a chance of putting an Italian prince on the throne of the new State, and so creating a vacancy at Parma or Modena which Victor Emmanuel might fill. But although he would have been glad to get one or two of the Italian Duchies for Piedmont, he was much more anxious to dislodge Austria from the Romagna. The main purpose, however, with

[1] Quoted by A. J. Whyte, *The Political Life and Letters of Cavour*, ii. 222, Oxford University Press, 1930. Dr. Whyte's account of the Congress is the best I have read.

which he went to Paris was to bring home to the assembled diplomatists of Europe the pitiable condition of Italy, more particularly of Naples and the Roman States, and to expose Austria to the world as mainly responsible for an intolerable condition of affairs.

The Treaty was actually signed, the Congress on the point of adjournment, before Cavour got his chance. It came at an extraordinary sitting of 8 April, when Lord Clarendon flung a bombshell into the Conference by denouncing, with a vehemence which Mr. Gladstone might have envied, the deplorable condition of Naples and the Papal States. Cavour wisely contented himself with a modestly and moderately worded speech in support of Clarendon. More was unnecessary. 'It would have been impossible', as Cavour wrote, 'for any Italian statesman to have formulated an indictment of the Roman Government more powerful or more accurate than that of the Foreign Secretary of Great Britain.' Lord Clarendon had been well coached.

Would his brave words be translated into resolute action? Would Great Britain support Piedmont with her fleet and army? After the Congress Cavour met Lord Clarendon and put the matter thus:

'That which has passed in the Congress proves two things: first, that Austria is decided to persist in her system of oppression and violence towards Italy; secondly, that the forces of diplomacy are impotent to modify that system. See the consequences for Piedmont. With the irritation on our side and the arrogance of Austria on the other, there are but two alternatives to take: reconcile ourselves to Austria and the Pope, or prepare to declare war at the Court of Vienna in a future not far distant. If the first part is preferable I must on my return to Turin advise my king to call to power the friends of Austria and the Pope. If the second hypothesis is best, my friends and I will not shrink from preparing for a terrible war—a war to the death.'

Would England support Piedmont? Cavour pressed Lord Clarendon on this point. 'Certainly, with all our hearts,' was the Englishman's reply. But with fleets and armies? In the exaltation of the moment Cavour imagined that he had obtained a pledge of armed assistance. Napoleon warned him: 'Austria will concede nothing; she will fight rather than let you take Parma; I cannot at the moment present her with a *casus belli*; but, don't worry, I have a presentiment that the actual peace will not last long.' At the same time the Emperor advised Cavour to go to England and see Palmerston.

He went; and though cordially received by the Queen and her ministers, he returned to Paris a wiser and a sadder man. England would support Piedmont with all their hearts—but with no more.

Nevertheless, an enthusiastic welcome awaited him at Turin. The King invested him with the Collar of the Annunciata and though he came home, as d'Azeglio observed, 'without even the smallest duchy in his pocket', his countrymen accurately appraised the value of his achievement. Cavour's own estimate of his work was characteristically modest yet precise:

'The Italian Question', he said, 'has become for the future a European question. The cause of Italy has not been defended by demagogues, revolutionists, and party men, but has been discussed before the Congress by the plenipotentiaries of the Great Powers.' And again: 'Two facts will remain, which are not without some importance. First, the stigma branded on the conduct of the King of Naples by France and England in the face of united Europe; and, second, the condemnation aimed by England at the Papal Government in terms as precise and energetic as the most zealous Italian patriot could have desired.'

The Pact of Plombières

After Paris, Plombières. 'Que peut on faire pour l'Italie?' was Napoleon's sincere but somewhat indiscreet question to Cavour in 1855. In 1856 Cavour had told him, and explained to him how it could be done. The seed was sown. The tender shoots were watered by the summer showers at Plombières. The harvest was reaped on the plain of Lombardy in 1859. The motives which inspired the Italian policy of Napoleon III have been frequently canvassed and still remain obscure. They would not have been Napoleon's had they not been complex and contradictory. He was not wholly the 'vulpine knave' depicted and denounced by Garibaldi. He was not wholly anything. But that he was genuinely sympathetic towards Italian aspirations is undeniable. Equally undeniable is the cleverness of Cavour. He dangled the bait before Napoleon's eyes with consummate adroitness. Had not the Italian campaign of 1796 revealed to Europe the military genius of the first Napoleon? What better field for the display of the genius of his nephew? Napoleon I had posed as the 'liberator' of Italy, and had actually gone far to promote its unity? Might not Napoleon III win still more enduring fame by accomplishing the purpose professed by his predecessor? Could the Third Empire be sustained without the perpetual glamour of successful war? And what foeman better worth the steel of a democratic Emperor than reactionary Austria?

The Orsini Conspiracy

The bait was swallowed; but the cordiality of the relations between the two men was temporarily interrupted by a painful episode. Early in 1858 Napoleon's life was attempted by some Italian exiles who had found refuge in England, where the conspiracy was hatched and the bombs prepared. Orsini's bombs killed ten and injured 150 people who awaited the Emperor's arrival at the Opera; the Emperor himself was untouched but unnerved. His anger blazed out fiercely against England; his army demanded to be led against the den of assassins; his Foreign Minister expressed to the English Government his opinion that France had a right to expect 'from an ally' that the guarantees against a repetition of such outrages should be more effectual.

To Count Walewski's dispatch no answer was returned; Lord Palmerston did, indeed, introduce a bill to amend the law in regard to conspiracy to murder, but the Government was defeated and resigned. Orsini was an Italian, but curiously enough it was England more than Italy that

Napoleon blamed, and on 21–2 July 1858 he met Cavour secretly at Plombières, a little watering-place in the Vosges. So closely was the secret kept that Cavour, mistaken for an Italian conspirator, barely escaped arrest at the hands of the local police, and Napoleon informed Cavour that Walewski had telegraphed to him the secret intelligence that Cavour was believed to be at Plombières. But important business was transacted by the exalted conspirators. The terms of an alliance were arranged. Austria was to be expelled from the Peninsula; and northern and central Italy were to be united under the House of Savoy. In return, Savoy, and perhaps Nice, were to be ceded to France and Victor Emmanuel was to give his daughter in marriage to the Emperor's not quite youthful and not too reputable cousin, Prince Napoleon ('Plon-Plon'). Both the sacrifices demanded from Victor Emmanuel were painful; but Cavour was convinced that the dead weight of the Austrian incubus could not be lifted without foreign help. England, though prodigal of sympathy, was not disposed to intervene; France was the only hope. Napoleon's terms were accepted.[1]

The Pact of Plombières

[1] For these crucially important negotiations between Napoleon III and Cavour (here treated with unavoidable brevity) cf. Trevelyan, *Garibaldi and His Thousand*, pp. 72–81, and Whyte, *The Political Life and Letters of Cavour* (Oxford, 1930), and in particular chapters vii and viii.

VIII

THE WAR OF ITALIAN INDEPENDENCE

The Union of North and Central Italy

Napoleon and Austria

IN January 1859 Europe was startled by the news that Napoleon, at his New Year's Day reception, had addressed the Austrian ambassador as follows: 'Je regrette que les relations entre nous soient si mauvaises.' It was a bolt from the blue. Still more startling were the words of Victor Emmanuel when, on 10 January, he opened Parliament at Turin:

'Our country, small in territory, has acquired credit in the Councils of Europe because she is great in the idea she represents, in the sympathy she inspires. The situation is not free from peril, for, while we respect treaties, we cannot be insensible to the cry of anguish (*grido di dolore*) that comes to us from many parts of Italy.'

The significance of the words was instantly apprehended: 'A rocket falling on the treaties of 1815,' was the vivid description given by Sir James Hudson, the English Minister at Turin. Massari,[1] an eyewitness of the scene in the Chamber, declares the effect of it to have been simply electric.

'At every period', he says, 'the speech was interrupted by clamorous applause and cries of *Viva il Rè!* But when the King came to the words, *grido di dolore*, there was an enthusiasm quite indescribable. Senators, deputies, spectators all sprang to their feet with a bound and broke into passionate acclamations. The ministers of France, Russia, Prussia, and England were utterly astonished and carried away by the marvellous spectacle. The face of the ambassador of Naples was covered with a gloomy pallor. We poor exiles did not even attempt to wipe away the tears that flowed unrestrainedly from our eyes as we frantically clapped our hands in applause of that king who had remembered our sorrows, who had promised us a

[1] Giuseppe Massari, the biographer of Victor Emmanuel II.

country. Before the victories the plebiscites and the annexations conferred on him the crown of Italy, he reigned in our hearts; he was our king!'

Europe was aghast at the prospect thus suddenly opened of another war. Diplomacy did its utmost to avert it. England, and especially the English Court, left no stone unturned to maintain peace. 'Be reserved,' wrote Lord Malmesbury, the English Foreign Secretary, to Hudson. 'We shall not support any party that begins the strife.' On 4 February 1859 Queen Victoria wrote a personal letter to the Emperor Napoleon, in terms unusually direct even for her.

'Your Majesty', she wrote, 'has now an opportunity either by listening to the dictates of humanity and justice, and by showing to the world your intention to adhere strictly to the faithful observance of treaties, of calming the apprehensions of Europe, and of restoring its confidence in the pacific policy of your Majesty, or, on the other hand, by lending an ear to those who have an interest in creating confusion, of involving Europe in a war whose extent and duration it is scarcely possible to foresee, and which, whatever glory it may add to the arms of France, cannot but interfere materially with her internal prosperity and financial credit . . . if anything could add to the sorrow with which I should view the renewal of war in Europe, it would be to see your Majesty entering upon a course with which it would be impossible for England to associate herself.'

The Emperor's reply, couched, of course, in the most courteous terms, contained an elaborate disavowal of any intention, on the part of France, to break the peace of Europe and an assurance—technically accurate—that he had discouraged Victor Emmanuel from 'an aggressive line of conduct and had promised to support him only if he were unjustly attacked'.[1]

England and Italy

No party in England contemplated the possibility of English intervention. Lord Palmerston had long ago

[1] The Queen's letter was in fact drafted by the Prime Minister, Lord Derby. Text of both letters in Martin, *Prince Consort*, iv. 366–71. Cf. also *Q.V.L.*, iii. 418 sq.

formed the opinion that Austria would have best consulted her own interests by withdrawing from Italy.

> 'Her rule', he wrote in 1848, 'was hateful to the Italians and has long been maintained only by an expenditure of money and an exertion of military effort which left Austria less able to maintain her interests elsewhere. Italy was to her the heel of Achilles, and not the shield of Ajax. The Alps are her natural barrier and her best defence.'[1]

Nevertheless, Palmerston, when in power, consistently pressed counsels of patience and moderation upon Sardinia. Lord Malmesbury, now at the Foreign Office, sent Lord Cowley on a mission of mediation to Vienna, and the Queen addressed a letter in a similar sense to the Emperor Francis Joseph.

It was all to no purpose. The treaties between France and Sardinia were definitely concluded in January 1859. On the 30th of that month Prince Napoleon, the son of Prince Jerome Bonaparte, was married to the Princess Clothilde of Sardinia. The 'deposit' stipulated in the contract was thus paid. Would Napoleon complete it? That he was still assailed by doubts and hesitations is certain; the dangers in the path along which Cavour was luring him were painfully obvious to him; he was acting in defiance of the public opinion of Europe; he was endangering his alliance with the French clericals; the Empress looked coldly on his adventure; Walewski's sympathies were, and always had been, wholly with Austria. Might he not, even at the eleventh hour, draw back? To Cavour he insisted that unless Austria attacked, Sardinia must expect no help from France.

Cavour

The strain imposed upon Cavour during the last three months had been terrible. That Italy could ever be either liberated or united without recourse to arms was, in his judgement, impossible. War with Austria was, as Mazzini had long ago maintained, inevitable. But in desiring it Cavour stood, among the statesmen and rulers of Europe,

[1] Palmerston to King Leopold of Belgium, 15 June 1848; Ashley, *Life*, i. 98.

absolutely alone. The responsibility was crushing, and at the eleventh hour he so far yielded to the combined pressure applied by France and England as to promise that, if Sardinia were admitted to the proposed Congress on equal terms, he would, though 'foreseeing the disastrous consequences this measure would have for Italy', consent to disarmament. On 19 April his consent was made known and produced an excellent effect in Europe at large. But would Austria be satisfied? Cavour was in a fever of apprehension lest she should be; but at the very last moment Austria played Cavour's game. France, it is true, had absolutely refused the proffered mediation of England; Austria accepted it, only on condition of the unconditional disarmament of Sardinia; and on 19 April Count Buol dispatched an emissary to Turin with a demand for the immediate and unconditional disarmament of Sardinia. On 23 April Cavour summoned an emergency meeting of the Chamber of Deputies, informed the members that the Austrian ultimatum was on its way, and asked that full powers should, during the crisis, be conferred upon the King to provide for the defence of the country.

His speech was hardly finished when the arrival of the Austrian messengers was announced. As Cavour left the Chamber to meet them he remarked: 'I leave the last sitting of the Piedmontese Parliament; the next I attend will be the Parliament of the Kingdom of Italy.'

The Sardinian reply to Austria was delivered on 23 April. It was a categorical refusal. The Austrian troops thereupon crossed the Ticino. The war of Italian independence had begun.

Lord Derby, speaking in the City, described Austria's action as 'hasty, precipitate, and (because involving warfare) criminal'. Queen Victoria, writing privately to 'Uncle Leopold', commented that the rashness of Austria had 'placed them in the wrong',[1] but at the same time reported

[1] That Queen Victoria was on the whole pro-Austrian is true, but Mr Thayer (*Life of Cavour*, passim) exaggerates the pro-Austrian bias of 'Victoria and Albert', as he is pleased to describe them.

'one universal feeling of anger at the conduct of France, *and of great suspicion'*. Nor did the suspicion lack justification; yet candour compels the admission that if Napoleon was a willing prey the tempter was in Turin.

Any way, the thing was done; *alea jacta est*, as Cavour remarked. 'We have made some history,' he added, 'and now let us have some dinner.'

King Victor Emmanuel promptly issued the following proclamation to his people:

'People of Italy. Austria assails Piedmont because I have maintained the cause of our common country in the councils of Europe, because I was not insensible to your cries of anguish. Thus she now violently breaks the treaties she has never respected.

So to-day the right of the nation is complete and I can with a free conscience fulfil the vow I made on the tomb of my parent by taking up arms to defend my throne, the liberties of my people, the honour of the Italian name. I fight for the right of the whole nation. We confide in God and in our Concord; we confide in the valour of the Italian soldiers, in the alliance of the noble French nation; we confide in the justice of public opinion. I have no other ambition than to be the first soldier of Italian Independence. *Viva l'Italia.*

'Victor Emmanuel'

On the 13th May the King met at Genoa the Emperor of the French, 'his generous ally', who had come to 'liberate Italy from the Alps to the Adriatic'.

The Italian War of Liberation

The welcome accorded to the Emperor was, naturally, enthusiastic. 'It was roses, roses all the way', writes one of Cavour's biographers, 'as befitted that May afternoon and the Maytime of hope in every Italian heart. Then, if ever, Napoleon might believe himself to be a benefactor of mankind.'[1] Exactly nine weeks later he started home again. 'Thank God he's gone,' was Victor Emmanuel's exclamation after bidding his ally farewell.

The campaign which intervened was represented at the time as a triumph of French arms. Superficially it had

[1] Thayer, *Cavour*, ii. 13.

that appearance. For a month the allies carried all before them: on the 4th of June they won a great victory at Magenta; on the 8th they entered Milan; on the 24th they won the double battle of Solferino and San Martino;—and then, the 'magnanimous ally' suddenly stopped short; the victor sought an armistice from the vanquished; Napoleon met the Emperor Francis Joseph at Villafranca, and personally negotiated with him, without the concurrence of Victor Emmanuel, the terms of an armistice.

The Armistice of Villafranca

Italy was to be free not to the Adriatic but only to the Mincio; Austria was to retain Venetia and the Quadrilateral; Lombardy up to the Mincio was to be handed over to Napoleon, who would, of course, transfer it to Piedmont. Leopold of Tuscany and Francis of Modena were to be restored to the thrones from which they had been driven by their respective subjects, 'but without the use of force'; Parma and Piacenza—being Bourbon not Hapsburg principalities—were annexed to Piedmont; Italy was to be united in a confederation under the honorary presidency of the Pope.

To King Victor Emmanuel and Cavour, to the peoples of Venetia, Tuscany, Modena, and above all of the Romagna, who had looked for the speedy termination of Papal rule, the news of the Armistice came as a terrible shock. Cavour could, at the moment, attribute its conclusion to nothing but deliberate treachery on the part of Napoleon.[1]

Cavour

On learning, not directly, but by way of Paris, of the negotiations for an armistice Cavour immediately set off for the front. On his arrival he had a stormy interview with King Victor Emmanuel, he denounced the treachery of Napoleon; begged his own Sovereign to refuse Lombardy; to carry on the war alone; to abdicate—to do anything rather than accept terms which involved a surrender of all the objects for which Piedmont and her Italian allies had taken up arms; which left Austria in possession of Venetia and the Quadrilateral and in a commanding posi-

[1] A judgement he subsequently modified

tion as a member of an Italian confederation; which denied the hegemony of Piedmont, which dissipated all hope of liberty for the States of central Italy; which thrust the Romagna back under the heel of the Papacy; above all, which frustrated all hopes of Italian unity.

Victor Emmanuel

Cavour's impeachment of the terms of the armistice was substantially accurate; but Cavour had for the moment lost his head, and when (12 July) he proffered his resignation, the King accepted it. Yet he bitterly resented his minister's desertion.

'For you gentlemen', he said, 'things always come right; for you settle them by resignation. I am the one who cannot get out of a difficulty so nicely. . . . I cannot desert the cause. We work together until there comes a difficulty, then I am left alone to face the music. I am the one who is responsible before history and the country.'[1]

The reproach was not undeserved; yet Cavour was right, in the interests not less of his country than of himself, to retire.

Nevertheless, to Europe as to Victor Emmanuel, his resignation seemed an attempt to evade responsibility. He himself justified his action partly on the ground that being the 'bête noire of diplomacy' Piedmont would be much stronger in the peace negotiations without him; partly because his retirement 'was necessary to attenuate the unhappy consequences of the peace'.

'You know', he wrote to his friend Emmanuel d'Azeglio the Piedmontese minister in London, 'that the policy of the Cabinet has been frankly national; that it had in view, not the enlargement of Piedmont, but the emancipation of Italy; the establishment of a wise liberal system throughout the Peninsula. If the present peace leads to the return of the old régime in Central Italy it will do more harm than good to the national cause. I could not take the responsibility for it.'

Cavour was right. Yet at this supreme moment in their country's fate the judgement of the King was sounder than that of his minister.

[1] Quoted *ap.* Whyte, p. 326.

Victor Emmanuel, though not less deeply chagrined, looked at the matter more calmly, and estimated more justly the benefits likely to accrue to Italy. 'The political unity of Italy,' he said, 'since Novara a possibility, has become since Villafranca a necessity.'

Napoleon's motives

Napoleon's motives in concluding the armistice have been endlessly canvassed. Cavour's bitter comment contains an element of truth: 'He was tired; the weather was hot.' Tired he was, and horrified by the awful carnage which he witnessed at Solferino. But there were other reasons; nor is it now disputed that they were substantial. French financiers were already grumbling at the enormous cost of the war; the politicians saw no adequate recompense in sight; the Austrians, though driven back behind the Mincio, were not really beaten, and the military outlook was less encouraging than Napoleon's critics have imagined; above all the diplomatic situation was difficult, and the attitude of Prussia was dubious not to say menacing. To his own disgust Napoleon found himself abetting the Revolution in Italy; to the dismay of the Empress and the French clericals his success in the north was endangering the position of the Pope; the courts of England, Belgium, and Prussia were regarding with increasing suspicion the Italian adventure of the French Emperor; Prussia was actually mobilizing with a view to an offer of 'mediation'. The last-named development was not less alarming to the Austrian Emperor than to Napoleon. It was, indeed, the determining factor alike in the offer and in the acceptance of the armistice. 'The gist of the thing is', wrote Moltke to his brother, 'that Austria would rather give up Lombardy than see Prussia at the head of Germany.'

Napoleon's own explanation, given on his return to Paris, was concise and conclusive: 'To serve Italian independence I made war against the wish of Europe; as soon as the fortunes of my own country seemed to be endangered I made peace.'

Attitude of Great Britain

The attitude of England, at this critical juncture, was of the greatest moral assistance to the Italian cause, and is still gratefully remembered in Italy. The British Government declared and maintained the strictest neutrality during the war, and made every effort to localize it; but public opinion, though profoundly mistrustful of the Emperor Napoleon, was unmistakably on the side of the Italians. Queen Victoria shared to the full her subjects' mistrust, and was now, as always, unrelentingly opposed to the disturbers of the peace of Europe. So long as the responsibility for war seemed to rest on Napoleon and the Italian 'revolutionaries', she was undoubtedly 'pro-Austrian'; on the other hand, when Austria's 'rashness' precipitated the rupture she unhesitatingly condemned it. In June 1859 Lord Derby's ministry was thrown out and Lord Palmerston, at the age of seventy-five, again became Prime Minister. Lord John Russell insisted on having the Foreign Office, and Lord Clarendon, whom both Palmerston and the Queen would have preferred, modestly stood aside.

The Prime Minister and the Foreign Secretary were, however, completely in accord in disapproval of the terms arranged at Villafranca. They were well calculated, so Palmerston insisted, to drive Italy to despair. *L'Italie rendue à elle-même*, he bitterly declared, must now be read, *L'Italie vendue à l'Autriche*. Lord Palmerston had already refused a suggestion made to him by Napoleon, before the conclusion of the armistice, that England should take the lead in proposing an armistice upon terms suggested by the French. Palmerston would have none of it.

'If the French Emperor is tired of his war and finds the job tougher than he expected, let him make what proposals he pleases, and to whomsoever he pleases; but . . . let him not ask us to father his suggestions and make ourselves answerable for them.'

Thus to Lord John Russell (6 July). To the Duc de Persigny he wrote (13 July), after learning the terms of the armistice, that England could never be a party to the creation of an Italian Confederation, in which Austria would have a place in virtue of Venetia. That, he declared, would be 'to deliver Italy, bound hand and foot, to

Austria'. England, so far from acquiescing in such an arrangement,

> 'might well deem it her duty to protest most emphatically and in the face of Europe against such an enslavement of the Italian peoples. Austria ought, on the contrary, to be strictly excluded from all interference, political or military, beyond her own frontiers. If that is not done, nothing is done, and the whole business will, in very short time, have to begin all over again.'[1]

Napoleon and Italy

Perhaps something less than justice has been done to Napoleon in regard to his Italian policy. Since 1870 there has been no party in Europe concerned to vindicate his memory. That his motives were, even more than usually, mixed is true; but that he had a real sentiment for Italy is unquestionable. What he desired to see, however, was Italy liberated but not unified. When urged by the Marquis Pepoli, just after the signature of the armistice, to allow the Central States to unite with Piedmont he retorted:

> 'If annexation should cross the Apennines, unity would be accomplished, and I will not have unity; I only want independence. Unity would make trouble for me in France, on account of the Roman Question; and France would not be pleased to see on her flank a great nation that might diminish her preponderance.'[2]

With the determination thus expressed his whole policy, precedent and subsequent, was consonant. A victory over Austria was popular in France; the destruction of the Papal power would have been profoundly unpopular. What Napoleon aimed at, accordingly, was a Confederation over which the Pope would preside, in which Austria as well as Piedmont would find a place, in which there would be a place also for a Central Italian Kingdom. The crown of that kingdom the Emperor hoped to place on the brows of his cousin Prince Napoleon.

Central Italy

Plainly, the key of the situation was to be found, not for the moment at Turin, but in the States of Central Italy

[1] Ashley, *Life*, ii. 162.
[2] *ap.* Thayer, op. cit., ii. 120.

and primarily in Florence. What was the situation in those States?

The Papal States

The attitude of Pope Pius IX was entirely uncompromising. He firmly refused, though urged by Napoleon, to become the Honorary President of an Italian Confederation, or to abate one jot or tittle of his claims on the allegiance of the Romagna, or any other portion of the Papal States. After Napoleon's victories in Lombardy the Austrians had evacuated the Legations and the Papal representative followed suit. A Provisional Government was then set up in Bologna, and not only the Romagna but the Marches adhered to it. At Perugia, also, a Provisional Government was set up for Umbria. The Marches and Umbria were, however, soon re-occupied by Papal troops, the re-occupation of Perugia being followed by an indiscriminate massacre of men, women, and children.

Romagna

The Romagna, on the contrary, maintained its independence, declared its adherence to Piedmont, and shortly afterwards united itself with Modena and Parma, under the dictatorship of Luigi Farini, one of the stoutest supporters of Cavour and an ardent Italian patriot.[1]

Modena

After the defeat of the Austrians at Magenta (4 June) Duke Francis V had withdrawn from Modena and his subjects placed themselves under the protection of Victor Emmanuel, who sent Farini to administer the Duchy as Piedmontese Commissioner (19 June).

Parma

Parma showed more hesitation, but the Duchess, after more than one feint, finally withdrew on 10 June, and the Parmesans accepted as governor Cavour's nominee Count Pallieri. The union of Parma and Modena with Piedmont was part of the bargain struck by Cavour with Napoleon at Plombières; but after the armistice their fate, still more the fate of Tuscany and the Romagna, hung for some time in the balance.

[1] L. C. Farini (1812–66), a native of Ravenna, had held office at Rome under Pius IX in 1848, but after 1849 retired to Turin; he edited *Il Risorgimento* and was elected to the Piedmontese Parliament; he was in d'Azeglio's cabinet, 1851–2.

On this question the English Government had very decided views, and the language employed by Lord Palmerston in correspondence with Lord Cowley, British ambassador in Paris, contained a very nasty hint to Napoleon, as well as to other recently crowned heads. 'The people of the Duchies', he wrote (22 August 1859), 'have as good a right to change their leaders as the people of England, France, Belgium, and Sweden; and the annexation of the Duchies to Piedmont would be an unmixed good for Italy, and for France and for Europe.'[1]

Lord John Russell's language was not less emphatic and even more picturesque: 'The disposal of the Tuscans and Modenese as if they were so many firkins of butter is somewhat too profligate.'

Tuscany

It was Tuscany that held the key of the position, and fortunate it was for Tuscany and for Italy that at this critical moment they could command the services of so strong a man, so disinterested a patriot, as Baron Bettino Ricasoli.[2] To get rid of the Grand Duke was not difficult. On the outbreak of the war he had declared his intention to remain neutral; but the Florentines were bent on co-operation with Piedmont, and on 28 April Leopold was compelled to withdraw from his Duchy—never to return to it. A Provisional Government was promptly set up and offered the Dictatorship to Victor Emmanuel, but, with the approval of Cavour and to the satisfaction of Napoleon, he declined it. Carlo Boncompagni, Piedmontese Minister at Florence was, however, nominated by Victor Emmanuel to act as 'Commissioner Extraordinary for the war of independence'. He presently appointed a ministry which included Ricasoli.

After the armistice the Piedmontese Commissioners were officially instructed to withdraw from the central Duchies, but Farini (privately urged thereto by Cavour) remained at Modena, and governed as dictator Parma and

[1] Ashley, *Life*, ii. 371.

[2] For an admirable sketch of Ricasoli see W. K. Hancock, *Ricasoli and the Risorgimento in Tuscany* (Faber, 1926).

the Romagna as well, now consolidated with Modena under the title of Emilia. Ricasoli, on the withdrawal of Boncompagni, was similarly dictator of Tuscany.

For all the States of Central Italy the problem was a difficult one; not least for Tuscany, though most of all for the Romagna.

In Tuscany, autonomist sentiment still remained strong, and in the absence of the Grand Duke there might have been some support for a Napoleonic kingdom. But in the breast of Ricasoli there burned the fire of a wider patriotism, and his influence sufficed to secure from the Assembly a unanimous resolution, not for annexation to Piedmont, but in favour of Tuscany forming 'part of a strong Italian kingdom under the constitutional sceptre of King Victor Emmanuel' (20 August).

The resolution was conveyed to Victor Emmanuel on 3 September, but the Peace Conference was still in session at Zurich, and the King's formal reply to the request for union was consequently guarded. In private, however, he used very different language to the delegates, who received an enthusiastic welcome from the populace both in Turin and Genoa. Emilia followed the example of Tuscany, and to the Emilian delegates Victor Emmanuel made a similar reply, promising to support their wishes at the Council Board of Europe, but uttering no word of annexation.

The Treaties of Peace were signed at Zürich on the 10th of November, the terms embodied therein being virtually identical with those agreed upon at Villafranca.

Almost simultaneously, however, the Central States elected as 'Regent' Prince Eugenio di Carignano. His election conveyed a threefold hint: the old rulers were not to be restored; Napoleon was not to create a Central Italian kingdom for his cousin; and the 'Regent' would presently give place to a king—Victor Emmanuel. The French Emperor, however, vetoed the appointment, and suggested that the settlement of the whole Italian question, including the future of the Papal States, should be referred to a European Congress. This suggestion was reinforced by a pamphlet which, issued towards the end of December under the title of *The Pope and the Congress*, was certainly inspired if not actually written by Napoleon. The main proposal was that the Pope, while retaining the Patrimony of St. Peter, should surrender the rest of the Papal States, which in their recalcitrance were a source rather of weakness than of strength to the Holy Father.[1] The Pope indignantly repudiated the suggestion; England saw in the proposed Congress one more attempt on Napoleon's part to induce Europe at large, and England in particular, to pull the chestnuts out of the fire for him; Austria would have none of it. The idea of the Congress dropped, and Napoleon's policy took yet another turn: Central Italy should be allowed to unite with Piedmont, but France must have its pound of flesh—Savoy and Nice.

Cavour in office

Such was the situation by which on his return to office (20 January 1860) Cavour found himself confronted. 'Let the people of central Italy themselves declare what they want and we will stand by their decision, let the consequences be what they may.' Such was Cavour's inflexible determination as regards Tuscany and Emilia. As to Savoy and Nice, if Italy were freed from the Alps to the Adriatic, the price would have to be paid. But the inevitable blow to Italian pride must be softened by the application of the same device as that invoked in the case of central Italy: the populations concerned must express their own wishes by means of a plebiscite. It was a highly ingenious suggestion. The rumour that Napoleon was to get Savoy and Nice had roused bitter indignation in England. 'In the opinion of Her Majesty's Government the King of Sardinia will besmirch the arms of the House of Savoy if he yields to France the cradle of his ancient and illustrious House.' So Lord John wrote to Sir James Hudson. But Lord John

[1] The 'Papal States' had long consisted of (1) The Patriarchate or Patrimony of St. Peter bounded by the Kingdom of Naples on the south and the Grand Duchy of Tuscany on the north; (2) Umbria with Perugia as capital; (3) The Marches—an Adriatic Province stretching from the river Tronto to San Marino; and (4) The Romagna, extending from San Marino to the mouths of the Po.

was notoriously more apt at homilies than at action: his words were generally braver than his deeds. Suppose that Cavour, in reliance on English support, had defied Napoleon, would England have supported him in arms? Those who recall the part subsequently played by the same Whig ministers in relation to the Danish Duchies will hesitate to give an affirmative reply. Any way, Cavour felt himself bound by the bargain of Plombières. The price must be paid.

Victor Emmanuel and Savoy

There was the King to be considered. To surrender to France the 'cradle of his race' was for Victor Emmanuel 'the sacrifice most painful to his heart'. But he had already sacrificed his daughter to the French alliance. As 'the child had gone, why not the cradle too?': such was his bitter comment on the transaction.

Mazzini and Garibaldi

Garibaldi and Mazzini regarded the cession of these provinces as a characteristic instance of Cavour's diplomatic chicanery. To them Cavour was a 'low intriguer'; Napoleon nothing better than a 'vulpine knave'. Garibaldi, a Nizzian by birth, particularly resented the cession of Nice. 'You have made me', he complained, 'a foreigner in the land of my birth.' But Cavour had no option. To defy France would be to invite attack from Austria. Only with the assent of France could northern and central Italy be united; but the assent of France had to be purchased by the sacrifice of the trans-Alpine Provinces.

On 11 March a plebiscite in the central States declared for union with the kingdom of Italy; on the 24th Cavour signed the Treaty for the cession of Savoy and Nice; on the 25th elections were held for the Italian Parliament; on 2 April the first Parliament, representing no fewer than 11,000,000 Italians, met at Turin.

'The last time I opened Parliament,' said the King in his first speech to the new Parliament, 'when Italy was sunk in sorrows and the state menaced by great dangers, faith in Divine justice comforted me and augured well for our destinies. In a very brief space of time an invasion was repelled, Lombardy liberated by the glorious achievements of the army, Central

Italy freed by the marvellous merit of her people; and to-day I have here assembled around me the representatives of the rights and of the hopes of the nation. . . . In turning our attention', he concluded, 'to the new order of affairs we invite all sincere opinions to a noble emulation that we may attain the grand end of the well-being of the people and the greatness of the country. It is no longer the Italy of the Romans, nor that of the Middle Ages; it must no longer be the battle-field of ambitious foreigners, but it must rather be the Italy of the Italians.'

Then came the one discordant note:

'In gratitude to France, for the good of Italy, to consolidate the union between two nations that have a common origin, principles and destinies—and finding it necessary to make some sacrifice, I have made that which has cost my heart dear. Subject to the vote of the people, the approbation of Parliament, and the consent of Switzerland, I have made a treaty for the reunion of Savoy and Nice to France.'

Three weeks later the 'vote of the people' was taken in Savoy and Nice; the vote was almost unanimous in favour of union with France. At the end of May the Italian Parliament, by an overwhelming majority ratified the Treaty.

Thus the curtain falls on the first act of the drama of Italian unification: Cavour's work was half done. The Scene of the next Act was in the south. Three days after the meeting of the Italian Parliament at Turin an insurrection broke out in Sicily.

IX

THE UNION OF NORTH AND SOUTH

Garibaldi, Victor Emmanuel, and Cavour

FOR the next act of the drama the stage was set in Sicily and Naples. The leading part was played by Garibaldi; though had it not been for the wise and prudent diplomacy of Cavour the act might well have ended not in triumph but in tragedy. As the action becomes at this point exceedingly complicated, it may be well at the outset to disentangle some of the main threads, and indicate, very briefly, the attitude of some of the leading actors.

Sicily and Naples

The first scene of the act was laid in Sicily, which, as we have seen, had long been restless under the rule of its Bourbon kings, and ardently desired autonomy and independence. In the Italian drama the Sicilians had little interest, and none whatever in the fate of the Neapolitans, whom they detested. The attitude of the Neapolitans cannot be indicated so simply or briefly. No worse government, except perhaps that of the Pope, was to be found in Italy than that of the Bourbon kings of Naples. But their rule, though infamous according to our standards, was not wholly intolerable. A more pitiable creature than Francis II, the last of the Neapolitan Bourbons, who succeeded his father, 'Bomba', in May 1859, has rarely occupied a throne. But his queen, a youthful Bavarian princess, was as spirited as she was beautiful. The Neapolitan peasants were too far sunk in superstition and ignorance to be conscious of political degradation; the army was loyal to the end. Discontent was, however, rife among the more educated middle classes, upon whom the hand of the tyrant pressed most heavily. But their aspirations were rather in the direction of Neapolitan liberty than of Italian unity. None could, however, be insensible to the gross misgovernment of which they were especially the victims.

'Naples and Sicily', wrote Sir Henry Elliot, 'were at that time entirely governed by an irresponsible police, uncontrolled by any form of law, and regardless of the most elementary considerations of justice. Men by hundreds were arrested, exiled, or imprisoned for years, not only without going through any form of trial, but often without being even informed of what, or by whom they were accused, or being allowed the opportunity of saying a word to explain or refute the accusation . . . while the police connived at ordinary criminals, their zeal and activity knew no bounds in hunting down supposed political offenders. . . . Another frightful abuse was the arrest and imprisonment of men on secret private denunciation, more especially on that of the priests. . . .[1]

Mr. Gladstone and Naples

It was with the unhappy fate of the political prisoners that Mr. Gladstone was particularly concerned when, in 1851, he addressed his memorable letters to Lord Aberdeen.[2]

It was with no idea of political investigation, still less of political propagandism, that Mr. Gladstone visited southern Italy in the winter of 1850–1. But he naturally met many of the foremost men in Naples, and was quickly enlightened by them as to the condition of affairs. He witnessed the trial of Carlo Poerio, a strict constitutionalist, a leading politician and an ex-minister of the Crown, who with Settembrini[3] and forty other political prisoners was sentenced to lifelong imprisonment under revolting conditions. He managed to visit some of the prisons; he saw refined gentlemen, imprisoned for no proved offence, chained two and two in double irons to common felons; his generous spirit was roused within him, and he was moved first to indignation then to vehement remonstrance. He was himself a Conservative, an ex-minister in a Conservative Government. He could not condone the misdeeds of

[1] Elliot, *Some Revolutions*, pp. 6–10. Sir Henry Elliot was British Minister at Naples from June 1859 to November 1860, and he is therefore a valuable first-hand authority for the events of that period.

[2] The full text of these Letters together with Mr. Gladstone's *Examination of the Official Reply of the Neapolitan Government* (1852) may (and should) be read in full in *Gleanings of Past Years*, vol. iv (John Murray, 1879).

[3] For admirable sketches of Poerio and Settembrini, cf. Countess Martinengo-Cesaresco, *Italian Characters*, i, ii.

an established government. He could not keep silence. For the step, admittedly unusual, which he was impelled to take he adduced three reasons:

'First, that the present practices of the Government of Naples, in reference to real or supposed political offenders, are an outrage upon religion, upon civilization, upon humanity and upon decency. Secondly, that these practices are certainly and even rapidly doing the work of republicanism in that country: a political creed which has little natural or habitual root in the character of the people. Thirdly, that as a member of the Conservative party in one of the great family of European nations I am compelled to remember that that party stands in virtual and real though perhaps unconscious alliance with all the established governments of Europe as such; and that according to the measure of its influence they suffer more or less of moral detriment from its reverses and derive strength and encouragement from its successes. This principle . . . is of great practical importance in reference to the Government of Naples, which from whatever cause appears to view its own social like its physical position as one under the shadow of a volcano, and which is doing everything in its power from day to day to give reality to its own dangers and fresh intensity together with fresh cause to its fears.'

'It is not', he goes on to say—'it is not mere imperfection, not corruption in low practices, not occasional severity that I am about to describe; it is incessant systematic deliberate violation of the law by the Power appointed to watch over and maintain it. It is such violation of human and written law as this, carried on for the purpose of violating every other law, written and eternal, temporal and divine; it is the wholesale persecution of virtue when united with intelligence, operating upon such a scale that entire classes may with truth be said to be its object; . . . it is the awful profanation of public religion, by its notorious alliance in the governing powers with the violation of every moral law under the stimulants of fear and vengeance; it is the perfect prostitution of the judicial office which has made it under veils only too threadbare and transparent, the degraded recipient of the vilest and clumsiest forgeries, got up wilfully and deliberately by the immediate advisers of the Crown for the purpose of destroying the peace, the freedom, and even if not by capital sentence the life of men among the most virtuous, upright, intelligent, distinguished and refined of the whole community; it is the savage and cowardly system of moral as well as in a lower degree of physical torture through which the sentences extracted from the debased courts of justice are carried into effect. The effect of all this is total inversion of all the moral and social ideas. Law instead of being respected is odious. Force and not affection is the foundation of government. There is no association but a violent antagonism between the idea of freedom and that of order. The governing power which teaches of itself that it is the image of God upon earth, is clothed in the view of the overwhelming majority of the thinking public with all the vices for its attributes. I have seen and heard the too true expression used, "This is the negation of God erected into a system of Government".'

It is impossible to follow in detail the minute evidence upon which the English statesman based this appalling but not exaggerated indictment. It may be read, together with an examination of the official reply put forth in the name of the Neapolitan Government, in the volume already cited.

The publication of these Letters, written by a man in Mr. Gladstone's position, caused an immense sensation, not merely in England, but throughout Europe. Lord Aberdeen was somewhat embarrassed, but Lord Palmerston gave his unequivocal support to Mr. Gladstone, and in 1856 both the British and French Governments took the unusual step of withdrawing their ministers from Naples as a protest against King Ferdinand's misgovernment. Three years later Bomba so far yielded to the storm as to liberate more than sixty of his prisoners with a view to their deportation to the United States. They managed, however, to get control of the ship in which they were sent off to America, and diverted its course to England, where a cordial reception awaited them.

Position of Cavour

That Cavour ardently desired the complete unification of Italy is undeniable. But he was too great a statesman to wish to see the process hurried. On the contrary, after the union of northern and central Italy, he would have called a temporary halt. That both the Two Sicilies and Rome would ultimately form part of a unified Italian kingdom he never doubted; but neither Italy nor Europe was, in his judgement, yet ready for this further move.

Attitude of the Powers

Austria, needless to say, was strongly opposed alike to the further aggrandizement of Piedmont, and to any further weakening of the principle of 'legitimacy' as represented by the Pope and the Neapolitan Bourbons. The Emperor of the French, less concerned about 'legitimacy' was equally anxious, for domestic reasons, to maintain the Temporal sovereignty of the Papacy and to prevent the union of southern and northern Italy. As late as July 1860 the French minister at Turin pressed Cavour to grant the eleventh-hour appeal of Naples for an alliance with Piedmont, while at Naples the French minister declared definitely that France would not allow annexation. But to the Neapolitan royalists Napoleon had himself declared a month earlier (12 June) that they must not look to him for active help against Garibaldi or against Piedmont. 'We French', he declared, 'do not wish for the annexation of south Italy to the kingdom of Piedmont, because we think it contrary to our interests.' He would be delighted, he added, if the Neapolitan Royalists defeated Garibaldi; but they must do it themselves. The victor of Solferino and the liberator of Lombardy could not oppose in arms the cause of Italian nationality in Naples. Rome was a different matter. 'The French flag', he pointed out, 'is actually waving on the Pope's territory, and then there is the question of religion.' If the Italians attacked Rome, he would be compelled to act; but Naples must defend itself—preferably by alliance, if they could still get it, with Piedmont.

Victor Emmanuel and Naples

Could they still get it? In May 1859 Victor Emmanuel had held out the hand of friendship to the young King of the Two Sicilies. It had been rejected. So late as 15 April 1860, on the very eve of Garibaldi's departure from Genoa, the offer was renewed—on terms.

'Italy', so Victor Emmanuel wrote to his 'dear Cousin' of Naples, 'can be divided into two powerful States of the North and the South which, if they adopt the same national policy, may uphold the great idea of our times—National Independence. But in order to realize this conception, it is, I think, necessary that your Majesty abandon the course you have held hitherto. The principle of dualism, if it is well established and honestly pursued, can still be accepted by Italians. But if you allow some months to pass without attending to my friendly suggestion, your Majesty will perhaps experience the bitterness of the terrible words—*too late*.'

Cavour must have been well aware, when he approved this letter, that the 'friendly suggestions'—internal reform and cordial alliance with Piedmont—would not be attended to. He and his master were cognizant of the fact that for months past Naples had been negotiating with the Papacy, Austria, and the exiled rulers of Parma and Modena, for a combined attack on Piedmont and for the restoration of the Romagna to the Pope, if not for the reinstatement of the former rulers in the Duchies.

Attitude of England

Nevertheless, the preference for dualism expressed by Victor Emmanuel may have been sincere. Cavour doubted whether the pear was yet ripe; so did foreign friends of Italy. Italian unity had no more ardent well-wishers than Sir James Hudson, the English minister at Turin, and Mr. Henry Elliot, who represented us at Naples. The attitude taken up by England in July and August 1860 was decisive; it gave Naples immediately to Garibaldi, and ultimately to Italy; but not until and after Garibaldi's conquest of Sicily were Hudson and Elliot converted to the idea of Italian unity. So late as 18 May Hudson had argued strongly against the fusion of north and south Italy; contending that the intervening Papal territory would make it difficult to rule Naples from Turin or Florence, and that the corruption of the Neapolitans was so abominable that 'their junction with north Italy, where honesty is the rule in public affairs, would merely produce a social decomposition, and then a political petrifaction'.[1] No one was

[1] Cf. Trevelyan, *Making of Italy*, p. 28, and Appendix A, where most interesting extracts are given from the correspondence of Hudson and Elliot respectively with Russell.

in closer touch both with the King and Cavour than Hudson, and in this passage he probably speaks their mind. Elliot wrote from the Neapolitan angle:

> 'At that time' [i.e. summer of 1859], writes Elliot, 'the strongest of the Neapolitan Liberals would have been found unanimous in repudiating with indignation the notion of their absorption into the comparatively small northern kingdom of Sardinia . . . it was not until after the extraordinary success of Garibaldi that all parties united in regarding incorporation with Piedmont as the only issue left open to them.'[1]

Garibaldi's Sicilian expedition was indeed the deciding factor, and to the story of it we now turn.

Garibaldi and the Thousand

The sequence of events is important, and even at the cost of repetition must be recalled. On 11 March the Central Provinces decided by plebiscite on union with Piedmont. On the 22nd Victor Emmanuel accepted their decision and appointed the Prince of Carignano as Viceroy, with Baron Ricasoli as Governor-General. On the same day Cavour learnt from Villamarina, his trusted agent in Naples, that a Papal envoy had visited Francis II with a view to promoting Neapolitan intervention in the Romagna. Three days later the elections were held for an Italian Parliament, which met for the first time at Turin on 2 April. On 5 April an insurrection, stimulated by Francesco Crispi—destined to play a great part in the politics of United Italy—and Rosolino Pilo, broke out in Sicily. On 15 April Victor Emmanuel wrote to Francis II of Naples the second of the two warning letters already referred to; on the 18th and 22nd the plebiscites, approving union with France, were taken in Nice and Savoy, and on the 26th the Parliament at Turin ratified by an overwhelming majority the Treaty which embodied the agreement for the cession of those provinces.

Meanwhile, Garibaldi having denounced in the Chamber a treaty which involved 'human traffic', and made him an alien in the city of his birth (Nice), sailed with his 'Thousand' volunteers for Sicily.

[1] Elliot, *Some Revolutions*, p. 8.

Attitude of the Government

Garibaldi waited for no leave from the Piedmontese Government. On 29 September 1859 he had written to the Sicilians:

'My brothers, the cause fought for by me and my comrades in arms is not the cause of a parish, but the cause of our Italy, from Trapani to the Isonzo, from Taranto to Nice. Therefore the work of the redemption of Sicily is the work of our own redemption, and we will fight for it with the same zeal with which we fought on the Lombard battle-fields.'[1]

He kept his word. On the eve of his embarkation at Genoa he wrote to the King:

'I know that I embark on a perilous enterprise. If we achieve it I shall be proud to add to your Majesty's crown a new and perhaps more glorious jewel, always on the condition that your Majesty will stand opposed to counsellors who would cede this province to the foreigner, as has been done with the city of my birth.'

The Piedmontese Government was, as a fact, in complete sympathy with the objects of the expedition, though had it been possible, they would have postponed it. On 30 March Cavour wrote to Villamarina at Naples:

'Evidently events of great importance are preparing in the south of Italy. . . . You know that I do not desire to push the Neapolitan question to a premature crisis. . . . It would be to our interest if the present state of things continued for some years longer. But . . . I believe that we shall soon be forced to form a plan which I would like to have had more time to mature.'[2]

Cavour was right; but he could control neither events nor Garibaldi. Cavour, indeed, understood Garibaldi better than Garibaldi understood him. Victor Emmanuel, even better than Cavour, understood him, and did all in his power, consistently with loyalty to his minister, to assist him. He contributed 3,000,000 francs out of his private pocket towards the expenses;[3] the public also subscribed

[1] *ap.* Trevelyan, p. 143.
[2] Chiala, *Lettere*, iii. 235–6 (quoted by Trevelyan).
[3] Elliot, op. cit., p. 80.

generously; the *National Society* supplied guns and ammunition, though not in adequate amounts; and the Government turned a blind eye to the enlistment of volunteers and other preparations which went on busily, almost ostentatiously, at Genoa.

Cavour and Garibaldi

Cavour had a difficult game to play, but he played it with consummate skill; so skilfully, indeed, that the Mazzinians, despite all the evidence to the contrary, have always asserted that he spared no pains to frustrate the objects of the expedition. Lord Acton describes his conduct as 'a triumph of unscrupulous statesmanship', and evidently regards Garibaldi as his catspaw and dupe. Lord Acton's verdict seems to be as far from the truth as that of the Mazzinisti. Mr. Trevelyan summarizes the facts with judicial impartiality: 'Mazzini and his friends instigated the expedition; Garibaldi accomplished it; the King and Cavour allowed it to start, and when it had begun to succeed, gave it the support and guidance without which it must inevitably have failed mid-way.'[1]

Conquest of Sicily

The 'Thousand' embarked at Quarto near Genoa on 6 May; on the 11th, after a very narrow escape from Neapolitan cruisers, they landed at Marsala. On the 15th Garibaldi defeated the Neapolitan forces at Calatafimi, and on the 27th successfully assaulted Palermo, which was finally evacuated on 6 June. There was some desperate fighting at Milazzo (20 July), but by the end of July Garibaldi was master of the whole island, except the actual citadel of Messina and a few of the Sicilian ports. The Neapolitan garrison was allowed to retain the citadel of Messina, but under a pledge of neutrality, which averted all danger to the future plans of Garibaldi, as far as the island was concerned. Soon after landing at Marsala Garibaldi had accepted the dictatorship of the island, immediately decreed conscription for the islanders, and imposed stern discipline alike on them and upon his own volunteers. Cavour attempted to induce Garibaldi to annex the island at once to the kingdom of Italy, but

[1] Op. cit., p. 162.

Garibaldi definitely declined to do so. His obstinacy served Cavour and Italy well. Had Victor Emmanuel become responsible for Sicily in July, Garibaldi would never have been allowed by the Powers to cross the Straits. The conquest and therefore the annexation of Naples might have been indefinitely postponed.

Attitude of the Powers

As it was, the diplomatic situation was intensely critical. The English Government alone made no secret of its sympathy with Garibaldi's enterprise; Napoleon III would do nothing to offend England. But the attitude of the eastern Courts was very different. 'A horde of pirates', 'bandits', 'desperadoes', 'dregs of the human race'—such were the least opprobrious of the descriptions applied to Garibaldi and his followers. Cavour had to bear the brunt of the attack, but he was not dismayed. 'Here things do not go too badly,' he wrote from Turin to La Farina, his agent in Sicily. 'The diplomatists do not molest us overmuch. Russia made a fearful hubbub—Prussia less': Cavour could write in this light vein; but his responsibilities were heavy. When, a few months later, he sped his king and the Italian army on the expedition to the south, he knew not whether they might not, on their return, find Turin in the occupation of the Austrians—or it might be the French. But courage, combined with prudence, earned its appropriate reward. We must not, however, anticipate events.

Cavour and the Two Sicilies

Cavour had failed, fortunately as it now appears, to get Sicily annexed to Piedmont. He was determined that if he could help it, Garibaldi should not be in a similar dictatorial position on the mainland. Down to the middle of July he was endeavouring to stir up an insurrection in Naples which would forestall Garibaldi's intervention. Before the end of July he had realized the hopelessness of doing this, and had changed his plans to meet the changed situation. Garibaldi must on no account be prevented from crossing to the mainland. But Napoleon was determined to stop him, if England would join in a blockade of the Sicilian coasts. The English Government were disposed to agree that Garibaldi had already been allowed enough rope, and must not be permitted 'to cross the Straits'.

On 27 July Garibaldi received two letters from his Sovereign. In the first, intended for publication to the world, Garibaldi was reminded that the King had *not* approved his expedition to Sicily and was advised 'to renounce the idea of crossing to the mainland . . . provided the King of Naples pledges himself to evacuate the island and leave the Sicilians free to decide their own future'. In a second and secret communication Garibaldi was bidden to refuse, with every expression of devotion, to obey his Sovereign. Garibaldi duly replied in the terms dictated (secretly) by the King. Meanwhile (25 July), Lord John Russell was induced to decline Napoleon's invitation, and to allow Garibaldi to cross to Calabria. Napoleon was dumbfounded, as well he might be, by England's *volte face,* but he was unwilling to take any action of which England disapproved; Garibaldi, with a handful of followers, crossed the Straits (18–21 August) and took Reggio by storm.

Francis II

Meanwhile, Francis II, in deference to the advice of Napoleon, and anxious also to conciliate English opinion, had (25 June) published a Liberal Constitution for Naples and promised to grant autonomy to Sicily under a prince of the Royal House. He also made humble suit at Turin for an alliance with Piedmont. It was too late. Carlo Poerio and other Neapolitan exiles were in Turin, and endeavoured to convince Cavour that Bourbon promises were made only to be broken; that Francis II was likely enough to stage anew the blasphemous farces performed by his predecessors in 1821 and 1848.

'The Neapolitan Government', said Poerio, speaking in the Chamber at Turin, 'has the tradition of perjury handed down from father to son. . . . I trust that the Ministers of Victor Emmanuel will not stretch out their hands to a Government which certainly is the most declared of the enemies of Italian independence.' (29 June.)

Cavour was placed in a cruel dilemma. His sympathies were all with the Neapolitan liberals; but he had the

Powers to consider. France had suggested the alliance; England officially supported France; Austria, Russia, and Prussia would have welcomed anything which would save legitimacy in Naples. 'If we consent to the alliance', wrote Cavour, 'we are lost. If we reject it what will Europe say? I was never, in my life, more embarrassed.' He endeavoured, as we have seen, to stir up revolution in Naples, until his agents there convinced him that only Garibaldi could do that. So Garibaldi must be allowed to cross the Straits.

Conquest of Naples

Garibaldi crossed; and in the first week of September was marching on Naples. On 6 September Francis II and his Queen quitted the capital and sailed for Gaeta. On the following day Garibaldi, hurrying on in advance of his army, entered Naples, proclaimed himself Dictator, and demanded confirmation of his Dictatorship from the Piedmontese Government. The Parliament at Turin had already, at Cavour's instance, approved the annexation of the Two Sicilies to the Italian Kingdom. Would Garibaldi respect that decision?

Garibaldi declared that he would not permit annexation until he could proclaim Victor Emmanuel King of Italy in Rome. Everything was now at stake: the life-work of Cavour; the life-work of Mazzini; the life-work of Garibaldi himself. To suggest that 'called upon to face an awful moment to which Heaven had joined great issues' Cavour was 'happy as a lover' would be affectation. He was distraught with anxiety; yet he was 'equal to the need'. By a masterly stroke of policy the control of the movement was taken out of the rash hands of the impetuous crusader, and confirmed in those of sober statesmanship. Cavour decided to dispatch a Royal army to the Roman Marches with the twofold object of warding off from the Romagna the attack threatened by the Papacy, and of obstructing, if necessary, the advance of the Garibaldians on Rome. 'If we do not arrive on the Volturno', he wrote to the Italian ministers abroad, 'before Garibaldi arrives at La Cattolica, the monarchy is lost. Italy will remain a prey to revolution.' Napoleon had given a qualified assent. 'If Piedmont', he said, 'thinks this move absolutely necessary to save herself from the abyss, be it so; but it must be taken at her own risk and peril.' It was. But, in truth, there was risk and peril either way. Austrian and Irish troops in the Pope's pay were holding Umbria and the Marches, and threatening the Romagna. French troops were defending the Patrimony of St. Peter. Austria was still in Venetia ready to pounce on Lombardy and Piedmont. Garibaldi was intent on attacking Rome.

Cavour decided that he had no alternative but to face the peril and take the risks. He summoned the Pope to dismiss his foreign levies. Pius IX very naturally refused (7 September). Accordingly, on the 11th, 35,000 Italian troops under General Cialdini crossed the frontier at La Cattolica, and on the 18th they inflicted a crushing defeat on the Papal army at Castelfidardo. On the 29th Ancona surrendered, and the Italians were masters of Umbria and the Marches.

Meanwhile, at the moment when Victor Emmanuel's army was marching south, Garibaldi and his Red-shirts were marching north. Mazzini, who had unfortunately gone to Naples (17 September), urged Garibaldi forwards. 'If you are not on your way towards Rome or Venice before three weeks are over, you will have lost the initiative.' Mazzini's warning was, from the republican standpoint, perfectly sound. Garibaldi, indeed, needed no urging. Fortunately, however, for Italy, for Cavour, and not least for Garibaldi himself, the situation was saved by the Bourbon. At the critical moment Bombino and the Neapolitan army played Cavour's game for him. For nearly a fortnight (19 September–1 October) they engaged Garibaldi on the Volturno without decisive issue. On 1 and 2 October, however, Garibaldi won a great victory; the Neapolitan army was scattered; King Francis II fled to Gaeta; and Garibaldi was left face to face with Victor Emmanuel, who had joined the army at Ancona on 3 October. 'Go to Naples,' was Palmerston's advice to

Cavour. Though all the rest of Europe was against him, he needed no bidding. He urged upon his sovereign 'infinite consideration' for Garibaldi, but expressed his belief that the latter 'will be overjoyed to lay his dictatorship at the feet of your Majesty'. He judged his 'fiercest enemy' aright. On 15 October the King and his army crossed the frontier into Neapolitan territory. On the 21st the plebiscite, on which Cavour had (in preference to the summoning of a parliament) insisted, was taken; and Naples and Sicily declared, with few dissentients, for annexation to the kingdom of Italy. Garibaldi then proved himself hardly less great than Cavour.

The Two Sicilies annexed to Italy

'To-morrow', he announced, 'Victor Emmanuel, the elect of the nation, will break down the frontier which has divided us for so many centuries from the rest of the country and . . . will appear amongst us. Let us worthily receive him who is sent by Providence. . . . No more political colours, no more parties, no more discords. Let Italy be one under the King *Galantuomo*, who is the symbol of our regeneration and of the prosperity of our country.'

On 26 October Garibaldi and Victor Emmanuel met; on 7 November they rode into Naples side by side. Garibaldi's work was done. He had added to his master's crown a 'new and more brilliant jewel'; he had commended his sovereign to his new subjects; and then, refusing all rewards and decorations, he went quietly away to his island home in Caprera. Well had it been for his fame and for his country's peace had he been content to remain there.

Capua had surrendered to the Italian army on 2 November, but Francis II held out for some months at Gaeta, where he was protected by a French fleet. On 13 February, however, Gaeta was at last surrendered; and the citadel of Messina on the 22nd. Exactly a month later the surrender of Civitella del Tronto marked the final extinction of Bourbon rule in Italy. Francis II found refuge in Rome.

Lord John Russell's Dispatch

At the critical moment the English Government had once again performed a signal service to the Italian *Risorgi-*

mento. Early in November a dispatch (dated 27 October) from Lord John Russell to Hudson was published in Italy.

'His Majesty's Government', wrote Lord John, 'can see no sufficient ground for the severe censure with which Austria, France, Prussia, and Russia have visited the acts of the King of Sardinia. H.M. Government will turn their eyes rather to the gratifying prospect of a people building up the edifice of their liberties and consolidating the work of their independence.'

From Naples Sir Henry Elliot wrote to his chief (12 November):

'For the last week Naples, and I believe Italy, have been more occupied about your dispatch to Hudson than about anything else. . . . Villamarina's first exclamation was that it was worth more than 100,000 men.'[1]

From Rome Mr. Odo Russell wrote to his uncle (1 December):

'Ever since your famous dispatch of the 27th, you are blessed night and morning by twenty millions of Italians . . . the moment it was published in Italian thousands of people copied it from each other to carry it to their homes and weep over it for joy and gratitude in the homes of their families, away from brutal mercenaries and greasy priests.'[2]

Cavour also wrote personally to Lord John expressing his profound gratitude for the service thus rendered to Italy.

The Italian Parliament

Cavour's own race was nearly run. Elections for Parliament were held in January 1861 and on 18 February a Parliament representing all parts of Italy, save Venetia and Rome, met at Turin. The union of north and south was thus formally cemented, and Victor Emmanuel reigned over 23,000,000 Italian subjects.

Unfortunately the harmony of these early days was marred by a vehement and bitter attack delivered by Garibaldi, from his place in Parliament, on Cavour. He declared, as he concluded an impassioned harangue, 'that it

[1] For dispatch in full see British Parliamentary Papers, pp. 125–7, and cf. also Trevelyan, op. cit., pp. 282–3 and 314.

[2] Walpole, *Life of Lord John Russell*, ii. 328.

would be for ever impossible for him to clasp the hand of the man who had sold his country to the foreigner or to ally himself with a government whose cold and mischievous hand was trying to foment fratricidal war.' Cavour was deeply hurt, but replied with superb self-control:

'I know, he said, that between me and the honourable Genera Garibaldi there exists a fact which divides us two like an abyss. I believed that I fulfilled a painful duty—the most painful I ever accomplished in my life—in counselling the king and proposing to Parliament to approve the cession of Savoy and Nice to France. By the grief that I then experienced I can understand that which the honourable General Garibaldi must have felt, and if he cannot forgive me this act I will not bear him any grudge for it.'

At the urgent entreaty of the King himself the two men subsequently met and a reconciliation was effected. Three months later (5 June 1861) Cavour passed away. Even his iron constitution succumbed at last to the superhuman exertions he had made; to the manifold and harassing anxieties he had undergone; to the alternations of exciting triumph and humiliating failure in which his last years had been passed. The King was with him to the end. His thoughts even in delirium were still with the country he had served so well. 'I will have no state of siege for the Neapolitans,' he cried, '*li lavi, li lavi, li lavi!*' Purify them, purify them, purify them! To his devoted parish priest, who had braved the decree of excommunication and administered the last rites of the Church, he whispered: 'Italy is made; all is safe.'

Not, however, to Cavour, nor to his immediate successors, was it given to solve the almost insoluble problem of Church and State. In 1929, however, it was solved, as we shall see, on lines which would have approved themselves to him. No less loyal to the Church than his master, Cavour never doubted that the change must come, with all its necessary consequences—that the new kingdom of Italy must eventually establish its seat of government in the ancient capital at Rome.

'The choice of a capital is determined', he said, 'by high moral considerations. It is the sentiment of the people that decides. Rome unites all the conditions, historical, intellectual, moral, which form the capital of a great state. . . . It remains to convince the Holy Father that the Church can be independent without the Temporal Power. "Holy Father," we will say, "the Temporal Power is for you no longer a guarantee of independence. Renounce it and we will give you that liberty which for three centuries you have in vain demanded from the great Catholic Powers. . . . We are ready to proclaim in Italy this great principle: *The Free Church in the Free State*."'

'We hold,' said Cavour, in one of his latest and most famous speeches (26 March 1861)—'We hold that the independence and dignity of the Supreme Pontiff, as well as the independence of the Church, will be secured by the separation of the two powers and by a large application of the principles of liberty to the relations between civil and religious society.'

He expressed, moreover, a fervent hope that this change might be brought about by amicable arrangement with the Vatican.

'But what,' he continued, 'what if in circumstances as fatal to the Church as to Italy the Pope should prove inflexible and persist in rejecting all terms? Then, gentlemen, we should still not desist from proclaiming loudly the same principles; we should not desist from declaring that whether or not an understanding precede our entry into the eternal city, Italy will no sooner have pronounced the forfeiture of the Temporal Power than she will emancipate the Church from the State, and secure the liberty of the former on the amplest foundations.'

It was not to be. For two whole generations every advance on the part of the Italian Government was met with the unvarying, inflexible *non possumus* of the Papacy. Yet it was in contemplation of the ideal of the Free Church in the Free State that Cavour passed away.

Fortunate it was for Italy that at the supreme crisis of her fate she should have brought forth two men, in character and training so diverse but endowed with gifts so perfectly complementary, as Garibaldi and Cavour. Without the faith and audacity of the adventurer, the great diplomatist might not have been able to move the mountains which obstructed the path to Italian unity. Without the prudent guidance of Cavour the enthusiasm engendered by Garibaldi's personality and leadership might have run to waste. Each was essential to the other.

One question, however, insistently obtrudes itself. Could not Cavour have advanced to his goal by a straighter path? Was the 'treacherous duplicity' deplored by our minister at Naples indispensable? Sir Henry Elliot would have liked to see Piedmont take the 'more manly and creditable course' and declare war openly on Naples. Had Cavour done so, would either Austria or France have remained neutral? Would not Napoleon III at least have claimed (as it was currently reported he had done) Genoa and Sardinia? If Piedmont was compelled to purchase the annexation of the central States by the cession of Nice and Savoy, might she not reasonably have been asked to give up Sardinia and Genoa in return for the great southern kingdom of the two Sicilies? Could England ever have permitted Piedmont to attack a friendly Power?

It is difficult for those who have seen Italy advance to the position of a Great Power to answer these questions without the risk of injustice to Cavour and Victor Emmanuel. 'If we had done for ourselves the things which we are doing for Italy, we should be great rascals.' So said Cavour in confidential talk with his friends. Could Italy have been made with less violence to the dictates of private morality? The putrefaction of Italy called for something more than the 'rose-water surgery' deprecated by Carlyle in the case of Ireland. To unite Germany was an easier task than to unite Italy; but Cavour was a tyro in diplomatic intrigue by the side of Bismarck. Moreover, Cavour was always a liberator. Bismarck achieved German unity at the expense of Danes and Frenchmen and Poles. Cavour accepted the calculated help of France. Bismarck, to attain his purpose in Germany, struck down Austria and bled France white. No more than Cavour did Bismarck seek personal ends; but while Bismarck desired to see Prussia dominate Germany and to see Germany dominate Europe, Cavour sought only to achieve the independence and unity of Italy, and to assert for a united Italy an honourable place among the Powers of Europe.

Cavour's work was not, however, fully accomplished when his life was cut short. In the two sides of Italy there were still two gaping wounds. By a curious historical coincidence those wounds were staunched by the policy of his Teutonic counterpart. Bismarck's war of 1866 gave Italy Venetia; the war of 1870 compelled France to withdraw from Rome and to make way for Italy.

X

VENICE AND ROME, 1861–71

Cavour and Venice

DURING the decade that followed the death of Cavour the fate of Italy rested on the lap of the gods at Berlin. Cavour himself had contemplated an alliance with Prussia, and had sent General La Marmora to Berlin to congratulate the new King William I on his accession (2 January 1861), and to discuss with Prussian statesmen the possibility of closer accord between their country and his own. But he had no desire to precipitate an attack on Austria. 'As to Venice,' he wrote to La Marmora, 'we have need of at least two years to put our fighting forces in order. It would be folly to declare war before then.' 'To provoke Austria at the present moment', he wrote to Victor Emmanuel at Naples,[1] 'would be an act of madness.' Venice must wait, Rome could not.

Ricasoli and Rome

Ricasoli, who succeeded Cavour as Prime Minister, was, in this matter, in complete accord with his predecessor. 'Without Rome', he said, 'Italy is nothing; for Venice we must wait; the day will come; for Rome we cannot wait.' After the union of the Two Sicilies with the Kingdom of Italy the enthusiasm of Italian nationalists throughout the Peninsula was wrought up to the highest pitch. Many of the clergy, especially the parish priests, were touched by it; the contagion had reached Rome itself; symptoms manifested themselves even in the Vatican.

Cavour's reiterated cry for a 'Free Church in a Free State' was not the mere mouthing of a rhetorical phrasemaker. On the contrary, he had formulated a definite scheme for the readjustment of the relations of Church and State, more or less on the model of the Siccardian legislation already enacted in Piedmont. The general principles of that legislation had already approved themselves to most liberal-minded laymen in Italy, and to not a few

[1] Whyte, op. cit., ii. 443–4.

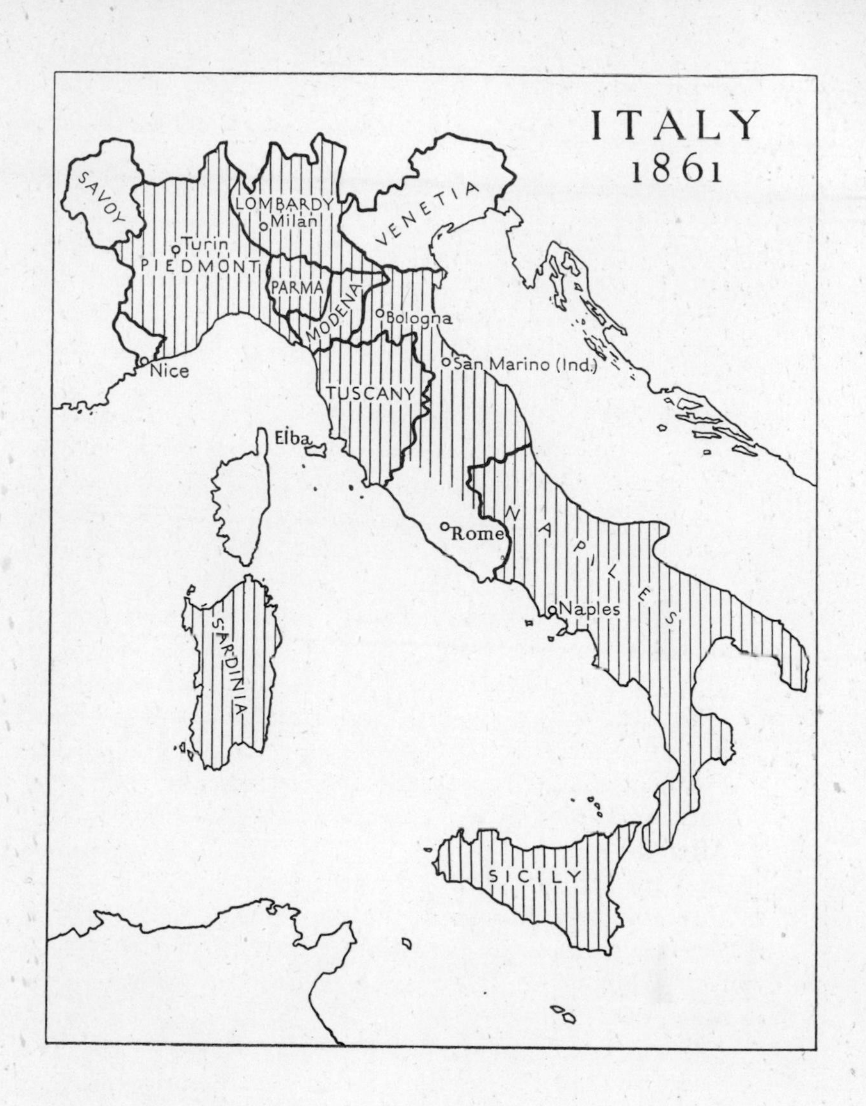
ITALY
1861
SAVOY
LOMBARDY
Milan
VENETIA
Turin
PIEDMONT
PARMA
MODENA
Bologna
San Marino (Ind.)
Nice
TUSCANY
Elba
Rome
NAPLES
Naples
SARDINIA
SICILY

clerics. Among the latter was a learned Jesuit, Father Passaglia, an ultramontane canonist, most tender of the Pope's universal supremacy, a theologian of profound erudition, who had been commissioned, with others, to formulate the dogma of the Immaculate Conception. Closely associated with Father Passaglia was a well-known Roman physician, Dr. Pantaleoni, a friend of Massimo d'Azeglio, and more than once expelled from the Papal States on account of his liberal views. These men worked assiduously during the winter of 1860–1 to bring the Papacy round to Cavour's views. 'A good Pope', declared Passaglia, 'will always be free, and the liberty of the Papacy is better served by the imitation of Christ than by the Temporal Power.' Pius IX seemed at one time inclined to compromise. Cardinal Antonelli, the real power behind the Papal throne, actually accepted, provisionally, the basis of compromise suggested by Cavour; moved thereto, perhaps, by the proposal that the cardinals should have the privileges of princes and seats in the Senate. Suddenly, however, Antonelli veered round. Perhaps he had never been sincere in negotiating; perhaps he was angered by the application of Siccardian principles in Naples and the recently annexed Papal States; perhaps he was encouraged by the Catholic Powers. The matter is still enshrouded in mystery. Anyway, on 21 March 1861, Dr. Pantaleoni was precipitately expelled from Rome. The negotiations were at an end.[1]

Cavour did not, even yet, despair of an accommodation with the Papacy. In his great speeches in Parliament at the end of March he reiterated, as we have seen, his conviction that without Rome Italy could not be constituted, and his equally strong conviction that Italy could go to Rome only 'in concert with France, and without subjecting the Church to the dominance of the State in spiritual matters'.

Napoleon III and Rome

To France, accordingly, he now turned. Prince Napoleon

[1] On the whole of this curious episode cf. Bolton King, *Italy*, ii. 200–10, and Whyte, *Cavour*, ii. 444 sq., and the authorities there cited.

was again an invaluable intermediary. The bases of a Treaty were virtually agreed. France was to evacuate Rome; Italy was to guarantee, against attacks from any quarter, the integrity of the Papal territory; France would then recognize the Kingdom of Italy. It was expected that the agreement would be concluded by 20 June. A fortnight before that date Cavour had passed away.

Garibaldi and Rome

After laying another crown at the feet of his King, Garibaldi, as we have seen, withdrew to Caprera. The imagination of the world was profoundly touched, more even than by his heroic feats in arms, by this act of simple and selfless renunciation.

> Not that three armies thou didst overthrow,
> Not that three cities ope'd their gates to thee,
> I praise thee chief; not for this Royalty,
> Decked with new crowns, that utterly lay low;
> For nothing of all thou didst forsake, to go
> And tend thy vines amid the Etrurian Sea;
> Not even that thou didst *this*—that History
> Retread two thousand selfish years to show
> Another Cincinnatus! Rather for this—
> The having lived such a life that even this deed
> Of stress heroic natural seems, as is
> Calm night, when glorious day it doth succeed,
> And we, forewarned by surest auguries,
> The amazing act with no amazement read.

But heroes, however pure-hearted, are, like saints, apt sometimes to be difficult to deal with in politics. Garibaldi affords a conspicuous illustration of this truth. He soon became restless at Caprera, and his restlessness was increased by the promises of Rattazzi, who displaced Ricasoli as Prime Minister in March 1862. Rattazzi had for some time been in communication with Garibaldi, and the latter was led to suppose, rightly or wrongly, that Rattazzi's government would oppose an advance on Rome in much the same sense as Cavour had hampered the expedition to Sicily.

'We had', writes Garibaldi, 'the veto of the Monarchy in 1860 and again in 1862. I think that overthrowing the Papacy was a work at least as necessary as overthrowing the Bourbons. In 1862 the task proposed to themselves by the red-shirts was that of knocking over the Papacy (assuredly the most inveterate and most dangerous enemy to Italy), and winning our natural capital without any other aim, without any other ambition than the good of our country. The mission was sacred, the conditions the same, and the noble Sicilians, with the exception of a few . . . replied with their wonted enthusiasm to the cry of "Rome or Death" proclaimed by us at Marsala.'

Aspromonte

But no Government, not even Rattazzi's, could permit a subject to defy its orders and act independently in so delicate a matter. Garibaldi, however, would listen to no reason. In July 1862 he collected a body of volunteers in Sicily, and with some 4,000 followers crossed to the mainland, and marched northwards through Calabria. On 29 August he encountered a Royal army at Aspromonte, near Reggio. The chief himself was wounded and carried a prisoner to Varignano, where, in honourable captivity, he proved a terrible embarrassment to a somewhat discredited government. His followers were scattered far and wide.

After the declaration of a general amnesty Garibaldi visited England. Palmerston and Russell had already incurred the opprobrium of the orthodox diplomatists of the Continent for their support of the Italian *Risorgimento*. 'Ce n'est pas de la diplomatie; c'est de la polissonnerie.' Such was Baron Brunnow's comment on British policy. Nevertheless, Garibaldi was assured of a warm welcome in this country. It proved to be enthusiastic to the verge of hysteria, but the visit was somewhat abruptly curtailed, perhaps on a hint from the Emperor of the French.

Annexation of Venetia to Italy

Meanwhile, in 1864, Napoleon III, partly perhaps in consequence of the unyielding attitude of the Papacy, had come to an agreement with the Italian Government. Italy was to protect what remained of the State of the Church from external attack; France was to recall all her troops within two years, and the Italian capital was to be transferred from Turin to Florence. This important step was taken in 1865. 'Of course,' said Drouyn de Lhuys, the

French Foreign Minister, 'you will eventually go to Rome, but a decent interval must elapse to relieve us from responsibility.' Bismarck saw to that. It was not to be his first service to Italy.

Bismarck and Italy

Bismarck was now completing his plans for the exclusion of Austria from the Germanic body. He had occupied the Danish Duchies; he had lured the Emperor Napoleon to a promise of neutrality by vague suggestions as to substantial compensation for France—perhaps, Luxemburg, perhaps the Palatinate, it might even be Belgium. To make assurance doubly sure he approached Italy with an offer of Venetia in return for her help in the war then imminent. Napoleon III had for some time been urging the Emperor Francis Joseph to abandon a troublesome dependency to Italy, and compensate himself by incorporating Bosnia and Herzegovina in the Hapsburg Empire. Francis Joseph refused. Venetia might be troublesome, but as recent events have made clear, Austria could not abandon Venetia (as understood by Italian irredentists) without sacrificing her position as a first-class Power.

On receiving Bismarck's offer Victor Emmanuel, with some magnanimity, gave Austria the first chance. In 1865 he offered to help Austria against Prussia in return for the cession of Venetia. The Emperor Francis Joseph declined the offer—not unnaturally, but the refusal cost him dear. In April 1866 Victor Emmanual concluded a treaty with Bismarck, and accordingly in the Seven Weeks War Italy fought on the side of Prussia. The German campaign was short but decisive. Within six weeks not Austria only but Germany lay prostrate under the heel of Prussia.

Italy gave but feeble assistance to her ally. She declared war on Austria on 20 June 1866; on the 23rd General La Marmora crossed the Mincio, and on the 24th Austria inflicted a crushing defeat upon him at Custoza. Garibaldi, called forth from Caprera to take command of a volunteer force to operate in the Tyrol, is bitter in his denunciation of the incompetence of the Italian commanders and their jealousy of the volunteers.

'The campaign of 1866', he writes, 'opened with the most brilliant prospects. The nation, though its resources had been exhausted by a rapacious government, showed itself rich in enthusiasm and self-sacrifice. The numerous fleet was to measure itself against an enemy inferior in numbers, and looked upon as already defeated; while our army—nearly double that of the Austrians in Italy—saw under its banner for the first time all the sons of the Peninsula, from Marsala to Mont Cenis, hastening, in eager emulation, to battle with the foe of centuries. It was only the insolent ignorance and incapacity of its leaders that could have brought about the disaster of Custozza.... Some good firearms reached us after the war ended: I say no more.'[1]

There was only too much truth in this scathing indictment.

Nor did the navy redeem the failure of the army. On the contrary: a month after the disaster at Custozza the Italian fleet suffered a crushing defeat off Lissa.

The war was not, however, decided in Italy or in the Adriatic. Two days after the decisive battle at Sadowa (Königgrätz) Austria ceded Venetia to Napoleon (5 July), on 22 July she concluded an armistice with Prussia, and a month later (12 August) with Italy. On the 19th the Austrians handed over Venice to France, and finally evacuated the city. On 3 October peace was signed between Austrian and Italy at Vienna. To satisfy the doctrinaire nationalism of Napoleon a plebiscite was to be taken before Venice was annexed to Italy. Thus the first article of the Treaty concluded at Vienna ran:

'His Majesty the Emperor of Austria having ceded the Lombardo-Venetian kingdom to H.M. the Emperor of the French, and H.M. the Emperor of the French having declared himself ready to recognize the union of the said province with the dominions of H.M. the King of Italy, on condition that the populations concerned assent,' &c.

The plebiscite yielded 642,000 votes in favour of union with Italy; 69 against. On receiving the plebiscite Victor Emmanuel declared: 'This is the greatest day of my life;

[1] *Autobiography*, ii. 256, 281.

Italy is made,' 'but', as he significantly added, 'not complete.' The Iron Crown of Lombardy, which in 1859 the Austrians had carried off to Vienna, was restored to the cathedral of Monza. On 7 November the King made his triumphal entry into Venice. Italy and her King had good cause to rejoice: yet the war of 1866 is not an incident in her national history which Italy can recall with pride. Garibaldi, indeed, regarded the whole episode as a national disgrace.

'She, Venice, emerges from foreign domination not through her own acts, but thanks to the courage of others. If only her liberty had been achieved by the valour of her brethren! But no, she was redeemed by the sword of the foreigner. Sadowa, the glory of Prussia, freed Venice, and the Italian nation does not even ask for a veil to hide this dishonour.'

Biting as Garibaldi's comment was, it was not wholly unjust.

Nor was he the only man to apprehend the significance of the events of 1866.

Bismarck's pound of flesh

The lamentable failure of Italy on land and sea—attributed by Garibaldi wholly to bad leadership—gave Bismarck an opportunity of exhibiting his contempt for an unprofitable ally and of conciliating the good will of a defeated opponent. Until Austria was expelled from Germany Bismarck would take no risks: once the hegemony of Germany was transferred to the Hohenzollern, he espoused the cause of the Hapsburgs in every other quarter. He would not dishonour his bond to Italy, but he took care that she should not get an ounce more than her pound of flesh. 'Venetia' was interpreted in the narrowest possible sense. The Trentino is geographically 'a prolongation of the plain of Lombardy and Venetia: all its gates are open to Italy'.[1] But the gates which Nature left open, Austria, with Bismarck's connivance, continued to shut. The new northern frontier of Italy was so drawn

[1] Virginio Gayda, *Modern Austria*, p. 15. For a fuller discussion of the problem of *Italia Irredenta* cf. Marriott, *European Commonwealth*, c. xiv, Oxford, 1919.

as to deprive Victor Emmanuel of 370,000 subjects who were Italian in blood and speech, to shut off the Trentini from their natural markets in the valley of the Po, and to thrust into the heart of an Italian province the military outpost of an embittered neighbour. Prussia and Austria reaped in 1915 the seed they sowed in 1866.

The Southern Tyrol

It is only fair to Bismarck and to Austria to add that though the Trentini are racially Italian, the southern Tyrol which they inhabit had never formed part of Italy except during the five years (1809–14) when Napoleon annexed it to his Italian Kingdom. Nor was it ever united with Venetia except during the periods 1797–1805 and 1815–66, when Venetia itself, the city and district, was an Austrian province.

The same is true of Trieste. But it was otherwise with the Venetian provinces to the east of the Adriatic, Istria and Dalmatia, and with the islands of the Archipelago. For four centuries at least the Venetian Republic had been dominant on the eastern coast of the Adriatic. Ardent irredentists based their claims indeed upon an even earlier title; but to claim for modern Italy all that ancient Rome possessed would raise complicated issues far beyond the region of the Adriatic. Be that as it may, Austria retained in 1866 not only Trieste, but the old Venetian lands to the east of it. Nevertheless, the gaping wound in Italy's eastern side was stanched.

Rome

The more septic wound in the western side still festered. Cautious physicians were content to await the results of diplomatic treatment. Garibaldi, on the contrary, was fretting with anxiety to apply the knife, lest he should die before his life-dream was fulfilled.

'I had good ground for imagining' (so he wrote in his *Autobiography*, ii. 283), 'that the time had come to give the final push to the tottering shanty of the Papacy, and win for Italy her own illustrious capital. . . . The French emperor's troops were no longer at Rome; were a few thousand mercenaries, the off-scourings of Europe, to keep a great nation at bay and prevent it from exercising its most sacred rights?'

The 'September Convention'

Under the Treaty concluded (15 September 1864) between Napoleon and Victor Emmanuel the former had agreed to withdraw his army from Rome as soon as the Papal army was reorganized, and at most within two years. Victor Emmanuel undertook, on his part, not, in the meantime, to attack Rome himself or allow any one else to do so, and to transfer his capital from Turin to Florence or Naples. Whichever city were selected the transference would be interpreted by the Catholic world as an abandonment of the idea of making Rome the capital, while to Italian nationalists the selection of Florence would mean a step towards Rome. The Turinese were bitterly affronted, and there was serious rioting in that loyal city. Nevertheless, the transference was effected in 1865, and on the 18th of November in that year the King opened his first Parliament in Florence.

France and the Papacy

Napoleon also was true to his engagements—in the letter—and by the end of 1866 the French army had evacuated the Holy City. Many French troops, however, took service in the Papal army, which was mainly commanded by French officers, whose service continued to be reckoned by the French War Office as service with the French colours. The Emperor Napoleon was in fact attempting, as he always did, to get the best of both worlds. In the event, as will be seen, he got the worst of both.

Mentana

Garibaldi saw in the official evacuation of Rome his opportunity, and he seized it. The Italian government, suspicious of his intentions, arrested him on the 23rd of September 1867 and deported him to Caprera, where a large flotilla of war-ships could keep him (it was thought) under observation. He managed, however, to elude their vigilance; suddenly reappeared in Florence on 20 October, and three days later crossed into Papal territory, where his son Menotti and bands of volunteers had for some time been carrying on guerrilla warfare. On the 25th the Red Shirts won a great victory over the Papal troops and captured Monte Rotondo. But a French army was by this time on its way to Rome.

The unhappy Emperor of the French was now heading fast for the catastrophe of Sedan. His own health was failing; the disastrous Mexican adventure had reacted most prejudicially on his position in Europe and in France; Bismarck, after playing with him at Biarritz, had ostentatiously refused any 'compensation' to France after the Prussian victory at Sadowa. Sadowa was, indeed, as a French marshal observed, less a defeat for Austria than for France. Apart from the crumbling of the diplomatic edifice, the Emperor's own position in France became daily more difficult. 'How can you expect my Empire to go on? The Empress is a Legitimist; Morny is an Orleanist; Prince Napoleon is a Republican; I am a Socialist; only Persigny is an Imperialist—and he is mad.' The question addressed in ironic humour to Rouher was none the less a searching one. The Roman question added immensely to his complications. The Empress, an ardent 'clerical', was constantly urging him to champion the cause of the Papacy: he himself was still in sympathy with the Italian ideal, and moreover he had to keep an eye on Berlin. Bismarck afterwards confessed that a war with France 'lay in the logic of history' after Sadowa. Napoleon could not but be aware of the logical working of Bismarck's mind. Could he afford to go to Rome? On the 17th of October he finally yielded to the importunities of the Empress. She might save the Papacy, but she had sealed the fate of the Second Empire.

On 29 October the French expedition landed at Civitavecchia, and on 3 November Garibaldi's ill-equipped forces were mowed down by the French chassepots at Mentana. The remnants of the Red Shirts were scattered; the French army reoccupied the Holy City. On 5 December Rouher uttered in the French Chamber his historic *Jamais*: never, never, would France allow Italy to destroy the Temporal Power or to make Rome its capital.

Mentana marked the end of the French alliance and the close of Garibaldi's Italian crusade. An army of occupation, dispatched by the government from Florence, was encamped on Papal territory, and before the battle of Mentana was fought, Garibaldi had issued to his volunteers a characteristic proclamation.

'The Government of Florence', it ran, 'has invaded the Roman territory, already won by us with precious blood from the enemies of Italy; we ought to receive our brothers in arms with love, and aid them in driving out of Rome the mercenary sustainers of tyranny; but if base deeds, the continuation of the vile convention of September, in mean consort with Jesuitism shall urge us to lay down our arms in obedience to the order of December 2 then will I let the world know that I alone, a Roman General, with full power, elected by the universal suffrage of the only legal government in Rome, that of the Republic, have the right to maintain myself in arms in this the territory subject to my jurisdiction; and then if any of these my volunteers, champions of liberty and Italian Unity wish to have Rome as the capital of Italy, fulfilling the vote of Parliament and the nation, they must not put down their arms until Italy shall have acquired liberty of conscience and worship, built upon the ruin of Jesuitism, and until the soldiers of tyrants shall be banished from our land.'

Mentana was a terrible blow not only to Garibaldi, but to Victor Emmanuel, who grieved bitterly, like the warm-hearted man he was, for the fate of his misguided but generous-hearted sons. 'Ah! those chassepots,' he would exclaim, 'they have mortally wounded my heart as father and as King: I feel as if the balls had torn my flesh here. It is one of the greatest griefs I have ever known.' Yet, rent by anguish as he was, he still maintained an attitude of unshaken dignity alike towards the French and towards his own rebellious sons. To the Emperor of the French he wrote an ardent appeal begging him to break with the clericals and put himself at the head of the liberal party in Europe, at the same time warning him that the old feeling of gratitude towards the French in Italy had quite disappeared. 'The late events have suffocated every remembrance of gratitude in the heart of Italy. It is no longer in the power of the government to maintain the alliance with France. The chassepot gun at Mentana has given it a mortal blow.' At the same time he could not overlook the offence of the Red Shirt rebels. Garibaldi himself was arrested, but after a brief imprisonment at Varignano was once more permitted to retire to Caprera.

Last days and death of Garibaldi

The tale of his last and rapidly declining years may be briefly told. In 1870, thanks not to Garibaldi but to Bismarck and Moltke, Italy went to Rome; Garibaldi was ageing fast and was racked by disease, but the sound of battle called loudly to the old chieftain, and after the fall of the French Empire he offered his services to the Republic. His quarrel had ever been not with France but with the 'vulpine knave' who had enslaved France and cheated Italy. Garibaldi's arrival in France was a great embarrassment to Gambetta, but he was given the command of a motley brigade to operate in the Vosges. It had been better for Garibaldi and no worse for France if he had not intervened in the historic conflict between France and Germany. Yet, despite accusations of military incapacity levelled against him, three French cities elected him as deputy to represent them in the Assembly at Bordeaux; but as a foreigner he was ineligible to enter it, and he resigned both his commission and his seat.

In 1874 he was elected deputy for Rome and took his seat in the Italian Parliament, but he refused the offer from the Minghetti government of a large grant (£40,000) and a pension. It is believed, however, that he subsequently accepted it from his friends of the Left. Not long before his death he revisited Genoa and Milan, where a monument was erected to the memory of those who had fallen at Mentana. On 2 June 1882 the end came rather suddenly in Caprera.

Mazzini had predeceased Garibaldi by ten years. Both men had long since accomplished all that it was in them to do for Italy. After 1849 Mazzini had been nothing but an obstruction to the cause of Italian independence and unity. The failures of the year of Revolution served only to accentuate his republican fanaticism, and so to render him incapable of further service to the cause he had so deeply and sincerely at heart.

Garibaldi's best service, on the contrary, was rendered between 1848 and 1866. It would have been well for his own reputation and not amiss for Italy had an Austrian bullet found him during his Tyrolese campaign in 1866. At all times he was something of an anxiety to any government he served: it needed all Cavour's diplomacy to turn Garibaldi's peculiar talents to the national advantage; to Cavour's successors he was a sheer embarrassment. Yet when all is said, the idealism of Mazzini and the heroic courage of Garibaldi were not less essential than the superb diplomacy of Cavour to the making of a united Italy.

Cavour did not live to witness the consummation of his work; Mazzini saw his ends accomplished, but by means exceedingly distasteful to him; Garibaldi, equally intent on the end, was less concerned as to methods. He could not forget Aspromonte; Mentana it was impossible to forgive. Yet he could rejoice wholeheartedly when his King entered Rome.

Italy in Rome

For the final denouement of the Italian drama the German attack on France was immediately responsible. After Mentana the French troops evacuated the Holy City, but remained in occupation of Civitavecchia. When the Emperor Napoleon saw the crisis coming in 1870 he turned to Austria and Italy for help. Victor Emmanuel, the soul of chivalry, could not refuse it; but he could not promise it so long as French troops remained on Italian soil. Austria would not come in without Italy. The Empress Eugénie would not, even to save France, desert the Papacy. Napoleon had perforce to go into the war without an ally.

After the initial defeats at Worth and Gravelotte he offered to give Victor Emmanuel a free hand as regards Rome. But the King could get no assurance that 100,000 Italians would suffice to save France. On 9 August, Italy declared herself neutral.

The French troops had been withdrawn from Roman territory; save for his mercenary army the Pope was defenceless. Once again Victor Emmanuel attempted, with all the earnestness and with all the tenderness at his command, to induce the Pope to come to terms and accept the position, at once dignified and independent, which the Italian Government was anxious to secure to him.

From Florence the King addressed to the Pope the following letter (8 September 1870):

'Most Blessed Father,—With the affection of a son, with the faith of a Catholic, with the soul of an Italian I address myself now, as on former occasions, to the heart of your holiness.

'A flood of dangers threatens Europe. Profiting by the war which desolates the centre of the Continent, the cosmopolitan revolutionary party increases in boldness and audacity and is planning, especially in that part of Italy ruled by your holiness, the direst offences against the monarchy and the papacy. I know that the greatness of your soul will not be less than the greatness of events; but I, being a Catholic King and Italian, and as such guardian by the disposition of Providence and the national will of the destinies of all the Italians, feel it my duty to take in the face of Europe and Catholicity, the responsibility of maintaining order in the peninsula, and the safety of the Holy See. . . . Permit me, your holiness, again to say that the present moment is a solemn one for Italy and the Church. Let the popehood add efficacy to the spirit of inextinguishable benevolence in your soul towards this land, which is also *your* country, and the sentiments of conciliation which I have always studied to translate into acts, that satisfying the national aspirations, the Head of Catholicity, surrounded by the devotion of the Italian people, should preserve on the banks of the Tiber a glorious seat independent of every human Sovereignty. Your holiness, by liberating Rome from foreign troops will take from her the constant danger of being the battle-ground of subversive parties. You will accomplish a marvellous work, restore peace to the Church, and show Europe, aghast at the horrors of war, how one can win great battles and obtain immortal victories by an act of justice, by one sole word of affection.'

But the Pope still unflinchingly adhered to the position he had taken up.

'I cannot', he wrote (11 September 1870), 'admit the demands of your letter nor accept the principles contained therein. I address myself to God and place my cause in his hands, for it is entirely His. I pray him to concede abundant grace to your Majesty, deliver you from every peril, and render you a participator in all the mercies of which you may have need.'

To the question at issue between the Church and the State we must return. Here it may suffice to say that the vast majority of Italians, ardent though most of them are in their devotion to the Catholic Church, were convinced that Rome was the only possible capital for United Italy. To that conviction a foreigner must needs defer. Yet concurrence in the justice of the national demand is not inconsistent with sincere admiration for the inflexible determination, for the unbroken consistency, with which the Pope maintained in all their integrity the claims of that sovereignty, compared with which, as Lord Macaulay justly said, 'the proudest royal houses are but of yesterday.'

Yet sympathize as we may and must with the dilemma of the Pontiff, reason compels us to approve the action of the King. General Cadorna, in command of 60,000 Italian troops, entered Papal territory on 16 September, and occupied Civitavecchia. On the 19th Rome was invested, but the Pope was determined to yield only to force. After a few hours' cannonade a breach was made near Porta Pia, and the Italian army, attended or followed by vast crowds, poured into the Holy City. General Cadorna intended to respect the Leonine City, but at the request of Cardinal Antonelli, the Papal Secretary, he occupied it, on the following day, to preserve order and protect the person of the Pontiff (September 20).

A plebiscite was promptly taken (2 October) and showed 133,000 in favour of the annexation of Rome to Italy; 1,500 against it.

The King himself paid a private visit to Rome at the end of the year (1870). A terrible inundation of the Tiber had taken place, and the King at once set off for Rome to demonstrate his sympathy with the distress of his new subjects. His demeanour and conduct at this time won him the respect and affection of many of those who had been the staunchest adherents of the Temporal Power. Not, however, until 2 June 1871 did the King make his triumphal entry into the capital. The seat of government was transferred to Rome, and a Parliament, for the first time representative of the whole of Italy, was opened by the King in a memorable speech.

'The work to which we consecrated our lives is accomplished. After long trials, Italy is restored to herself and to Rome. Here where our people, scattered for so many centuries, find themselves for the first time reassembled in the majesty of their representatives, here where we recognize the home of our thoughts, everything speaks to us of grandeur, but at the same time everything reminds us of our duties. . . . We have arisen in the name of liberty, and in liberty and order we ought to seek the secret of strength and conciliation . . . the future opens before us rich in happy promise; it is for us to respond to the favours of Providence by showing ourselves worthy to represent amongst the great nations of the earth the glorious past of Italy and of Rome.'

XI

UNITED ITALY

WITH the entry of Victor Emmanuel into Rome the drama of the Italian *Risorgimento* reached its climax. The main purpose of this book is therefore accomplished. The half-century which followed upon unification represented an anti-climax. Yet the political lessons to be learnt from the study of that period are so important that an epilogue, despite the risks proverbially attendant on that device, would seem to be demanded.

Disillusionment

Periods of high tension are invariably followed by relaxation; the accomplishment of a splendid task often involves subsequent disillusionment. Italy did not escape the common fate. The extent of the disillusionment is strikingly illustrated, and the causes of it are in some degree explained, by a passage from the pen of one who was a detached and trained observer and at the same time an ardent lover of Italy. In 1896 Mr. Lecky could still write with enthusiasm, as we have seen, of the Italian *Risorgimento*, as 'the one moment of nineteenth-century history when politics assumed something of the character of poetry'. Yet even then he was constrained to add that the spell was already broken, that 'the glamour' had 'faded'. Much more decided was the disillusionment when, in 1899, he published a second edition of *Democracy and Liberty*.

> 'It is impossible', he then wrote, 'to deny that the events of the last years have filled the well-wishers . . . of Italy . . . with profound misgiving. The furious and sanguinary riots almost amounting to civil war that have taken place in Italian towns; the crushing and ever-growing weight of taxation; the steady growth of Socialism; and the manifest incapacity of a democratic parliament to command the confidence of the Italian people are signs that it is impossible to misread.'

Mr. Lecky's observations did not lack justification, but the moment at which he made them was an unfortunate one for scientific diagnosis. Italy was going through a very difficult time.

The 'unity' achieved in 1871 was palpably superficial. Impatient idealists like Mazzini might complain of the slow pace of the unification movement, but for the mass of Italians the pace was much too fast. As d'Azeglio strikingly put it: 'We have made Italy; now we have to make Italians.' That was a work that called for patience, and in such work Mazzini could have no part. The prophet himself passed away in 1872, but he had already lost his influence in his own country. His cosmopolitan influence waxed rather than waned, especially in England, but he left few disciples in Italy. *Il Dovere* (the organ of Mazzinian doctrine) ceased publication in 1878, and though efforts were made to reanimate the creed they hopelessly failed. In Italy, as elsewhere, Socialism was attracting the urban wage-earners in large numbers, and to Socialism the true Mazzinisti, like their master, were stoutly opposed.

The 'land of cities'

The naked truth is that the *Risorgimento* itself was the work of a small minority of enlightened patriots; and even to many of the *intelligentsia* 'liberty' meant primarily municipal independence. The idea of unity had never penetrated the mass of the citizens, much less the peasantry. Consequently, when they were called upon to pay the price of unity and independence there was grave discontent. Nor was the price light a one. Italy, owing partly to physiographical conditions, partly to historical accidents, always has been and is pre-eminently the 'land of cities'. The centres from which the *Risorgimento* radiated were, as Mr. Trevelyan has observed, the various cities of Italy. 'The Italian revolution of 1848 was the sum of its municipal revolutions.'[1] That is profoundly true and explains much that has happened in Italy since 1870, and not least what has happened since 1919.

Parliamentary Government

Once more, Italy found itself saddled, after 1870, with a parliamentary Constitution, fashioned on the English model, in the working of which Italians had no experience,

[1] *Historical Causes of the Present State of Affairs in Italy* (1923).

and for which they had little natural or inherited aptitude. The traditional form of Italian democracy is not representative, but direct. It derived not from England, but from the City-States of ancient Greece, whence it was imported into the medieval municipalities of Italy. Cavour, as we have seen, had made a first-hand study of parliamentary government in England. He had guided Piedmont through the early stages of that difficult experiment with consummate adroitness. In Victor Emmanuel he found a patriotic sovereign who was prepared to adapt himself to the exotic methods of a 'constitutional' monarchy. Perhaps at heart the King was more in sympathy with Garibaldi's methods than with Cavour's, but loyalty was the core of his character, and his confidence once given was not lightly withdrawn.

Could Cavour have worked the parliamentary system in a united Italy from Rome? None can say. Two things may, however, be affirmed with some assurance of certainty: first, that if Cavour's hands had not been forced by Garibaldi, the work of unification would have proceeded much more gradually, and the parliamentary system would not, in infancy, have been exposed to the premature strain which ultimately shattered it; secondly, that if Cavour could not have established an English constitution in Italy, no one else could. Between the death of Cavour and the advent of Signor Mussolini Italy produced no statesman of the first rank, with the possible exception of Francesco Crispi; and Crispi, a Sicilian by birth and a republican by tradition, was bitterly opposed to Cavour and all his ways. But, elected to the first Italian Parliament in 1861, he soon shed his republicanism and broke with Garibaldi, whose advance on Rome in 1867 he strongly disapproved. After the death of Victor Emmanuel (1878) he proved himself, in difficult days, a staunch supporter of the dynasty, being convinced, as he frequently said, that 'only the Monarchy can unite us; the Republic would divide us'. Cavour, however, had left the Monarchy no choice but to be 'constitutional' in the English sense, and

Crispi, therefore, like other Italian politicians, had to accommodate himself as best he could to the parliamentary mould. But Italy never really fitted into it; and the misfit was one of the causes of the reaction which followed on the triumph of the *Risorgimento*.

There were many others. The most persistent and pervasive was the antagonism between the old Church and the new State; but that obstinate problem demands and will receive more detailed treatment presently. Here it must only be emphasized that the persistent rivalry between the Vatican and the Quirinal accentuated the difficulties inherent in many other problems by which the young Italian State was confronted. Pre-eminently was this true of popular education.

Education and illiteracy

'The real Quadrilateral that has stopped us', said Villari after the campaign of 1866, 'is our seventeen million illiterates and five million dilettanti.' At that time the percentage of illiteracy was said to be 78 in the whole country and over 90 in Naples. Even at the close of the century Italy was said to be, next to Portugal, the most illiterate country in western Europe. Elementary education was indeed made compulsory in the north in 1859, and throughout the kingdom in 1877; but it applied only to children between six and ten years of age, and attendance was not really enforced. After unification matters steadily, though slowly, improved, but only in the north did the communes show any genuine enthusiasm for education. Excellent commercial schools were established at Genoa and Venice, and Milan and Turin made a beginning in adult education on the lines known in England as 'University Extension'.

Local authorities were not bound to provide religious instruction unless it was demanded by the parents; but in practice, Italy being an essentially Catholic country, religious instruction was given, except in Milan, in a large majority of schools, and not infrequently by priests.

Poverty

Hampered by illiteracy, the progress of Italy was also greatly retarded by lack of material resources. So long as manufacturing industry was dominated by coal and iron, Italy, poor in both, was bound to be left hopelessly behind in the industrial struggle. Harbours are few and inconvenient; on the east coast, indeed, there are no good harbours between Venice and Brindisi. The acquisition of Trieste and Pola (1919) was from this point of view very important to Italy's position on the Adriatic. Nor were internal means of communication at all adequate. Roads were bad and until the latter part of the nineteenth century the railway system was ill-developed and chaotic. Agriculture, too, was relatively almost as backward as industry and commerce. Until the advent of the electrical era Italy possessed, indeed, few, if any, natural advantages, and her people consequently were poor.

The disappearance of the petty princes and their courts, the concentration of government in a single capital, the unification of services, ought, it might be supposed, to have made for simplicity and economy. It was quite otherwise. The people found themselves burdened by Parliament with a load of taxation such as the dethroned despots had never imposed. High taxation naturally intensified poverty and poverty evoked discontent. Liberty might be glorious, but it was undeniably expensive. Moreover, the machinery of government becoming daily more complicated there was an increased demand for skilled craftsmen to work it. The best administrators were found among those who had been trained in Austrian methods. Piedmont also could supply a certain number of fairly competent officials. But the supply was quite unequal to the demand; and the public services were in consequence gravely lacking in efficiency.

Corruption

Nor did the parliamentary régime promote purity of administration. On the contrary, the virus of corruption increasingly permeated the body politic. Parliamentary government, for its efficient working, implies party organization, and the party system cannot be improvised; party creeds are the product of evolution, and party affinities are the work of time. Sir Robert Walpole, the first man to become Prime Minister of England by virtue of a parliamentary majority, and the first minister to resign because he lost it, declared that every man had his price. Until parties are organized, and when they begin to disintegrate, the maxim, though cynical, is apt, in one sense or another, to be true. In the matter of parliamentary government Italy tried to run before she had learnt to walk; and the result for her was as unhappy as, under parallel circumstances, it has proved elsewhere.

The ministerial system was hopelessly unstable. The 'Right' was in office continuously until 1876; but between that date and 1891 there were no fewer than thirteen ministries; and their precarious existence could not be maintained save by means which did not make for the purity of public life. The deputies were the nominees of powerful constituents who wanted contracts and other privileges; ministers could exist only by satisfying the greed of deputies.

Of the politicians of that day Agostino Depretis was the most typical, and in a parliamentary sense the most successful. A high authority describes him as 'for eleven years Dictator of Italy'.[1] He was never that. Between 1876, when he came in as leader of the 'Left', and his death in 1887, this old Mazzinian was Premier more often than not. But he was adroit rather than strong, and contrived to continue in office by the system known as *trasformismo*, that is, by taking into his Cabinet men from the 'Right' to-day, from the 'Left' to-morrow, according to the shifting gusts of wind in the Chamber. And the wind, generally a noisome one, shifted according to the necessity of conciliating this locality or that; of getting government favours for influential constituents in Genoa or Bologna as the case might be. Small wonder, then, that ministries were unstable and that the whole parliamentary system was permeated by corruption.

Parliamentary corruption had its counterpart, perhaps its origin, in local government, which after 1871 was necessarily reorganized, with an increasing tendency to-

[1] L. Villari.

wards bureaucratic centralization. But the outstanding and persistent problem by which the young State was confronted was that of finance. In the fifteen years after unification the national revenue increased threefold; but even that proved insufficient to meet the rapid growth of expenditure.

Finance

The building of a new State is an expensive process. Italy, as we have seen, was poor. Economically, socially, educationally, it had an immense amount of leeway to make up. A national army, a national navy, a national system of railways—all these had to be created. Piedmont could and did provide a nucleus; but what had sufficed for Piedmont was quite insufficient for Italy. By 1873 Italy had a standing army of 350,000 men; the navy was greatly improved; naval arsenals were re-equipped; and the navy was reinforced by the creation of a mercantile marine—subsidized, of course, by the State. But all these things cost money; and an Italy not yet completely industrialized, though committed to extravagant expenditure for public works, some necessary, others the product of 'graft', could ill afford to furnish it. The need for increased taxation was indeed imperative; whether it was wise to raise so large a proportion of it by indirect taxation, and in particular by taxes imposed on the food of a poverty-stricken peasantry, is questionable. Apart, however, from taxation, recourse was had to every device known to profligate politicians and unprincipled financiers: to currency inflation, compulsory conversion of loans, partial repudiation of interest obligations, and the like.

It is, however, only fair to admit that without money it was impossible for the young State to attain that position in the high society of Europe to which a United Italy naturally aspired.

Foreign Policy

That was the real crux of the situation. Had Italy been content, for a generation, to nurse her resources, to gather economic strength; had circumstances permitted her to do so, the path of domestic administration would have been much smoother and many of the worst evils, diagnosed by Mr. Lecky and other sympathetic observers, might have been avoided.

Unfortunately, United Italy inherited from the *Risorgimento* period a profound mistrust of France. True the Second Empire had fallen, but throughout all the vicissitudes of domestic politics, and despite all changes of dynasty and polity, France has remained singularly constant in adherence to certain fixed political traditions—*les mœurs politiques*, as one of the most brilliant of her historians has phrased it.[1] Not least consistent was she in her Near-Eastern and Mediterranean policy. Napoleon I bequeathed to the Legitimists and the Orleanists, not to mention the Imperialists, that keen interest in the Levant, Syria, and Egypt which he had himself inherited from the *ancien régime*. France had been foremost in encouraging the ambitious designs of Mehemet Ali of Egypt (1830–40); the conquest and organization of Algeria (1830–47) was the one outstanding achievement of the Orleans monarchy; and in 1881, at the instigation of Bismarck and with the approval of England, France occupied Tunis.

Italy had in 1876 been advised by Austria and Russia to take Tunisia, but she feared French opposition. She was consequently seriously perturbed by the action of France in 1881; she entered a strong protest against it, and appealed, but in vain, to the Powers. Bismarck's designs were, indeed, precisely fulfilled: the attention of France was diverted from Alsace; strife was stirred up between Italy and France, and Italy was brought, as the third partner, into the Triple Alliance.

Crispi

Crispi, though his public career was chequered by domestic irregularities, was for nearly twenty years (1876–1896) the outstanding personality in Italian politics. A real patriot, but not unsusceptible to the flatteries of Bismarck, he was a staunch advocate of the Triple Alliance. But he consistently maintained that that alliance in no way impaired the traditional friendship of Italy for England. Italy, indeed, would like to have brought England

[1] Albert Sorel.

in as a fourth partner. Nor was the idea so fantastic in 1882 as it seemed twenty years later. From both France and Russia, England was at that time bitterly estranged, and until the conclusion of the Anglo-French Entente (1904) the inclusion of England in the Triple Alliance was always a possibility, even if a remote one. Austria, we now know, would, almost at any time, have welcomed her admittance with eagerness. Bismarck, however, always mistrustful of a foreign policy liable to be deflected by the vicissitudes of party fortunes, firmly declined the suggestion, though he agreed that ministerial 'declarations', explaining that the alliance was not 'in any case to be regarded as directed against England', should be annexed to the Treaty.

The Triple Alliance

The Treaty was of immense significance for Italy. Germany and Austria-Hungary bound themselves, in the event of an unprovoked attack upon Italy by France, to assist her with their whole military strength. Italy was reciprocally bound to assist Germany against France, but only to benevolent neutrality if either Germany or Austria-Hungary were attacked single-handed by Russia. On the other hand, the Treaty evidently closed the door on Italy's ambitions in the Adriatic.

Bismarck was, of course, aware of this flaw in his diplomatic structure, and as early as 1883 warned the Crown Prince Rudolph of Austria that they could not confidently count on the support of Italy if war were to break out with France or Russia.

Italy and England

Crispi, though out of office in 1882, strongly urged his Government to accept England's invitation to co-operate with her in Egypt in that year. Failing co-operation, Italy nevertheless promised to support England in Egypt, and England promised support to Italy 'at every other point whatsoever in North Africa, and in particular in Tripolitania and Cyrenaica'. When in 1887 the Triple Alliance was renewed for a further period Germany virtually bound herself to promote the extension of Italian territory at the expense of France. At the same time Italy and Austria-

Hungary mutually undertook to maintain the *status quo* in the Balkans, the Adriatic and the Aegean Sea, or, should that prove impossible, reciprocally to communicate their intentions to each other.

Colonial policy of Italy

It is, then, manifest that so long as Italy was willing to postpone the realization of her irredentist ambitions the Triple Alliance was an invaluable buttress to her diplomatic position in Europe. As a fact, her irredentist claims were, of necessity, postponed owing to disastrous complications in another quarter.

The early 'eighties saw the beginning of that scramble for Africa which, in the ensuing years, led to the exhaustive partitioning of the whole continent among the European Powers. United Italy could not afford to be left behind, and in 1882 the Government took over as a Crown Colony, Assab, north of the Straits of Bab-el-Mandeb, which, some twelve years previously, had been acquired as a coaling station by an Italian steamship company. In 1885, primarily as a retort to the French occupation of Tunis, but partly at the instigation of the British Government, Italy announced her intention to 'pick up the keys of the Mediterranean in the Red Sea' and occupied Massowah on the Abyssinian coast. That was the beginning of a disastrous adventure for Italy. When in 1887 the Italians advanced from the coast into the hinterland the Negus of Abyssinia called upon them to withdraw, and on their refusal, attacked and cut to pieces an Italian column at Dogali. The Italians could not, of course, sit down under this reverse, and in 1889 their stations on the Red Sea were consolidated as the Province of Eritrea and an Italian Protectorate was proclaimed over part of Somaliland. By the Treaty of Uccialli concluded (September 1889) with Abyssinia Italy recognized Menelik as Emperor of Ethiopia, and Menelik recognized the Italian Colony of Eritrea.

In 1891 Great Britain recognized Abyssinia as within the Italian sphere of influence, and four years later Crispi, who had returned to power in 1893, occupied Adowa, the capital of Tigré, a little state tributary to Abyssinia. The

Abyssinian Sultan Menelik thereupon attacked, with a greatly superior force, the Italians in Adowa, and the latter lost, in killed and wounded, no fewer than 10,000 out of a total force of 14,000. This disaster dissipated the dream of colonial expansion in East Africa.

Domestic difficulties

It also gravely accentuated the difficulties of a domestic situation already sufficiently serious. Ever since 1871 Italy had been straining her exiguous resources to the uttermost. Her means were not yet equal to the position she was attempting to assert for herself. Financial disaster and social unrest were a part of the price she had to pay for o'er-vaunting ambition. During the two decades which preceded the outbreak of the World War Italy was almost continuously a prey to industrial and agrarian unrest and social disorder.

Socialism

'The very rapid growth of Socialism, its appearance as a parliamentary party, its absorption of much of what is best in national life and thought, is the master fact of Italian politics to-day. A movement that barely existed ten years ago, is now their most living force.' Thus wrote two close and competent observers of Italian life in 1900.[1] But 'Socialism' is often loosely used; it covers a large variety of opinions. Strong opponents often fail to distinguish between Socialism on the one hand, and Syndicalism, Communism, and even Anarchism, on the other. Socialists themselves maintain that the Socialism of the ballot-box has nothing in common with the Syndicalism that favours direct action, still less with Anarchism. The methods are undoubtedly different; whether the ultimate goal is distinguishable is more questionable. Be that as it may, there is no doubt that Socialism of various hues developed rapidly in Italy after the attainment of unity.

Nor can it be doubted that the spread of socialistic doctrine was, in part at least, responsible for the social disorder which disfigured Italy and gravely retarded its economic progress.

Social disorders

Of that disorder there were frequent manifestations,

[1] Bolton King and T. Okey.

particularly in the two decades between 1890 and 1910. The first was, characteristically, in Sicily. The trouble there was due partly to general discontent with a Government which appeared to the Sicilians, as to others, as 'a tyrant who swallowed everything, robbed at his will, and disposed of property and persons for the benefit of a few'. Primarily, however, Sicilian discontent was agrarian in character. The Socialists had since 1891 organized throughout the island a network of more or less revolutionary unions (*fasci*). Similar in their objects and methods to the branches of the Irish Land League, the *fasci* incited the peasants to seize the property of the landlords (frequently absentees) and to farm the land on their own account. Giovanni Giolitti, a professed Democrat, who in 1892 had formed the first of his five ministries, showed lamentable weakness in dealing with the situation; Crispi (who succeeded him in 1893) erred almost as gravely in the opposite direction. Sicily was governed under martial law for more than six months, and nearly 2,000 Sicilians were transported to semi-penal settlements in the islands. Troubles broke out again, however, in 1898. During the earlier months of that year there were sporadic outbreaks in Southern Italy, in Parma and Piacenza, and in the Romagna; and early in May there was a still more menacing insurrection in Milan. It is difficult to determine its exact character as between a mere riot and an incipient revolution. But the authorities, rightly or wrongly, took a grave view of it; for three days the mob was master of the city, and order was restored only after considerable loss of life.

Murder of King Humbert

The assassination (29 July 1900) of King Humbert, who in 1878 had succeeded his father Victor Emmanuel, gave pause to the less extreme Socialists, but the political and economic situation was, in the opening years of the new century, exceedingly grave. Unrest was endemic; but the causes which provoked it varied considerably. There was in many of the outbreaks an element of anarchism, mostly imported from abroad. There was legitimate discontent with the failure of the parliamentary régime, both in foreign and in domestic affairs. The disasters to Italian arms in Africa were enhanced by repeated revelations of scandals, financial and political, at home. Ministers came and ministers went, but the common folk could see little to choose between them. The cost of living was high, expenditure extravagant, taxation heavy, and corruption rampant. And behind all this there were the fundamental difficulties inseparable from the transition from one industrial system to another. The process is always a painful, not infrequently a dangerous one. The Chartist Movement in England was the product of the new industrialism; so was the Revolution of 1848 in France; Bismarck, warned of the danger, mitigated the severity of the attack in Germany by large doses of State Socialism. Italy had no Bismarck; not even a Peel. There is therefore no cause for wonder if, in the bankruptcy of statesmanship, Italy should have failed to adjust herself with rapidity to the new conditions of an industrialized State which lacked many of the requisites for successful industrialization. Small wonder, also, if to half-educated artisans and illiterate peasants the first effects of the general use of machinery, both in industry and in agriculture, should have appeared to threaten the interests of the wage-earners.

Strikes

During the first two years of the new century there were no fewer than fifteen hundred sectional strikes, involving about one million wage-earners. In September 1904 a general strike was proclaimed. In Milan, particularly, it quickly assumed the character of an anarchist insurrection, and in Rome, Florence, Naples, Genoa, and Venice there were very grave disturbances. Giolitti, however, called out two classes of the Reserves and the movement collapsed. Anarchy reared its head again in 1907. From June until October the whole country was in a state of unrest: disturbances among the agricultural labourers of the Romagna; anti-clerical demonstrations followed by reprisals in all parts; agrarian disorder in the south. In October the general strike was again proclaimed in Milan and spread thence to other cities; the railways, however, had in the meantime been nationalized, the employees had become civil servants and been deprived of the right to strike, and the dismissal of the ringleaders brought about the collapse of the movement.

Nature, too, made a large contribution to the tribulations of this unhappy country. An eruption of Mount Etna in 1906, followed by a terrible earthquake in Sicily at the end of 1908, caused a loss of life and a damage to property more serious than all the anarchist insurrections put together. Not that the anarchists desisted from their relatively puny efforts. The syndicalists raised trouble in 1908; but the Libyan War (1911) diverted attention from class warfare at home; an anarchist attempt on the life of Victor Emmanuel III (March 1912) evoked widespread demonstrations of devotion to the Monarchy, and at the Socialist Congress that was held at Reggio in the ensuing summer an unbridgeable chasm revealed itself in the party. The revolutionary wing organized numerous outbreaks in 1913, and not even the intervention of Italy in the World War availed entirely to exorcize the spirit of anarchy. The munition-workers made trouble at Turin in 1917, and after the war there was still more serious and more general disturbance. To that we must return in due course. The relation of Italy to the general diplomatic situation of Europe demands prior attention.

XII

ITALY AND HER NEIGHBOURS (1887–1914)

FEAR and suspicion of France drove Italy, as we have seen, into an alliance with Germany, and, consequently, into an alliance with Austria-Hungary. But the connexion was eminently one *de convenance*, not of affection. Italy was, indeed, scrupulously careful to insist that friendship with the Central Empires was not, under any circumstances, to involve hostility to England; and, apart from that, there was a fundamental antagonism of interests between Italy and the Hapsburg Empire, while, on the other hand, the maintenance of cordial commercial relations between Italy and France was especially important to Italy. Nevertheless, despite inherent elements of weakness, the Triple Alliance was of substantial value to Italy at a most critical period of her national history.

The Triple Alliance

The formal diplomatic relations between Rome and Berlin were further improved by the personal intercourse of sovereigns and statesmen. Crispi paid at least three visits to Berlin and established very friendly relations between himself and Bismarck. Victor Emmanuel II and the Emperors of Austria and of Germany had interchanged visits in 1875; a most cordial welcome was given to the young Kaiser when he visited Rome in 1888; and King Humbert, accompanied by Crispi, went to Berlin in 1889.

In 1891 the Triple Alliance was renewed for a period of six or (unless denounced with twelve months' notice by any of the contracting parties) twelve years. It was in fact renewed in 1902, and once more in 1912, but even before the earlier date its significance had been gravely impaired. Bismarck's fall in 1890 was the first blow to it, and in 1896 Baron Blanc, the Italian Foreign Minister, addressed to Berlin and Vienna a strongly worded memorandum emphasizing the importance of a good understanding between the Triple Alliance and Great Britain. In 1898 Italy and

France renewed the Commercial Treaty, and thus brought to a close the disastrous tariff war which had ever since 1887 so gravely disorganized Italian trade. A visit paid by the French Mediterranean Fleet to Cagliari in 1899 was reciprocated by a visit of the Italian Fleet to Toulon in 1901. Meanwhile (1900) the two countries had concluded a friendly arrangement by which each recognized the dominant interests of the other in Morocco and Tripoli respectively. When, in 1902, negotiations for a renewal of the Triple Alliance began, Italy pressed her allies on three points: first, for the insertion of a clause to the effect that Italy had undertaken no engagements that could prove dangerous to France; secondly, that Austria should expressly sanction in advance an Italian occupation of Tripoli; and, thirdly, that Germany should bind herself to the unconditional maintenance of the *status quo* in the Near East—in plain English to the defence of the Straits against Russia. On none of these points could Italy obtain any satisfaction, though Austria did, in a separate declaration, undertake not to oppose Italy's designs on Tripoli. Italy and Austria had already (1900) agreed to maintain the *status quo* in Albania, and, if and when that should prove no longer possible, to endeavour to obtain autonomy for it. Italy would have been glad to see these further stipulations inserted in the Treaty, but her allies refused. As a fact, renewal of the Triple Alliance was no sooner completed than Italy formally intimated to Paris that the treaty contained nothing which bound Italy to take part in any attack upon France, or to threaten her security or peace.[1]

The diplomatic edifice so carefully constructed by Bismarck was evidently developing ominous fissures. They were to widen in the years ahead. The welcome accorded to King Victor Emmanuel and Queen Elena when, in 1903, accompanied by Signor Tittoni, the Foreign Minister, they visited Paris was not less warm and spontaneous than that

[1] On these negotiations cf. Pribram, *Secret Treaties of Austria-Hungary*, ii. 241 seq.; and Brandenburg, *From Bismarck to the World War*, pp. 187 seq., and the original documents there cited.

which they naturally received in London. That was sufficiently significant, but much more significant was the welcome of President Loubet in Rome (1904). If the visit completed the rupture between the Vatican and the French Republic, it confirmed the accord between the Republic and the Quirinal.

Writing of Italy, where he was in charge of the British Embassy in 1902, Sir Rennell Rodd says:

'Time had modified the conditions which had antagonized France and Italy. France had had an anti-clerical phase, and the possibility of intervention on behalf of the Holy See no longer gave preoccupation. Public sentiment in Italy had grown more reconciled to the French Protectorate over Tunis, where Italian settlers prospered. Crispi was dead, and the Triple Alliance was regarded as the particular work of a statesman who had led the country into a policy of adventure at that time beyond her powers . . . the feeling became appreciable that the guarantees of the alliance were dearly bought at the price of the permanent hostility of France and a pernicious tariff war.'[1]

Italy and France

The conclusion of the Anglo-French agreement in 1904 helped further to a good understanding between the French Republic and Italy, nor could the latter be blind to the significance of the agreement reached between Great Britain and Russia in 1907. Plainly, a diplomatic re-adjustment of the highest importance was in process of accomplishment. Meanwhile, the Conference at Algeciras (1905–6), on which Germany had confidently counted to destroy, in the eyes of the world, the significance of the Anglo-French *entente*, had actually demonstrated its solidarity. Moreover, it had served equally to expose to public gaze the widening breach in the structure of the Triple Alliance. Prince von Bülow had already (1903) been warned by the German representative in Rome that the Irredentist movement was rapidly gathering momentum. On the Austrian side General Conrad von Hötzendorff, from the moment of his appointment (1906) as Chief of the Staff, insisted that war between the Hapsburg

[1] *Social and Diplomatic Memories*, iii. 4.

Empire and Italy was inevitable, and that the right policy for Austria was to anticipate it. When in 1911 Italy involved herself in the Tripoli Expedition, Austria might, in her own interests, have been wise to follow his unscrupulous advice; but the old Emperor would not hear of war against his 'ally'.

The Balkan Crisis, 1908–9

Meantime, a good deal had happened to embitter relations between them. In no European capital, not even in London, did the Balkan crisis of 1908–9 cause graver perturbation than in Rome. In July 1908 the Young Turks had raised the standard of revolt at Salonika, and in April 1909 had occupied Constantinople and deposed the reigning Sultan, Abdul Hamid. On 5 October 1908 Prince Ferdinand of Bulgaria proclaimed the independence of Bulgaria, and in the ensuing April it was formally recognized by the Turkish Government. On 12 October 1908 the Cretan Assembly decreed the union of the island with the kingdom of Greece. On the same day that Ferdinand proclaimed the independence of Bulgaria, the Emperor Francis Joseph announced the formal annexation of Bosnia and the Herzegovina to the Hapsburg Empire.

The news came as a bombshell to Europe. The German Emperor was hardly less upset than King Edward VII. The latter saw in the events of 1908 the first steps towards the precipice over which Europe plunged in 1914. The Kaiser was bitterly angered by Aerenthal's duplicity, which was likely to lead to the dismemberment of Turkey, one of the sleeping partners in the Triple Alliance. Serbia, the power most directly concerned, would have appealed to arms had Russia been in a position to support her. But Russia, fresh from her defeat at the hands of Japan, dared not disregard the warning of Germany, that war with Austria meant war with her. For roundly as the Kaiser might objurgate Aerenthal in private, he publicly supported his Austrian ally. So complete, indeed, was the diplomatic isolation of Germany that he had no alternative. Berlin was, in fact, in the toils of Vienna.

Italy was, by now, most anxious to escape from them.

The events of 1908 finally opened her eyes to the inherent contradictions involved in her adherence to the Central European alliance. True, Austria had promised support in regard to Tripoli, but even nearer to the heart of Italians than expansion in North Africa was the hope of redeeming the 'unredeemed' districts in the southern Tyrol and on the Adriatic. The Austrian Government had not shown the slightest desire to conciliate Italian opinion in that quarter. On the contrary, everything was done in the 'Italian' provinces of the Hapsburg Empire to eliminate Italian influence, even to the extent of encouraging Slav immigration and enterprise. To that as to every other case of the kind there were, doubtless, two sides, but, making all necessary deductions, the picture drawn by Signor Virginio Gayda is appalling:

'Where possible, as in Dalmatia and at Trieste, they have tried directly to eliminate the Italian race, repressing their economic life and their political liberties, substituting foreigners—Germans or Slavs—for Italians in the Italian cities, in order to impoverish the Italians, reduce their number and destroy the national unity of the country. Where, as in the Trentino, Friuli, and Istria, such direct action was impossible . . . they have attempted a slow and insidious method of moral and spiritual disintegration. They have sought to exhaust the national sentiment by continual persecution. . . . By violence and machination a Government has coldly and deliberately worked for forty years for the material and spiritual destruction of a subject people. It has not succeeded—no people can be suppressed at the will of a Government. But the drama of the Austrian Italians has been a bloody business and there have been cruel martyrdoms.' [1]

Tripoli

But whatever the provocations offered by Austria, the unredeemed provinces would have to wait a more favourable international situation. In Tripoli, on the contrary, the pear was almost ripe. Some subsequent events suggest that Italy might, and perhaps should, have seized the opportunity offered by the Balkan crisis of 1908–9 to

[1] *Modern Austria*, p. 19.

assert her claims upon that portion of the southern Mediterranean littoral still open to her. 'North Africa will belong to Italy.' Such was Mazzini's prophecy long before Italy herself was made. The opening years of the twentieth century saw Egypt, Tunisia, and Morocco in the grip of European Powers whose superiority at sea Italy could not hope to challenge. The events of 1905–11 made it clear that a third naval Power, Italy's own ally, was not prepared to accept, without protest, the Franco-British ascendancy in North Africa.

Morocco

In April 1911 a French expedition was dispatched to Morocco and in May occupied Fez, the Moroccan capital. In view of the agreement concluded (8 February 1909) on the Moroccan Question between France and Germany it was not unnatural that these events should have aroused suspicion at Berlin. 'Should France find it necessary to remain at Fez,' said von Kiderlin-Wächter, the German Foreign Secretary, 'the whole Moroccan Question will be raised afresh, and each signatory of the Act of Algeciras will resume entire liberty of action.' The French troops did not remain at Fez; they commenced their retirement in June; but with each stage of the retirement the tone of Germany became more and more menacing, and on 1 July France was officially informed that the *Panther*, a German gunboat, had been dispatched to Agadir, an open roadstead on the Atlantic coast of Morocco.

France angrily protested that her recognized paramountcy in Morocco was impugned by this action; it looked like war; but England definitely supported France; and though for nearly three months peace hung by a thread, an agreement was eventually patched up between France and Germany.[1]

The European war was postponed; but the 'Agadir' incident convinced Italy that she must act at once in Tripoli. On 29 September she declared war on Turkey.

Tripoli

The claims of Italy had, as mentioned above, been

[1] For details of the Agadir Crisis see Marriott, *History of Europe from 1815 to 1923* (Methuen, 1931), c. xxi.

already acknowledged by France and Austria, and Italy herself had, for years past, been consistently pursuing a policy of economic penetration, and with conspicuous success. That the pear, when fully ripe, would fall into their laps, without further effort, was the general expectation.

The Young Turk revolution at Constantinople completely altered the situation. Its repercussions were felt throughout the whole Ottoman Empire. Not least in Tripoli. The advance-guard of the Italian occupation—the merchants, bankers, engineers, and the like—found themselves suddenly, and to their amazement, thwarted at every turn by newly appointed Turkish officials. The whole economic fabric, carefully erected in Tripoli by Italians, was threatened. The Young Turks saw no reason why a valuable province of the Ottoman Empire should be allowed to pass, without protest, under the domination of Italy. The Italian flag was, accordingly, treated with ostentatious contempt; Italian citizens were insulted, and every such 'incident' was sedulously reported, not without exaggeration, in the Italian press. Thus public opinion in Italy was carefully prepared for decisive action at the appropriate moment.

Meanwhile, German archaeologists and geologists had of late years been showing renewed activity in the pursuit of their scientific investigations in Tripoli. Italian suspicions were aroused. Could there be any connexion between the reawakened fanaticism of Moslem officials and the scientific enthusiasm of Teutonic professors? That Turkey, like Roumania, had become a sleeping partner in the Triple Alliance was more than suspected at Rome. That a great German soldier-scholar, Baron von der Goltz, had devoted many years to the reorganization of the Turkish army on German lines was, of course, known to the world. The conjunction between Germans and Young Turks in Tripoli wore, on this account, a more sinister aspect at Rome.

The Racconigi Agreement

Another conjunction had, meanwhile, created more than a momentary excitement among the high diplomatists of

Europe. In October 1909 the Czar Nicholas of Russia, smarting under the humiliation lately imposed upon him by the 'knight in shining armour' at Potsdam, paid a ceremonial visit to Victor Emmanuel III at Racconigi.

Italy and Russia

The two sovereigns agreed to maintain, as far as possible, the *status quo* in the Balkans, or, failing that, to encourage the development of the national States of the Balkans to the exclusion both of Austria and Italy. Russia consented to maintain a benevolent attitude in reference to Italy's designs on Tripoli and Cyrenaica; Italy promised to reciprocate this attitude towards the ambitions of Russia in reference to the Bosphorus and the Dardanelles. Russia communicated the terms of this agreement not only to the other members of the Entente, France and Great Britain, but also to the Balkan States, and on the invitation of Russia, England and France agreed to adhere to the Racconigi Agreement. The arrangement had, as Professor Brandenburg has pointed out, a twofold significance: it registered the first united move of the Entente Powers in regard to the Near-Eastern Question, and it marked the further progress of Italy from the Triple Alliance towards the Triple Entente.[1]

Nevertheless the Triple Alliance remained formally intact. In December 1909 Aerenthal concluded a fresh agreement with Italy in regard to the Balkans: neither Power was to come to terms with a third Power without informing the other, and Austria-Hungary specifically bound herself not to reoccupy the Sanjak of Novi Bazar without having previously arranged with Italy for suitable compensation to her. The alliance possessed in truth one element of reality: it was founded on common hostility to the Balkan Slavs: 'It would be far more advantageous to Italy', declared the Marquis San Giuliano, 'to have a strong Austro-Hungarian Monarchy as its neighbour than if a purely Slavic group were to be formed in the Balkans and

[1] Brandenburg, op. cit., pp. 355–6, who quotes the text of the Racconigi Agreement as communicated to France *ap.* Stieve's *Schriftwechsel Iswolski*, ii. 363.

to exercise its influence upon the provinces of the Dual Monarchy that border on Italy.'[1]

Turco-Italian War, 29 September 1911 to 18 October 1912

Those rights were now menaced from an unexpected quarter. The scientific interest which German geologists and archaeologists had lately developed in Tripoli aroused grave suspicion at Rome; and the descent of the *Panther* upon Agadir convinced Italy that unless she was prepared to forgo for all time her reversionary interests in North Africa, the hour for claiming them had struck.

The Racconigi Agreement completed the isolation of Turkey. Accordingly, when, two years later, Italy decided that the time had come for the occupation of Tripoli, she was secured against interference by any of her European neighbours. On 27 September 1911 she suddenly presented to Turkey an ultimatum demanding the consent of the Porte to an Italian occupation of Tripoli under the sovereignty of the Sultan, and subject to the payment of an annual tribute. A reply was required within forty-eight hours, but already the Italian transports were on their way to Tripoli, and on 29 September war was declared.

Italy and the Porte

Italy found in Tripoli no easy task. She occupied the coast towns of Tripoli, Bengazi, and Derna without difficulty, but against the combined resistance of Turks and Arabs she could make little progress in the interior. The Porte, trusting that international complications would supervene and once again, as so often in the past, extricate it from its difficulties, obstinately refused to make any concessions. But between her two allies Germany was in a difficult position. She was indignant that Italy should, without permission from Berlin, have ventured to attack the Turks; but, on the other hand, she had no wish to throw the third partner in the Triple Alliance into the arms of the Triple Entente. Italy, however, was not to be diverted from her predetermined purpose. In the spring of 1912 her navy attacked at several points: a couple of Turkish war-ships were sunk off Beirut; the forts at the entrance to the Dardanelles were bombarded on 18 April; Rhodes and the

[1] Pribram, op. cit., p. 149.

Dodecanese Archipelago were occupied in May. To the bombardment of the Dardanelles Turkey retorted by closing the Straits. This proved highly inconvenient to neutrals, and after a month they were reopened. Throughout the summer the war went languidly on, entailing much expense to Italy and very little expense or even inconvenience to the Turks.

In two ways the war was indeed advantageous to the policy of the Young Turks. On the one hand, 'by reconciling Turk and Arab in a holy war in Africa, the Tripoli campaign healed for a time the running sore in Arabia which had for years drained the resources of the Empire.' On the other, the naval operations of Italy in the Aegean aroused acute friction between the Italians and the Greeks, whose reversionary interests in the islands were at least as strong as those of Italy upon the African littoral. That friction would be likely to increase, and in any case could not be otherwise than advantageous to the Turk.

Treaty of Lausanne

Then suddenly a new danger threatened the luckless Turk. The Tripoli campaign was still dragging its slow length along, and seemed as though it might be protracted for years, when the conflagration blazed up to which Tripoli had applied the first match. In view of the more immediate danger the Porte at last came to terms with Italy, and the Treaty of Lausanne was hastily signed at Ouchy on 18 October. The Turks were to withdraw from Tripoli; Italy from the Aegean Islands; the Khalifal authority of the Sultan in Tripoli was to remain intact; he was to grant an amnesty and a reformed administration to the islands; Italy was to assume responsibility for Tripoli's share of the Ottoman debt. The cession of Tripoli was assumed *sub silentio*. The withdrawal of the Italian troops from the islands was to be subsequent to and consequent upon the withdrawal of the Turkish troops. The latter condition has not been fulfilled, and so Italy remains in Rhodes and the Dodecanese. Her continued occupation has not injured the Turks, but it has kept out the Greeks.

On the same day that the Treaty of Lausanne was signed

Greece declared war upon the Ottoman Empire. She was not alone. The miracle had occurred. The Balkan States had combined against the common enemy.

The Balkan Wars

With the Balkan wars (1912–13) Italy was concerned only so far as they might affect the future of the Adriatic littoral and in particular of Albania. Hardly had the Balkan League entered on its wonderful career of victory, when Serbia received a solemn warning from the Powers that she would not be permitted to retain any port on the Adriatic. Montenegro, however, was determined, whatever Europe might decree, that she would take Scutari. As far back as December 1912 the Powers had decided that Albania should be an autonomous State under a prince selected by them, and that she must retain Scutari. Montenegro persisted in defying the Powers, and despite a blockade by an international squadron of the Montenegrin coast, captured the town. But Montenegro's triumph was brief. King Peter was compelled to bow to the will of the Powers and to surrender Scutari to an international force landed from the warships. For the Powers an autonomous Albania might solve many difficulties; it might stifle the incipient and conflicting pretensions of Italy and Austria-Hungary; it might frustrate inconvenient claims of Greece on 'northern Epirus', and interpose a powerful barrier between the Southern Slavs and the Adriatic. The man selected for the difficult task of ruling the wild highlanders of Albania was Prince William of Wied, German Prince, Russian soldier, and nephew of the Queen of Roumania. But his position was impossible, and after a turbulent reign of six months (March–September 1914) he abandoned the hopeless task. When the European war broke out no central authority existed in Albania. A Turkish Pasha ruled Durazzo; Greece took possession of 'northern Epirus'; in October 1914 the Italians occupied the islet of Saseno, and in January 1915 the town and harbour of Valona.

But we anticipate the sequence of events. On the conclusion of the second Balkan War the Emperor William congratulated his cousin of Roumania on their 'mutual co-operation in the cause of peace'. If the Kaiser had truly laboured in the interests of peace, his august ally in Vienna had done his utmost to enlarge the area of war. Austria was deeply chagrined by the success achieved by the Serbians in the Balkan wars, and on the eve of the signature of the Treaty of Bucharest (10 August 1913) she communicated to Germany and Italy 'her intention of taking action against Serbia and defined such action as defensive, hoping to bring into operation the *casus foederis* of the Triple Alliance.'[1]

Italy and Austria

Italy refused point-blank to recognize the contemplated attack of Austria upon Serbia as a *casus foederis*; Berlin also exercised a restraining influence upon Vienna; but the tension between Austria-Hungary and Serbia was not relaxed; the murder of the Archduke Franz Ferdinand on 28 June 1914 provided a fresh ground of offence; the outbreak of the world-war had been postponed by the action of Italy for less than twelve months.

What would be Italy's attitude when war actually came? That was a matter of profound concern both to the Entente and to her allies in the Triple Alliance. Three courses were open to her: intervention on the side of the Central Empires; neutrality; or intervention on behalf of the Entente.

Austrian offers to Italy

On 3 August 1914 Italy formally declared her neutrality, but Germany made desperate efforts to prevent an actual rupture of the alliance and brought all possible pressure to bear upon Austria-Hungary in order to induce her to make larger and larger concessions to the ever-increasing demands of Italy. All to no purpose. Italy was determined to use the opportunity to get all that she had been denied by Prussia and Austria in 1866, and perhaps something more. 'Italy', said Signor Salandra, the Premier, 'has legitimate aspirations to affirm and sustain.'[2] The world now knows what they were.

[1] Telegram quoted by Giolitti in the Italian Chamber, 5 December 1914 (*Collected Diplomatic Documents*, p. 401).

[2] December 1914. Cf. Sir James Rennell Rodd, *Social and Diplomatic Memories* (Third Series), c. ix.

On 8 April 1915 Italy informed Austria that the price of her neutrality was: the Trentino, the valley of the Isonzo, the formation of Trieste and north-western Istria into an independent State, certain islands of the Adriatic archipelago, and a free hand in Albania. That Austria would make such concessions unless she had been beaten to her knees was not to be expected. The proposal was in fact an ultimatum. Austria refused it, and on 3 May Baron Sidney Sonnino, who in October had become Foreign Minister, notified the Ballplatz that Italy 'resumes from this moment complete liberty of action, and declares as cancelled, and as henceforth without effect, her treaty of alliance with Austria-Hungary'.

Treaty of London

A week earlier Italy had concluded with Great Britain, France, and Russia the Treaty of London. By that treaty, which was 'secret', Italy undertook to put all her strength into the war against the enemies of the Entente. In return she was to obtain the district of the Trentino, the southern Tyrol up to the Brenner Pass, Trieste, the countries of Gorizia and Gradisca, the whole of Istria up to the Quarnero, including Volosca, and the Istrian archipelago, the province of Dalmatia in its existing frontiers, together with most of the islands in the Adriatic (including Lissa), and she was to retain Valona and the Dodecanese.[1] Italy also stipulated for a loan of £50,000,000 on easy terms and that the Pope should have no say as to the final terms of peace. Italy at the same time agreed that large accessions of territory, including Fiume, should be assigned to Croatia, Serbia, and Montenegro.

Italy declared war against Austria-Hungary on 24 May, against Turkey on 21 August, and a few weeks later against Bulgaria. Not, however, until 27 August 1916 did she declare war against Germany.

The intervention of Italy was, both in a moral and a material sense, of immense service to the Entente. But it was not secured without great efforts on the part primarily of Sir James Rennell Rodd, the British ambassador in

[1] *British and Foreign State Papers*, 1919, vol. cxii, pp. 973 seq.

Rome, who was strongly backed by Baron Sidney Sonnino, the Foreign Minister, and by the Marquis Imperiali, Italian ambassador in London.

On the other side powerful forces had been operating in favour of neutrality: the clericals heartily disliked the idea of fighting on the side of 'godless' France and 'orthodox' Russia; the socialists did not want to fight any one except capitalists; the old-fashioned conservatives were averse to a complete breach with the autocracies of Central Europe; Giolitti also threw his great though waning influence into the same scale. Giolitti's influence was, however, more than balanced by the adhesion to the interventionist party of a leading socialist, Benito Mussolini, who, late in 1914, founded *Il Popolo d'Italia* to popularize the cause he had so zealously espoused.

For Italy the choice made in April 1915 was one of the most momentous in her history. But advantageous as her decision was for the Allies, it introduced considerable complications into the diplomatic situation. The Serbs were gravely perturbed by the adhesion of a Power whose notorious ambitions threatened to frustrate the dream of a Greater Serbia. The terms of the 'Secret' Treaty of London were soon known to Serbia, and the knowledge caused a bitter pang. Rather than see Italy firmly established east of the Adriatic many Serbs would have preferred to leave the Hapsburgs in occupation.

The price demanded of the Entente by Italy was undoubtedly a heavy one; they had, however, little option but to pay it, albeit largely at the expense of a gallant and hard-pressed ally. In the end, the intervention of Italy proved of immense importance to the Greater Serbia to be.

XIII

THE WAR AND THE PEACE

Italy in the War

ITALY was ill-prepared for war. The Giolitti Government had left the army deplorably deficient in munitions, particularly in heavy artillery and machine guns, in equipment, and in stores of every kind. Of aircraft Italy had practically none. Nor did the material resources of Italy permit of the rapid improvisation which wrought such miracles in England and France. Totally devoid of coal, she was, as we have seen, poorly provided with iron and other raw materials. She was short also of tonnage, and the poor accommodation and inadequate equipment of her ports made it difficult for her Allies to supply her deficiencies from abroad. On the outbreak of war the General Staff was taken unawares. Threatened by the thrust of the Trentino salient, Italian soldiers had based their strategical plans on the supposition that Italy would act on the defensive. Suddenly to adapt their plans to the demands of offensive warfare was by no means easy, especially in view of the fact that on the north-eastern frontier Austria almost enveloped Italy.

Campaign of 1915

Accordingly, General Cadorna, who commanded the Italian army, leaving a subsidiary force to contain the Austrians on the Trentino sector of his widely extended front, made his main attack on the Isonzo front, with Trieste as his objective. The capture of Trieste would have been of inestimable value, both in a moral and a military sense, to Italy, but it was not to be. At the cost of nearly 280,000 men, killed (66,009), wounded, and prisoners, Italy had gained in the campaign of 1915 little except 'hard experience'. General Cadorna had, indeed, diverted the attention of some 800,000 Austrian troops from Russia, and the initial campaign had, according to an Italian account, yielded 'satisfactory evidence of the men'. On the other hand it had revealed still more clearly the need of better material, especially heavy guns, and of new methods in military organization.

The Campaign of 1916

The campaign of 1916 somewhat improved the position of Italy. The Austrian offensive in the Trentino was repulsed; repeated attacks were launched against the Austrians on the eastern or Isonzo front, and considerable forces were dispatched to Albania in March and, later in the year, to Salonika. Though the taking of Gorizia was encouraging, the territorial advance was insignificant, but the detention of large Austrian forces on the Italian front was of great service to the allied cause, though the Italians had again to deplore losses amounting to nearly double those of 1915.

Conference of Rome

In January 1917 an allied Conference was held in Rome at which a proposal was mooted that British and French forces should be sent to co-operate with the Italians in a determined effort to 'knock out' Austria. Mr. Lloyd George, who had just succeeded Mr. Asquith as Prime Minister, favoured the idea, but it was rejected by his military advisers and by the French High Command. Italy, however, attacked repeatedly in the summer of 1917, though with results miserably disproportionate to the terrible punishment inflicted on her gallant troops.

The defection of Russia, gravely as it affected the whole position of the Allies, was particularly menacing to Italy, since it enabled Austria to concentrate her efforts against Italy. The military situation of Italy was further weakened by the development of a *Defeatist* movement behind the lines, and by the outbreak (August 1917) of revolutionary riots in Turin. From the first there had been not only a considerable pro-German party among the upper classes, but a very strong section of 'internationalists' among the socialists of the industrial towns. 'Next winter not another man in the trenches' was the *mot d'ordre* issued by a socialist deputy named Treves, and there was considerable response to it among the socialists. Nor did economic conditions, and especially the increasing shortage of food, tend to diminish the force of the appeal, though it was the petted and over-paid munition workers who were primarily responsible for the outbreak at Turin. The slogan of the socialists was reinforced by the Church. In August 1917 Pope Benedict XV, in a pontifically impartial manifesto, made an earnest appeal for the cessation of 'useless slaughter' and for the conclusion of peace on terms fair to both parties.

Defeat at Caporetto

These things naturally reacted on the morale of the troops, and on 24 October 1917 the enemy, reinforced by six German divisions and advised by a German Army Staff, discovered a weak spot in the Italian line, due to treachery or cowardice; 180,000 prisoners and 2,300 guns were captured by the enemy in three weeks; the Italians were soon in full retreat; the retreat became a rout, and the rout of the Second Army involved the retreat of the Third. Only a magnificent stand made by the Fourth Army on the Piave saved Italy from disaster. Had that army broken the enemy would have at once taken Venice, Verona, and Vicenza. The moment was intensely critical, and the allied commanders realized it. Six French and five British divisions were promptly dispatched to the Italian front; Marshal Foch and General Robertson went off in hot haste to Italy, met Cadorna in consultation at Treviso on 30 October, and on 4 November an allied council was held at Rapallo. Mr. Lloyd George, Sir Henry Wilson, General Smuts, Marshal Foch, and M. Painléve conferred there with Signor Orlando (who had just succeeded Boselli as Prime Minister) and Baron Sonnino. Important decisions were reached as to the future conduct of the war. Henceforward there was to be unity of command under a French *generalissimo*. General Diaz replaced Cadorna as Commander-in-Chief of the Italian forces, which, under his leadership, made a wonderful recovery on the Piave.

Vittorio Veneto

The defeat at Caporetto proved to be, even before the allied reinforcement could arrive, a moral no less than a military crisis for Italy. Italy emerged from it purged and purified. The voice of faction was hushed; the 'defeatists' hid their heads in confusion; the spirit of the best days of the *Risorgimento* revived. Soldiers and civilians worked as one man to reorganize and re-equip the army during the winter of 1917–18; the Italian defence was stiffened by the arrival of French and British reinforcements; and when in June 1918 the Austrians somewhat tardily renewed the attack they were gallantly repulsed. In October a re-equipped Italian army under General Diaz and a mixed British and Italian force under Lord Cavan, with the aid of a French contingent under General Graziani, combined in a final offensive, known as the battle of Vittorio Veneto, and in a brief but brilliant campaign chased the Austrians out of Italy. The scale of the operations may be measured by the fact that nearly 600,000 prisoners and 7,000 guns were captured. On 2 November Austria begged for an armistice. The war on the Italian front was over. In Italy, as elsewhere, sunshine had during the war years alternated with shadow, and if in the Tyrolese mountains and on the Isonzo shadow seemed to predominate, Ludendorff himself testified to the effect on the general situation of Italy's tenacious grip upon the throat of Austria. With British sea-power unbroken, and streams of American reinforcements pouring over to the help of the war-wearied armies of England and France, Germany could hardly, in any case, have emerged victorious from the terrific struggle. But had Italy not come in to contain and finally to break Austria, the struggle might have ended in stalemate. The value of Italian help must be measured, therefore, not by spectacular feats of arms, but by the attrition of the Austrian armies.

Italy at the Peace Conference

Under the terms of the armistice concluded with Austria, the latter agreed to evacuate not only all Italian territory, but also all the territories assigned to Italy by the Treaty of London. These were promptly taken over by Italian forces, and at the request of the inhabitants, Fiume, Landeck, and Innsbruck were also, in the interests of public order and the security of property, occupied.

At the Peace Conference in Paris Italy was represented by Signor Orlando, an able lawyer and experienced politician, who since Caporetto had been Prime Minister, and by the Foreign Secretary Sonnino.

The views of Sonnino and Orlando were not in complete accord: Sonnino would have stood simply by the Treaty of London; Orlando wanted to get Fiume in addition. Nevertheless, the case of Italy was in reality a relatively simple one. No Power had entered the war with aims more clearly defined. Precise promises, embodied in a Treaty, had been made to her by the Allies. The time had come for their fulfilment.

But there were two complications.

The Adriatic Problem

The Jugo-Slavs were insistent on reasonable access to the Adriatic, and quite immovable on the question of Fiume. With Trieste and Pola in the hands of Italy, Fiume affords the only outlet for the trade of Carinthia, Carniola, and Styria. Without it, Croatia-Slavonia is virtually landlocked. Moreover, in President Wilson the Jugo-Slavs found a powerful champion of their claims. Unfortunately for Italy, and perhaps for the world, Mr. Wilson went to Paris possessing little first-hand acquaintance with European politics, and less with European politicians, but, nevertheless, fixedly determined to adhere to his own rather pedantic formulas. Partly out of genuine sympathy for the Serbs, whose gallantry in holding the gate against the Central Empire entitled them to, and obtained for them, the fullest consideration from all the Allies, partly in protest against the 'secret diplomacy' of the Treaty of London, Mr. Wilson throughout offered stout and persistent opposition to the claims of Italy. The ninth of his 'Fourteen Points' had indeed promised 'a readjustment of the frontiers of Italy along clearly recognized lines of nationality', but that promise was a good deal less precise than the terms of the Treaty of London, and was complicated by the provision (Point 11) that 'Serbia [should be] accorded free and secure access to the sea', and also by the large and vague promise of Point 10: 'The peoples of Austria-Hungary, whose place among the nations we wish to see safeguarded and assured, should be accorded the first opportunity of autonomous development.'

The Adriatic problem threatened more than once to dissolve the accord between the Allies in Paris. England and France, while anxious to deal fairly both with Jugo-Slavia and with Italy, were strictly bound by the terms of the Treaty of London, and never betrayed the slightest wish to evade specific performance of their engagements. But, hampered though they were by Wilson's obstinacy and pedantry, they were most anxious to avoid a breach with the representative of the United States, the man to whom they owed so largely the Covenant of the League of Nations.

The Supreme Council gave close attention to the consideration of the Adriatic Question in April 1919, and some concessions to the Italian claims were wrung from President Wilson, but in the opinion of the Italians they were quite inadequate, and on the question of Fiume Wilson and Orlando were irreconcilable. 'Fiume', wrote Colonel House (15 April), 'was the main difficulty. If we could get over that hurdle the rest would be settled in a canter.' But they could not. On 20 April Wilson withdrew from the discussion, and three days later took the very strong step of publishing a Memorandum on the Adriatic question. He contended that since the date of the Treaty of London, for which he had no responsibility, 'the whole face of circumstances had been altered. But not even in that Treaty was Fiume assigned to Italy, for the very good reason that "it must serve as the outlet of the commerce not of Italy but of the lands north and north-east of that port". The partition of the Adriatic was intended to make Italy secure against Austria-Hungary. Austria-Hungary no longer exists.'

There was force in the contention, though the publication of the Memorandum was highly indiscreet, and was bitterly resented in Italy.

On the day following publication (24 April) Orlando,

having issued a vigorous reply to Mr. Wilson, left Paris abruptly for Rome, where he received an enthusiastic welcome. His attitude at Paris was endorsed in the Chamber by 382 votes to 40. France cordially supported the claims of Italy, and an open rupture was averted only by the tact of Mr. Lloyd George. Early in May, Orlando returned to Paris in order to join the Allies in presenting the Peace Treaty with Germany to the German delegation. Discussions on the Adriatic question were resumed, but no agreement could be reached, and on 19 June Orlando, having returned to Rome still empty-handed, was defeated in the Chamber and resigned. He was succeeded by Signor Nitti, an expert in finance but a weak administrator, who equally failed to secure a settlement of the Adriatic problem, and after a year of office in turn gave way to Giolitti (June 1920). But the Adriatic problem continued to baffle each successive ministry.

On 9 December 1919 England, France, and the United States had agreed on a Memorandum to be presented to Italy,[1] but the Italians refused to accept the proposals, and claimed the fulfilment of the Treaty of London. England and France were then, as always, ready to honour their bond, and on 14 January 1920 actually went beyond it, and offered to allow Fiume to remain under Italian sovereignty.

d'Annunzio

Meanwhile, another grave complication had entered into the problem. Early in September d'Annunzio—one of the most romantic figures in Italian life, a great poet and an ardent patriot—had with a body of enthusiastic volunteers occupied Fiume, and defied alike the Italian Government and the Jugo-Slavs to turn him out. The Italian Government was on the horns of a dilemma: they were threatened with revolution if they attempted to expel d'Annunzio: they were threatened by the wrath of the Powers if they did not. Nor was the position much easier for the Jugo-Slav Government. Their claim to Fiume, whether based

[1] Cf. Correspondence relating to the Adriatic Question (Cmd. 586 of 1920).

on geography, ethnography, or economics, was irresistible. The Treaty of London[1] had reserved for Serbia, Croatia, and Montenegro, the Adriatic coast from the bay of Volosca to the northern frontier of Dalmatia, including Fiume and the whole coast then belonging to Hungary and Croatia, together with the ports of Spalato, Ragusa, Cattaro, Antivari, Dulcigno, and San Giovanni di Medua, and several of the islands. But Fiume was the key of the position. Among the Southern Slavs there was increasing indignation at the delay in effecting a settlement.

San Remo Conference

So matters stood when, towards the end of April 1920, the English, French, and Italian Premiers met at San Remo. M. Trumbitch, the Foreign Minister of Jugo-Slavia, was invited to the San Remo Conference, but was unable, owing to a political crisis at home, to reach it in time, and proposed that the matters in dispute should be settled by direct negotiation between Italy and Jugo-Slavia. Signor Nitti assented to the suggestion, and Mr. Lloyd George and M. Millerand cordially concurred. Accordingly, about a month later, M. Pashitch and M. Trumbitch met Signor Scialoja at Pollenza. Italy was in a complaisant mood. Signor Nitti, indeed, was hardly less anxious for a final settlement of the Adriatic problem than were the Jugo-Slavs themselves; and negotiations, therefore, proceeded favourably. Unfortunately, before they could be concluded they were broken off by a political crisis in Rome, and although Signor Nitti weathered the storm for the moment, his Ministry foundered on the nationalistic rocks, and Signor Giolitti, as we have seen, took office, with Count Sforza as Foreign Secretary.

Treaty of Rapallo

No government, however, could ignore a situation which daily became at once more menacing and more grotesque. Early in November negotiations were resumed at Rapallo, and there, on 12 November 1920, a treaty was signed. Fiume was recognized by both parties as independent,

[1] For text of Treaty of London cf. White Paper Miscellaneous, No. 7 (1920) and *History of the Peace Conference*, vol. v, appendix iii, where all the important documents relating to Fiume are printed in full.

under the guardianship of the League of Nations, with the addition of a narrow strip of coast territory north-westwards, towards Volosca, thus giving Italy direct access to the independent State; but Sushak with Porto Baros was to remain in the hands of Jugo-Slavia. Zara and its adjacent communes were assigned to Italy, together with the islands of Cherso, Lussin, Lagosta, and Pelagosa, with the adjacent islets and rocks. Dalmatia, on the other hand, was given to Jugo-Slavia, with Lissa and the rest of the islands. D'Annunzio and his Legionaries were ejected, and replaced by Italian regular troops (January 1921), who in their turn began to give trouble, but were at last induced to evacuate Porto Baros and the Delta which they had occupied. Tedious negotiations as to the delineation of frontiers ensued, but the frontier line between the two States in the north-east was ultimately drawn in a sense favourable to Italy, while it left some 500,000 Slavs under the Italian flag. On the whole, a reasonable compromise seemed to have been reached. But the troublesome business of Fiume was not, even now, quite finished. Not until after the accession of Signor Mussolini to power (October 1922) was the matter finally settled. Italy and Jugo-Slavia were by this time in a less unfriendly mood. The independent State of Fiume was partitioned. Porto Baros and the adjacent Delta were assigned to Jugo-Slavia, which also obtained a fifty years' lease of a basin in the main harbour of Fiume. The rest of Fiume, with the coastal corridor somewhat narrowed, passed to Italy. This sensible arrangement was embodied in an Agreement signed in Rome (January 1924), and a *Pact of Cordial Collaboration* (July 1924) further strengthened the accord at long last arrived at between the two Adriatic Powers.

Summary

From the prolonged negotiations thus summarized Italy emerged far from satisfied. Yet the definition of her northern and eastern frontiers, and the settlement ultimately reached on the Adriatic question, fell little, if at all, short of her largest claims, indeed her wildest ambitions. The territorial settlement left her, apart from the complicated position in Fiume, in a very strong position.

The Brenner Pass constitutes her north-eastern frontier; she retains, accordingly, the southern Tyrol, including Bozen and Trent. Gorizia, Trieste, Istria all fell to her, with the islands of Zara and the adjacent communes, together with the islands of Cherso, Lussin, Lagosta, and Pelagosa, and the adjacent islands. Yet she was not content. The proceedings at the Peace Conference in Paris had outraged Italian sensibilities. The Italians felt that the sacrifices she had made in the common cause were imperfectly appreciated by her Allies, and were in consequence inadequately rewarded. She was annoyed to find (as a gifted Italian writer put it) that 'her Allies grudged her a very considerable part of the extremely limited ex-Austrian territories claimed by her, now advancing ethnographic reasons, now the necessity that Adriatic ports be given to other States for whom they would be useful.'[1] Another grievance was that a large portion of Asia Minor, including Smyrna, definitely promised to Italy under the agreement concluded (17 April 1917) at St. Jean de Maurienne was, as the same writer says, 'assigned to Greece who had only intervened at the end of the war, unwillingly coerced into it by France and Great Britain'. The text of the St. Jean de Maurienne agreement has since been published, but the course of events deprived it, as a matter of fact, of any practical importance; yet Italy could point to Article IX of the Treaty of London (of 1915) where, 'Generally speaking, France, Great Britain, and Russia recognize that Italy is interested in the maintenance of the balance of power in the Mediterranean, and that in the event of a total or partial partition of Turkey-in-Asia she [Italy] ought to obtain a just share of the Mediterranean region adjacent to the province of Adalia'. This phrase was understood by Italy to indicate a zone of some 70,000 square miles. That the agreement was ultimately invalidated by the course of events was no fault of the Allies;

[1] Villari, *Italy*, p. 312.

but that Smyrna should have been assigned to Greece was a source of legitimate complaint on the part of Italy. She would be more than human if she had not found some consolation in the failure of Greece to retain it.

The German Colonies

Italy's most serious grievance was, however, the failure (as alleged by Italy) of her Allies to implement the 13th Article of the Treaty of London, whereby she had been led to expect a share in the confiscated colonies of Germany in Africa. The Article ran as follows:

'In the event of France and Great Britain increasing their colonial territories in Africa at the expense of Germany, these two Powers agree in principle, that Italy may claim some equitable compensation, particularly as regards the settlement in her favour of the questions relative to the frontiers of the Italian colonies of Eritrea, Somaliland, and Libya and the neighbouring colonies belonging to France and Great Britain.'

To ask whether the Allies could have effectively urged the plea that Italy was 'equitably compensated' elsewhere is not perhaps to the point. But it is pertinent to ask why, as a fact, the Italian representatives at the Peace Conference allowed attention to be concentrated on the Adriatic problem, to the entire neglect of the extra-European claims of Italy. Be the answer what it may, Signor Villari undoubtedly expresses the prevalent view in contemporary Italy that it was unjust that 'a rapidly expanding nation of 35,000,000 to 40,000,000 inhabitants should remain for ever restricted within the narrow limits of Italy, whereas other less prolific races had unlimited spaces in which to expand'.[1] Nor is the grievance purely material. The memory of the colonial disasters in the last years of the nineteenth century still rankles: Italy would gladly erase them from the national consciousness of her people; and Signor Villari hints, not obscurely, that she will take the first opportunity of doing so by asserting for herself a substantial place in the tropical sun.

[1] Ibid.

ITALY
1931
TRENTINO
LOMBARDY
Milan
VENETIA
Trieste
Fiume
Turin
Venice
PIEDMONT
Pola
Parma
Modena
EMILIA
Bologna
Genoa
San Marino (Ind.)
LIGURIA
Florence
Leghorn
MARCHES
TUSCANY
UMBRIA
Elba
ROME
ABRUZZI
MOLISE
Rome
APULIA
CAMPANIA
Naples
BASILICATA
Brindisi
SARDINIA
Cosenza
CALABRIA
Messina
Palermo
Reggio
SICILY
Catania

XIV

POST-WAR ITALY

Fascismo

THE history of Italy since the war can be summed up in one word—*Fascismo*. The official birthday of the Fascist movement was 23 March 1919. On that day Signor Benito Mussolini, ex-soldier, ex-socialist, and at that time editor of *Il Popolo d'Italia*, founded at Milan the *Fasci di combattimento*, which may be provisionally described as the Italian British Legion. It was, or soon became, much more than that. It was founded at the moment when, as we have seen, the Italian question was approaching a crisis in the Peace Conference at Paris; but the genesis of the movement is to be sought in the general conditions which prevailed in Italy before, during, and after the war.

The Genesis of Fascism

From the day when Italy entered Rome, down to the day on which she declared war on Austria-Hungary, the country, for reasons already analysed, was in a state of almost continuous unrest. In that unrest, due on the one hand to discontent with social and economic conditions, due, on the other, to disillusionment at the political results of unification, to disgust at parliamentary ineptitude and corruption, and, most of all perhaps, to humiliation evoked by the sorry figure cut by Italy in oversea adventure and international politics, Fascism was born.

The War

All the causes which gave birth to Fascism were accentuated by the war and the peace. The strain imposed by the war upon a country relatively poor and almost wholly unprepared was, as we have seen, terrific. The tales of suffering and sacrifice endured by the men at the front; the restrictions and privations imposed—widely though not impartially—upon the civil population; the humiliation of Caporetto and the immense effort needed to wipe out the stain of that shameful defeat—all these things tended to undermine a political and social structure none too substantially built.

The Peace

After the conclusion of peace all the belligerent countries and some of the neutrals were plunged into turmoil. Italy did not escape the common fate. But in Italy, as we have seen, other causes of much longer standing co-operated with conditions directly attributable to the war to produce a crisis which threatened the very existence of the State. The hostility of large sections of the city populations was directed, with paradoxical impartiality, against the 'profiteers' who had made money out of the war, and the soldiers who had endured all its hardships. 'Defeatist' assaults on men in uniform, especially if they wore war decorations, were of common occurrence. 'The national colours', writes Mr. Trevelyan, 'could not safely be shown: an anti-patriotic "terror" was established'.[1]

> 'After the war', wrote Signor Mussolini, 'Bolshevism was sowing its seeds here, strikes were becoming numerous, our money was worth little, and while the stated causes of agitation were always economic, in truth they were political, and the aim was to undermine the State's authority, with the idea of establishing Soviets.'[2]

Italy called aloud for a Saviour of Society. Signor Mussolini responded to the call.

Mussolini

Benito Mussolini was born on 29 July 1883 at Dovia in the province of Forlì. His father was a blacksmith, strongly imbued with hatred of all forms of religion, and devoted to the cause of international revolution. His mother was a school-teacher of deep religious convictions, and to his mother Mussolini, like all men who have attained eminence, owes everything; and to her memory he is devoted. The boy was educated for the scholastic profession and qualified as a teacher, but soon abandoned teaching and went off to Switzerland, where he studied at the universities of Lausanne and Geneva, maintaining himself the while by manual labour of various kinds. He

[1] Sidney Ball Lecture, p. 15.
[2] Interview in *Evening Standard*, 11 December 1930.

was not a tranquil sojourner in Switzerland. He got into close touch with the Labour movement in that country and encouraged its extreme socialistic tendencies. As a result he was expelled from one Canton after another, and ultimately from the Swiss Confederation. Having returned to Italy he served his period of military service and then took up again his teaching career. But he quickly found himself in trouble with the police, was sentenced to a short term of imprisonment for his part in certain Labour troubles in the Romagna, and went off to the Tyrol. He became (1908) Secretary of the local Chamber of Labour at Trento, and did a good deal of journalistic work for various Socialist papers. He soon made the Austrian Tyrol, like Switzerland, too hot for him, and after his expulsion from the Tyrol returned to Italy, where he published a brochure, *The Trentino as seen by a Socialist.* He had already imbibed Irredentist sentiments, but had by no means shed his Socialism. Yet he was evidently drawing away from the materialistic philosophy of Marx and Lassalle, and was strongly attracted by the syndicalist philosophy as preached by Georges Sorel and others. Thus did he come to contemn Parliamentary Government, and to favour the idea of direct action.

In 1911 Mussolini found himself in opposition to the Imperialists who were responsible for the Tripoli Expedition and did his best to impede recruitment for the army. In June 1914 he again came into prominence during the Communist disturbances in the Romagna, but was sorely disillusioned by the conduct of some of his comrades in that unhappy enterprise.

The World-War

When the War broke out Mussolini was strongly opposed to intervention on behalf of the Central Powers, but whether from aversion to war in general or detestation of the Central Powers was not as yet apparent. Anyhow, he was asked to resign the editorship of *Avanti*, the official organ of the Italian Socialists, and thereupon founded his own paper, *Il Popolo d'Italia.* In November 1914 he was formally expelled from the Socialist Party, but warned his late comrades that though they might ostracize him and try to silence him to-day, he was determined to make himself heard, and with prophetic assurance he added: 'In a few years the masses of Italy will follow and applaud me when you will no longer be heard and cease to have a following.'

When, in May 1915, Italy declared war on Austria Mussolini enthusiastically espoused the cause of patriotism and took service as a private in the Bersaglieri. 'From to-day onwards', he declared, 'we are all of us Italians and only Italians.' During the campaigns of 1915–17 he fought with desperate courage and was promoted to non-commissioned rank, but in February 1917 was very badly wounded and compelled to abandon further participation in the war. He resumed the editorship of *Il Popolo d'Italia*, and consistently preached the vigorous prosecution of the war to a triumphant conclusion.

The war was to Mussolini a veritable 'Mount of Transfiguration'. With prophetic vision, quickened by many hardships endured for Italy, he saw arising on the ruins of war a new Italy purified as by fire, and purged of the corruption which, ever since 1870, had tainted the political life of his country, and clogged the wheels of administrative and economic progress. He also saw Italy restored to the territorial limits assigned to her, as Italians think, by history and by nature, and taking her rightful place in the councils of Europe.

The Fascist Gospel

It was to youth he made his primary appeal; but, as a fact, he has enlisted under his banner not only the young in years but men of all ages who have youth in their hearts. His creed is as stern as that of the apostle Paul: 'Endure hardness.' His followers were bidden not to look for *panem et circenses*—the dole and the cinema. He preached the gospel of work, discipline, sacrifice. His was the idealism of Mazzini, combined with the practical statesmanship of Cavour and the heroic temper of Garibaldi.

The Need of Italy

It was for such a man that post-war Italy cried. Of all the allied countries Italy, perhaps, stood in greatest peril of revolution during the difficult post-war years. There was, as we have seen, a pervasive spirit of disillusionment, and on that spirit Bolshevism fatally wrought. It was primarily to combat Bolshevist propaganda that in March 1919 Mussolini organized the *Fasci di combattimento* at Milan. The *Fascio* had already become a designation for all those who in the War were united in the cause of Italy, and opposed first to the neutralists and then to the defeatists. The oath which Mussolini prescribed to his followers was as follows: 'In the Name of God and Italy, in the Name of those who have died for the greater glory of Italy, I swear that I will consecrate myself, entirely and for ever, to live for the good of Italy.' His first disciples were, for the most part, personal friends, ex-combatants like himself, and mostly ex-Socialists, who were disgusted, on the one hand, by the miserable treatment meted out to ex-soldiers by the Government, on the other by the derision and contempt which was poured on them by many of the urban artisans, and most of all, perhaps, by what they regarded as the ineffectual defence of Italian interests made by their representatives at the Peace Conference in Paris. The Fascisti were naturally attracted to the banner of d'Annunzio, who was at that time in occupation of Fiume, and showed themselves opposed to a government which could neither protect Italian interests abroad, nor combat the forces of Bolshevism at home.

Anti-Fascist Forces

Fascism, however, was regarded with considerable suspicion by all the established parties in Italy: by the Conservatives, who mistrusted Mussolini as a revolutionary Socialist; by the Liberals, who still clung to the idea of a Parliamentary régime; and by the Socialists, who saw in Mussolini only the Imperialist and the enemy of Bolshevism. Consequently, the progress made by the new movement was, at first, disappointingly slow. At the General Election of 1919 the Fascists ran a number of candidates, but not one of them was returned, Mussolini himself being heavily defeated at Milan. *L'Avanti* contemptuously described him at that time as 'a corpse waiting for burial in a ditch'. Shortly after the election, Signor Nitti arrested Mussolini on the charge, arising out of his connexion with d'Annunzio, of an armed conspiracy against the security of the State. But he was speedily released. It may occasion surprise that when Labour troubles broke out at Milan in the spring of 1920, and the factories were actually seized by the operatives, the movement was not opposed by the Fascists. The explanation is that they regarded the movement as a syndicalistic experiment; but the experiment was soon seen to be a ludicrous fiasco, and in the Municipal Elections of the autumn of that year the Fascists combined with the other anti-Socialist Parties to defeat the Communists.

The *Squadre*

In November 1920 Mussolini initiated an important step in organization. In order more effectively to fight Bolshevism the Fascists were organized in *Squadre*. They were mostly armed only with cudgels, though some of the ex-combatants had their revolvers, and a few had carbines, but one of their most effectual weapons was castor-oil. During the next two years, while Bolshevism was at the height of its influence in Italy (1920–2), there were perpetual conflicts between the Fascists and the Bolshevists; no fewer than two thousand Fascists were killed, many of them in treacherous ways, and not a few after being subjected to brutal torture. That there should have been bitter reprisals on the part of the Fascists can hardly excite surprise. The life was a life of hardship and danger, yet the ranks of the Fascists were rapidly recruited, not only from among the upper and middle classes, who were frightened by the spectre of Bolshevism, but by large numbers of working-men, some of whose unions joined the Fascist movement *en bloc*.

Parliamentary Fascism

The growth of the movement was clearly demonstrated at the General Election of 1921 when Mussolini himself and thirty-seven other Fascists were returned, and in conjunction with the Nationalist Party began to play a prominent part in Parliament. In November of the same year Fascism was organized definitely as a political party

(*Partito Nazionale Fascista*), with the avowed object of making a clean sweep of the older political parties and of the incompetent and corrupt rings which had hitherto monopolized political office.

Fascist Programme

It was about this time that the Fascist programme was definitely formulated. It repudiated the Liberal, Socialist, and Democratic theories of the State, but proclaimed that while the functions of the State must be strictly limited, its prestige as representing the nation must be at all costs restored; the individual was to exist for society, not society for the individual, though individualism was by no means to be crushed but encouraged. Parliament was to survive, but only as the organ for dealing with questions concerning the individual in his political capacity; all economic and industrial questions were to be remitted to the control of technical or vocational councils; production was to be in every way stimulated but was to be left, like distribution, to individual enterprise. The Trade Unions were to be protected so far as they were a help to production, but not to be permitted to impose restrictions on production or labour. Organizations, both of workmen and employers, were, on similar terms, to be legally recognized and invested with responsibility. No strikes were to be permitted in public services, and all class conflicts were to be submitted to the arbitrament of the State. Private property was to be recognized, and the State was to hand back to private enterprise all such undertakings as it had proved itself incapable of managing successfully. The finances were to be restored, and the duty of economy to be emphasized. The press was, temporarily at any rate, to be placed under strict censorship, and opposition was not to be allowed any opportunity of manifesting itself. The Army and Navy were to be maintained in a state of the highest efficiency: 'Always', said Mussolini, 'it is the musket that wins; I want to make of you a nation of warriors.' Education, though always on the Aristotelian principle of conformity to the ideal of the State, was to be promoted; and an increase in population was to be encouraged. Without a larger population Italy, thought Mussolini, could never assert her rightful place in the economy of Europe and the world. 'As regards foreign and colonial affairs, Italy must reaffirm her right to complete historic and geographic unity and fulfil her mission as the bulwark of Latin civilization in the Mediterranean.' Italy must claim her place also in the colonial field; her Dependencies must be peopled by Italians.

The General Strike

Fascism had to meet its first great crisis in the General Strike which was proclaimed on 1 August 1922. On its proclamation, the Fascist Directorate ordered a general mobilization, and issued a manifesto calling on the workers to shake off the yoke of the politicians by whom they were led, and giving the Government forty-eight hours in which to prove that it could control its own employees and those who were attempting to destroy the whole machinery of the State. On the expiry of that time Fascism would assume all the functions which the State proved itself incompetent to perform. In Milan, the Fascists volunteered to perform the work of the electricians, fire brigade, transport workers, and men employed in other essential services; in other towns, they took over the whole municipal administration. In twenty-four hours the strike was called off, and by 4 August order was completely restored.

The march on Rome

The Fascist organization had broken the General Strike; and when, in the month following, Mussolini publicly proclaimed himself a supporter of the monarchy, recruits from all classes and in great numbers enlisted under his banner. In October 1922 the Fascists held an important Congress at Naples. No fewer than 40,000 Fascists paraded through the streets and loudly proclaimed that unless the Government was conferred on them, they would seize it by marching on Rome. The Prime Minister, Facta, thereupon drafted a decree proclaiming martial law, but the King refused to sign it; Facta resigned (27 October), and Signor Salandra, who was entrusted with the formation of a new Cabinet, invited Mussolini to join it. Mussolini, however, dissatisfied with the proposed composition of the new Government, declined, and on 28 October the Fascists made their peaceful entry into Rome. Their movement, they declared, was not directed against the King, or the Army, or the Police, or the productive *bourgeoisie*, or the masses who worked in fields and offices, but only against the politicians, 'a class of weaklings and defectives, who for four years have proved themselves incapable of governing'. On the 29th the King, on Salandra's advice, sent for Mussolini. The latter, on leaving Milan for Rome, declared: 'To-morrow, Italy will have not a ministry but a Government.' From that day to this, a Government—if not a Ministry in the parliamentary sense—Italy unquestionably has had. On 30 October Mussolini reached Rome, and immediately submitted his Cabinet list to the King. The new Cabinet included men of all parties, except the anti-Nationalists, and the first act of the new Government was to order all the Fascist *Squadre* to leave Rome. In November Mussolini asked for and obtained from Parliament dictatorial powers to carry through a number of pressing reforms; in December the *Squadre* were disbanded.

The Dictatorship of Mussolini

Since that date Signor Mussolini has been continuously in power. The time has not yet come to pronounce a verdict on the interesting experiment which he initiated, and for nearly a decade has carried on with unremitting energy, with rare self-devotion, and, so far as contemporaries can measure results, with amazing success. History will some day place the experiment in true perspective. Yet some things are plain enough even to casual observers. Italy has been rescued from the very edge of the precipice at the foot of which lay a chaotic abyss. Liberals persistently assert that Italy was never in any real danger of a Bolshevik revolution; that the Italian people are naturally averse to violence; and that the wide diffusion of proprietary rights in the soil effectually guarantees their country against the fate of Russia. It may be so; but it is certain that in less than a decade the whole face of the country has been transformed to the evident advantage of the sojourner, and presumably of the permanent inhabitants. Order and discipline have been restored; squalor has been replaced by decency; cleanliness and a reasonable standard of sanitation prevail where previously there was filth and disease; means of transport, whether by road or rail, have been improved out of recognition; new buildings of imposing design adorn the cities; new domestic dwellings attest by their profusion the higher standard of comfort attained by the lower and middle classes; notwithstanding an immense development in the hydro-electric industry, the consumption of coal is said to have increased by 50 per cent.; there is no 'dole', yet unemployment, until the advent of the world-blizzard, did not exist; peace is enforced in industry, and agriculture has benefited by improved methods and the development of the means of transit. But have not all these advantages been attained at the price of that which is more precious than rubies, the enjoyment of liberty, personal and political? The answer to that question depends on the definition of 'liberty'. 'Liberty', said Mussolini, echoing Mazzini, 'is not a right but a duty.' Parliamentary democracy—and all that the phrase implies to an Englishman—has unquestionably been superseded by a dictatorship: the press is muzzled; Parliament has been reduced to the position of a debating society, without the power to legislate, and has no control whatever over the Executive; the new electoral methods seem (at any rate to an Englishman, so far as he can comprehend them) a mere travesty of representative government. Despite many elaborate devices, all real power is concentrated in the Fascist Grand Council and its President.

Fascism and Imperialism

All this may be admitted, without establishing any conclusive indictment against the Fascist régime. Fascism derives from a curious blend of Imperialism, Nationalism, and Syndicalism. 'You call us Imperialists,' said Signor Mussolini some years ago, 'well and good: Imperialism is the eternal and immutable law of life. It is but the natural need, desire and will for expansion which every individual and virile people have within them. Italy has need of expansion, and expand she will, despite the selfish embargo placed on her ambitions by the older colonizing Powers at the Peace Conference! Nationalism is the core of the Fascist creed. The nation is above all its nationals, it comprehends all classes, and while respecting (in its own interest no less than in others) the rights both of capital and labour, of employers and employed, it requires them to walk in step for the common good.'

Fascism and Syndicalism

On the other hand, the Fascist creed approximates to the root idea of Syndicalism, in that it subordinates politics to industry. Modern industry, the Fascist insists, has outgrown the machinery of parliamentary democracy. Certain observations recently addressed by Mr. Winston Churchill to academic audiences seem to suggest that his mind is moving in the same direction as Signor Mussolini's. They are both, consciously or unconsciously, inspired by Syndicalist doctrine. The control of industrial policy, so Mussolini has repeatedly contended, cannot be entrusted to a miscellaneous crowd of politicians elected to a seat in Parliament by people as untrained in the technique of industry as themselves. The conduct of modern business, the economical employment of great masses of manual labourers, the buying of raw materials, the marketing of finished goods, the improvement of machinery—all these matters call for highly trained experts whose labours must not be liable to frustration by well-meaning but inexperienced politicians. Vocation, not locality, must therefore be the basis of representation. Society must be organized by industries. Such, it would seem, is the creed of Signor Mussolini and of the quasi-military organization —still military despite the dispersal of the *Squadre*—which he has inspired with his own idealistic faith.

Many questions will occur to the philosophic historian whose business it may be to chronicle the events of this post-war period in Italy. But the time, even for formulating them, much less for answering them, is not yet. *Finis coronat opus.* We must await results. Meanwhile, Englishmen who are disposed to pronounce hasty judgement will do well to recall the history of their own political evolution.

The Tudor Dictatorship

When the Tudors ascended the English throne they were confronted by a state of things comparable to that which existed in Italy at the close of the World War. The nation had not recovered from the effects of the long conflict with France, of the sporadic contests at home between baron and baron, this shire and that, the adherents of the White Rose and the Red. Socially, the country was distraught; politically, it had outgrown its strength; economically, it was anaemic. So backward were we in matters of commerce and shipping that we could take no advantage of the great discoveries which at the close of the fifteenth century opened to Portugal and Spain the path of Empire. The Tudor sovereigns established a virtual dictatorship. Constitutional forms were, indeed, scrupulously observed; parliaments met with increasing regularity; growing towns were enfranchised; local government was reorganized; shipping and commerce were, in every way, encouraged; a regular navy was created; schools for the scientific study of seamanship were set up; above all, order and discipline, so grievously lacking under Lancastrians and Yorkists, were restored; the 'overmighty subject' of the fifteenth century found a master in the Crown; the more ambitious nobles—especially if they had any royal blood in their veins—lost their heads.

Elizabethan England, with its exuberance of national spirit manifested in fifty directions, testified to the value of Tudor discipline. The success of the Puritan Revolution proved that a dictatorship may well be a prelude, perhaps an indispensable prelude, to a period of constitutional advance. The Tudors prepared the way for Pym and ultimately for Walpole. Parliamentary democracy—the curious device of a responsible Cabinet under the aegis of a 'constitutional' king—was the ultimate product of the dictatorial rule of the Tudor sovereigns.

It is not suggested that Fascist Italy affords a precise parallel with Tudor England. Such parallels are pitfalls for the unwary commentator. But Englishmen who can read aright the lessons of their own past, will certainly be less ready to pass judgement on the present phase in Italy.

There remains to be noticed one outstanding achievement which would by itself entitle Signor Mussolini to a pre-eminent position in Italian history. But the Lateran Treaty deserves a separate chapter, with which this brief history of the Italian *Risorgimento* may fitly conclude.

XV

CHURCH AND STATE

The Lateran Treaty

Cavour and the Church

LIBERA chiesa in libero stato. If those were not the last words uttered by Cavour, they undoubtedly represented his ideal of the relations which should subsist between Church and State in Italy. In this, as in many other respects, Cavour was true to the tradition of nineteenth-century Liberalism. That tradition is now virtually extinct in Italy, as elsewhere. But Cavour's words not only gave expression to his own fervent aspiration, they testified also to his painful consciousness that he had left the very difficult problem unsolved. Moreover, that problem, as he must have realized, was in large measure the product of his own life-achievement. A contemporary writer stated the matter very clearly:

'There can be no question that the existence of an effective Italian power must involve a material modification in the condition of the Court of Rome. A King of Italy and a Sovereign Pontiff, both ruling or laying claim to rule over any considerable portion of Italian territory, are a contradiction pregnant with irreconcilable opposition. . . . The King of Italy can never become the supreme head of a national government so long as the Pope continues to claim temporal and sovereign dominion in the Peninsula; for the authority of the Crown would be exposed to perpetual antagonism within the pale of its own civil jurisdiction. On the other hand, it is also certain that to obtain from the Court of Rome the necessary concessions for obviating such collisions with the royal authority involves what may well appear the hopeless task of modifying the most tenacious and unrelaxing of human constitutions.'[1]

Victor Emmanuel and Pope Pius IX

A hopeless task it proved to be. The annexation of the Legations, the Marches and Umbria, to the kingdom of Italy, was not accomplished, as we have seen, without

[1] *Edinburgh Review* (July 1861).

fulminations from the Vatican, and these culminated in the ban of excommunication pronounced against Victor Emmanuel. The King was not greatly inconvenienced by the Papal anathemas, but as a loyal and even devoted son of the Church he was deeply hurt. Again and again he addressed himself to the Pope, begging him to recognize the national movement, and to accept the position which the new kingdom of Italy was anxious to assign to him. Affirming his sincere attachment towards the Church and its august Head, he pointed out that it was not his intention to curtail the rights and authority which the Holy See exercises on earth by Divine commission from Heaven, but that he also had duties to fulfil towards the people whom Divine Providence had confided to his government.

'As an Italian Prince', he wrote, 'I wished to liberate Italy, and I thought it my duty to welcome to participation in the National War all the peoples of the Peninsula. . . . The universal vote for annexation[1] to the Constitutional Monarchy of Piedmont was reconfirmed with such solemnity that I had to accept it definitely for the sake of the peace and welfare of Italy. . . . To the same end I am anxious to pay homage to the high sovereignty of the Apostolic See, nor do I feel that as a Catholic Prince I offend against the immutable principles of that religion which, with filial and unalterable devotion, I glory to profess.'

As to the sincerity of the King there can be no question, and there can be as little about the consistency with which the Pope repelled all these advances.

Friction between Pope and King, created by the events of 1860, was naturally intensified by the annexation of the Two Sicilies to the kingdom of Italy; it culminated when, in September 1870, 'Italy entered Rome'. Victor Emmanuel renewed, with increased emphasis, his appeals to the Pope. All to no purpose. From 20 September 1870 down to 11 February 1929 (the day which witnessed the signature of the Lateran Treaty) there was a complete estrangement between the Vatican and the kingdom of Italy.

The problem presented by the position of the Papacy was

[1] See *supra*, c. viii.

threefold. The first raised the oecumenical position of the Papacy as head of the Roman Catholic Church throughout the world. The second concerned the relations between the Pope as temporal sovereign over a portion of Italian territory and the King of united Italy. That problem was evidently peculiar to Italy. The third concerned the relations between the State and the Church in Italy. This differed from the problem common to all Christian States only in so far as it was complicated in the case of Italy by the two problems aforesaid.

The Temporal Power

As regards the first. Is an independent territorial sovereignty essential to the faithful discharge of the Pope's functions as head of the Universal Church? That question, though implicitly answered by the Lateran Treaty, is of less immediate concern to the historian of the Italian *Risorgimento* than the others. For the moment we may accept the answer of so learned and liberal a Catholic as Dr. Döllinger:

'The Church', wrote Döllinger, 'by her nature can very well exist and did exist for seven centuries without the territorial possessions of the Popes; afterwards their possession became necessary, and in spite of great changes and vicissitudes, has discharged in most cases its function of serving as a foundation for the independence and freedom of the Popes. As long as the present state and arrangement of Europe endures, we can discover no other means to secure to the Holy See its freedom and with it the confidence of all. But the knowledge and power of God reach farther than ours. . . . Let no one lose faith in the Church if the secular principality of the Pope should disappear for a season, or for ever. It is not essence, but accident; not end, but means; it began late; it was formerly something quite different from what it is now. It justly appears to us indispensable, and as long as the existing order lasts in Europe it must be maintained at any price, or if it is violently interrupted it must be restored. But a political settlement of Europe is conceivable in which it would be superfluous, and then it would be an oppressive burden.'[1]

[1] Dr. Döllinger, *Kirche und Kirchen*, 1861; *ap*. Acton, *History of Freedom*, pp. 303 seq.

Dr. Döllinger, then, writing in 1861, was clearly of opinion that while the Temporal Power, under existing conditions, was essential to the Papacy as an institution, the fact that it could be maintained only under the protection of the Emperor of the French rendered a temporary surrender of that power advisable. In that judgement Lord Acton, the most erudite of Catholic historians, concurred. Nor is it for a Protestant historian to dissent from it.

Of much more immediate concern to Italy were the two other problems enumerated above.

Church and State

The relations between Church and State had been more or less strained ever since the time when the King of Sardinia began to stand forth as the champion, not merely of Italian independence but of Italian unity. Reference has already been made to the Siccardian legislation, by which clerical pretensions were curtailed in Piedmont.[1] With the unification of Italy the laws of Piedmont became the laws of the united State, and the problem, raised on a relatively small scale at Turin, was transferred to the ampler stage at Rome. One of the first acts of the Parliament of United Italy, sitting in Rome, was to pass the Law of Guarantees (May 1871).[2] This Law was based on a draft found among Cavour's papers after his death; yet it is doubtful whether, if Cavour's life had been prolonged for another ten years, he would have made such ample concession to the Papacy without a substantial *quid pro quo*. Nothing of the kind could, however, be obtained by any of his successors. This famous Law guaranteed to the Pope all the diplomatic privileges of a territorial sovereign; the exclusive use of the Vatican and Lateran palaces and some other buildings in Rome; his own independent Court; and the right to send and to receive diplomatic representatives from other sovereign States. No Government official was to intrude on Papal territory without the leave of the Pope; the Pope was to have his own Guards, his own

Law of Guarantees (1871)

[1] *Supra*, c. vi.

[2] For the almost simultaneous declaration of Papal Infallibility see Marriott, *History of Europe, 1815–1923* (Methuen, 1931), pp. 4, 267.

separate postal and telegraphic communications with foreign countries, and was to receive a dotation of £125,000 a year, though on each Papal vacancy the unclaimed arrears were to revert to the State. As regards spiritual matters, the Law of Guarantees provided that the Pope should have full freedom in the exercise of his spiritual functions, and that there should be no interference on the part of the State with ecclesiastical conclaves or other assemblies, or with freedom of communication between the Pope and Ecclesiastical Authorities in Italy and in other countries.

Patronage

In the matter of patronage, the Law of Guarantees surrendered the right of the State to appoint to bishoprics and other benefices, though it retained the rights which the Crown had inherited in Piedmont, Sardinia, Sicily, and other parts of divided Italy. Further, the Law relinquished the Royal *exsequatur* and *placet*—the necessity of obtaining the Royal assent to the publication and execution of ecclesiastical Acts and Bulls. This renunciation did not extend to the temporalities of the Church, and as a fact the nominees to bishoprics and other benefices were still required to obtain the Royal *exsequatur* and *placet* before they could get possession of the temporalities. The State thus did, in fact, retain a veto over ecclesiastical appointments, though this was due not to the terms of the Law of Guarantees, but to the refusal of the Papacy to acknowledge or accept that legislation.

Spiritual Jurisdiction

As regards ecclesiastical courts, the Law provided that there should be no appeal to the State Courts against spiritual judgements; but such judgements could not claim the support of the secular arm to enforce them until the Civil Courts had declared them to be in conformity with the laws of the State and the rights of citizens.

The Papacy, as already hinted, persistently declined to acknowledge the validity of the Law of Guarantees, holding that a unilateral instrument of this kind was inconsistent with its own sovereign rights. On the face of it, the Law of Guarantees would appear to have offered a generous settlement of the points at issue. It was, in fact, opposed by Crispi and the politicians of the left, as being far too favourable to the Church, and it is very doubtful whether Cavour himself would have made such ample concessions, except in return for the Papal recognition of the kingdom of Italy and the abandonment of its position as a hostile political Power, planted on Roman soil under foreign diplomatic protection. The refusal of the Pope to accept the Law of Guarantees must, indeed, be largely attributed to the influence of France and the ultramontane party in general. Croce defends the attitude of the Papacy:

'For the Papacy,' he writes, 'an international political institution, it was impolitic and even impossible to come to an agreement on these terms, for fear of increasing in the eyes of the world its already conspicuously Italian character; it behoved it rather to assume the role of one who has yielded to force, of the downtrodden victim, and to continue to protest at first angrily, and later less angrily but no less consistently, never abandoning the assertion of its violated rights.'

Such was, in fact, the attitude of the Papacy, and it was maintained with complete consistency. Not only did the Pope refuse to recognize the Italian kingdom, but by the decree *non expedit* he prohibited Catholics from accepting the elementary rights and performing the elementary duties of citizenship. They were neither to vote for Members of Parliament nor to accept parliamentary seats or political office. This inhibition was in fact very loosely observed. Not that the ordinary citizen in Italy is anti-Papal or anti-Catholic. Quite otherwise. Italy is whole-hearted in its acceptance of Roman Catholicism; all but a very small minority of the people conform regularly to the ordinances of the Roman Catholic Church and respect the Pope as its head. Nor can it be said that in the sixty years between the occupation of Rome and the conclusion of the Lateran Treaty, the State showed itself, on the whole, otherwise than respectful towards the Papacy, and sympathetic towards the religious sentiments of the people. Croce himself admits that the position was decidedly more favourable in fact than in theory. On the one hand, even the Liberals abstained from provocative measures which could hurt Catholic sentiment: for example, Crispi himself, when Home Secretary, guaranteed freedom and security to the Conclave which assembled on the death of Pope Pius IX, and the guarantee was scrupulously fulfilled; on the other, Catholics took a much more active part in politics than the *non expedit* prohibition implied. The ban on political activity was gradually relaxed, especially during the pontificate of Pius X (1903–14), and in 1913 the *non expedit* was altogether withdrawn.

Ecclesiastical Property

Tithes were abolished in 1887; charities were transferred to the State in 1890; and although all Church property was taken over by the State, nearly one million a year is paid out by the State to the Church Fund. On two other and very delicate matters a large measure of compromise was reached, even before the conclusion of the Lateran Treaty.

Marriage and Education

The civil code of Italy prescribed civil marriage, but there was nothing to prevent the performance of the religious ceremony as well where it was desired. Similarly in regard to education. The Local Authorities were not bound to provide religious instruction in the elementary schools, unless it was demanded by the parents; but, as a fact, religious instruction was generally given, and not infrequently by priests.

The World-War

The War might well have provoked a crisis in the relations between the Italian kingdom and the Papacy. It was averted by the exercise of tact on both sides. The position of the Papacy was admittedly difficult, and it was rendered more so by Prince von Bülow, who made it known in Rome that the Central Empires had decided to restore the States of the Church to the Pope at the close of the War. It was for that reason that, as we have seen, Italy inserted in the Pact of London a provision that the Papacy was to be excluded from any European Congress to arrange terms of peace. There was a good deal of defeatest agitation carried on by the Italian clericals during the War, but there is no evidence that the Papacy lent itself to this agitation, and it is the unquestionable fact that, throughout the War, successive governments in Italy maintained a respectful attitude towards the Holy See. It is also the fact that, though on the Pope's advice the diplomatic representatives of the enemy powers left the Vatican, a considerable number of German and Austrian priests remained.

Fascismo and the Papacy

The effect of the Fascist Revolution was far from detrimental to the Papacy. On the contrary, Signor Mussolini showed himself, from the first, anxious to bring about a settlement of the long-standing difficulties. His disposition was manifested in matters which, though they may seem relatively trifling, were not insignificant. Religious processions, for example, were freely permitted; a service of army chaplains was re-established; the Crucifix was replaced not only in all elementary schools but on the Capitol, in the Colosseum, in the Courts of Law, and in certain other public places; and religious instruction, hitherto voluntary, was made universal and compulsory. In 1926 the Duce himself initiated, though with great secrecy, negotiations for a comprehensive and final settlement. It may well be that negotiations were facilitated, as one critic has pointed out,[1] by certain psychological affinities between the Duce and Pope Pius XI, by the ambition of both men to leave behind them a record of concrete and positive achievement. Nor is it disputable that there is much more in common between Fascism and Catholicism than between either of those creeds and Liberalism. The basis of Government in both cases is not contractual but authoritarian; 'The Pontiff', said the Pope in addressing the parish priests of Rome on the day when the Lateran Treaty was signed, 'has no need either of assent, or of consent, or of guarantees.' As the Pope asserts the Divine Right of the head of the Catholic Church, so Signor Mussolini asserts the Divine Right of Fascism. 'Let no one presume to deny the moral character

[1] A. J. Toynbee, *Survey of International Affairs* (1929), p. 443. Oxford, 1930.

of the Fascist State; for I should not have the face to speak from this tribune were I not conscious of representing the moral and spiritual force of the State.' So spake the Duce in the Chamber on 13 May 1929. As Fascism and Catholicism have philosophical affinities, so they have common political antagonisms; they are united in opposition to Freemasonry—the lodges were dissolved by Mussolini in 1928, to Socialism, and to Liberalism.

No good Fascist and no good Catholic would, however, admit that such common affinities or common antagonisms were of more than secondary or incidental importance as contributing to the success of the treaty negotiations. Pope and Duce were inspired, they rightly insist, solely by regard for the permanent well-being of the people for whom they were, in their several ways, responsible. The prolonged dispute between State and Church was inflicting irreparable injury alike upon the cause of good government and upon that of religion. 'Let it be ended; let good men come together; let the allegiance of good Italians be no longer divided.'

The great settlement of 1929 gave effect to these aspirations. It consisted of three parts: a Political Treaty, a Financial Convention, and a Concordat. The first settled and eliminated the Roman question; the second regulated the financial relations between the Holy See and Italy; the third defined the conditions governing religion and the Church in Italy. These instruments were severally signed at the Lateran Palace by Cardinal Gasparri, Papal Secretary of State, and by Signor Mussolini, on 11 February 1929, and after the completion of the ceremony the following official communiqué was issued:

'The Holy See considers that with the Agreements signed to-day it possesses the guarantees necessary to provide due liberty and independence to the spiritual government of the dioceses of Rome and of the Catholic Church in Italy and the whole world. It declares the Roman question definitely and irrevocably settled, and therefore eliminated, and recognizes the Kingdom of Italy under the dynasty of the House of Savoy, with Rome as the capital of the Italian State. Italy, on its side, recognizes the State of the Vatican City under the sovereignty of the Supreme Pontiff.

'The Law of Guarantees and any other Law or Act contrary to the present Treaty is abrogated.'

These instruments were formally ratified at the Vatican on 7 June, and in the following December the King and Queen paid a ceremonial visit to Pope Pius XI, who in the same month visited St. John Lateran. He was thus the first Pontiff to set foot on Italian territory since the day (20 September 1870) when Italian troops occupied Rome.

The Political Treaty

The Political Treaty consists of twenty-seven articles. By the first article 'Italy recognizes and reaffirms the principle embodied in the *Statuto* of 4 March 1848, whereby the Catholic, Apostolic, Roman religion is the sole religion of the State'. By the second, 'Italy recognizes the sovereignty of the Holy See in the international field as an attribute inherent in its nature, in accordance with its traditions and the requirements of its mission to the world'. By the third, 'Italy recognizes the full ownership, exclusive dominion, and sovereign authority and jurisdiction of the Holy See over' a defined territory to be known as the Vatican City. This independent State includes only (in the Pope's own words) 'the minimum territory necessary for visible temporal Power'. Statistics are eloquent. Before the changes effected in 1860 the Papal States had consisted of twenty Provinces with a population of over 3,000,000 people. The 'Patrimony of St. Peter', which alone remained to the Papacy after 1860, contained five Provinces with some 680,000 people. By the terms of the Treaty of 1929 the Vatican City comprises about 108 acres and is inhabited by 528 people; but there are in addition thirteen buildings situated in different parts of Rome which enjoy extra-territorial privileges.

There follow a number of detailed agreements as to a separate railway station in the Vatican; through coaches on the State railways for Papal passengers; direct telegraphic, telephonic, wireless, broadcasting, and postal connexions with other States; water-supply, and so on. Cardinals were to have free access to Conclaves, and to enjoy immunity from custom duties levied at Italian ports. The Holy See was to have the right to accredit and receive diplomatic representatives, and was to enjoy all the usual diplomatic privileges and immunities; and specific provision was made for the appointment of an Italian ambassador to the Holy See and of a Papal Nuncio to the Court of Italy. The Vatican City was to be permanently neutralized.

Then, at last (under Article XXVI), came the turn of the State. That article was reproduced almost verbally in the proclamation already quoted.

Financial Convention

Under the Financial Convention the Holy See accepted 750,000 lire in cash and 1,000,000,000 lire in 5 per cent. Italian bonds, in liquidation of all claims of the Holy See on the Italian kingdom.

The Concordat

The Concordat, described in the preamble as the 'necessary complement' of the Treaty, is a much more lengthy document than the Treaty itself, consisting, as it does, of no fewer than forty-five articles. Signor Mussolini, not unnaturally, regarded the Treaty as the more important document of the two. The Pope, on the contrary, held that it was the Concordat which 'explained, justified and recommended the Treaty'; and was 'inseparably bound up with it'. It was designed (again in his own words) 'to regulate suitably the religious conditions in Italy which, for so long a season, had been rough-handled, subverted and devastated by Governments which were either sectarian or else bound to the chariot wheels of the enemies of the Church, even when they were possibly not her enemies themselves'. The Pope naturally congratulated himself and the Church that the Concordat was not, like the Law of Guarantees, a unilateral settlement, imposed by a sovereign on a subject, but an agreement between two independent Powers, negotiating on an equal footing.

The Concordat dealt in minute detail with every point of difficulty which had arisen between the Ecclesiastical and Secular authorities since the formation of the Italian kingdom, and provided a comprehensive and, it is hoped, a permanent settlement.

In the first place, Italy assured 'to the Catholic Church the free exercise of spiritual power, and the free and public exercise of its worship, as well as jurisdiction in ecclesiastical matters'. It further undertook, 'in consideration of the sacred character of the Eternal City, the Episcopal See of the Supreme Pontiff, centre of the Catholic world, and goal of pilgrimage . . . to keep Rome free from anything which should be inconsistent with such character, and to guarantee to the Holy See free and independent communication with the Bishops, clergy, and the whole Catholic world'. Clerics were to be exempt from military service, save in the case of general mobilization, and were then to wear the habit, 'in order that they may exercise their sacred office among the troops'. The secrets of the confessional were to be respected by the State, and clerics and members of religious orders were to be exempted from jury service. Criminous clerks, to use a phrase familiar in England from the days of Henry II, were to be subject to State tribunals, but their Ordinaries were to be kept informed of any sentence passed upon them, and in other ways special treatment was to be accorded to them. Similar respect was to be shown to ecclesiastical buildings. The State undertook to recognize all Sundays as Festivals and nine other specially sacred days; but on such days prayers were to be said 'for the prosperity of the King of Italy and the Italian State'. Dioceses were to be rearranged so as to correspond as far as possible with provinces. On the vexed question of patronage it was agreed that appointments to bishoprics and other benefices should lie with the ecclesiastical authorities, who, however, were confidentially to communicate to the Italian Government the name of the proposed nominee so as to make sure that there was no political objection to the nomination. Nominees were to be Italian-speaking Italian citizens; but (in view, doubtless, of the spiritual needs of the recently annexed provinces in 'unredeemed' Italy) Italian coadjutors who could speak the 'tongue locally used' were, when necessary, to be appointed to work under them. The *Exsequatur*, the Royal *Placet*, and the 'Sovereign prerogative of Royal Patronage' were finally renounced by the State. An accommodation was also reached on the two most delicate and most difficult of all questions at issue—religious instruction and marriage. As to the latter, the State 'being desirous of restoring to the institution of marriage, which is the basis of the family, that dignity which is in keeping with the Catholic traditions of the Italian people' recognized 'the sacrament of marriage as legal for civil purposes when administered according to Canon Law'. Cases of judicial separation were to be tried by the Civil Courts, but the Ecclesiastical Courts were to have exclusive jurisdiction in matters of divorce, though the decisions were to be reported to the Supreme Tribunal of the *Segnatura*, and by it transmitted to the Court of Appeal, which was, on being satisfied as to procedure, to register them for civil purposes. On the education question, the State 'considering the teaching of Christian doctrine in the form admitted by Catholic tradition to be the basis and the apex of public education', agreed that religious instruction, already universal in the elementary schools, should be extended to the secondary schools, and be given either by priests or the 'religious', and supplementarily by laymen holding a certificate from the Ordinary. Only books approved by the ecclesiastical authority were to be used in the instruction. All seminaries and colleges for the training of ecclesiastics were to be solely under the jurisdiction of the Holy See.

This Concordat, so comprehensive and so clear, evidently represents a very remarkable achievement, a veritable triumph of good sense and high statesmanship both on the part of the Vatican and on that of Signor Mussolini. The months succeeding the conclusion of the agreements embodied in the three Instruments witnessed considerable activity in what the Duce happily and humorously described as the 'polemics of adjustment'. Such adjustments are the necessary and inevitable concomitants of the settlement of an historic quarrel. Partisans on both sides bitterly complained that too much had been conceded; but, on his side, the Duce made it clear that while in the Vatican City the Pope has sole and exclusive sovereignty, in Italy the Church is definitely subject to the laws of the State and to the special provisions of the Concordat.

Signor Mussolini is understood to be, like most great men, a close student of the career and policy of Napoleon. Of Napoleon's dealings with the Papacy a distinguished French historian has recently written: 'Napoléon croyait être Constantin, l'empereur protecteur de l'Église, garant du dogme, l'empereur-sacerdote.' Signor Mussolini is much better entitled than the great Corsican to the title of a second Constantine; nor, assuredly, will the future historian find himself constrained to add: 'L'Église ne voyait en lui qu'un Dioclétien un persecuteur. Ceci était plus exact.'[1] On the contrary, History will see in him a man who has justly apprehended the part that religion must play in the ordering of any well regulated State, and has also been wise enough to understand that the relations between the Church and a State whose only possible capital is Rome, cannot be finally adjusted on terms appropriate and applicable in any other country. Italy is in a unique position. A State so literally within a State may be logically inconsistent with the Fascist theory of the State: it may be out of harmony with the ideas generally prevalent in the modern world as to the respective spheres of religion and politics, as to the distinction between the things that are Caesar's and the things that are God's. But it is the mark of the highest statesmanship not to follow precedents, but to create them. The precedent of the Lateran Treaties can never be exactly followed elsewhere; no parallel to the conditions of the Italian problem exists. If by conceding to the Vatican its demand for 'visible independence and a territorial sovereignty', however circumscribed, Signor Mussolini has been able to purchase immunity from the menace of 'a potentially hostile organization'

[1] Driault, op. cit., p. 672.

permanently entrenched in the State capital of Italy, will any one deny to him the guerdon of wisdom and courage?

As to his success, in this as in other spheres, History alone can testify. The contemporary commentator must be content to record facts, and to express the hope that the reward appropriate to accurate diagnosis and skilful manipulation may not ultimately be withheld.

The Lateran Treaty closes a great era in Italian history. It crowns the work of the architects of Italian unity: of Mazzini and Garibaldi, of Cavour and Victor Emmanuel. To each of these men, Prophet and Crusader, Statesman and King, United Italy owes a debt which exceeds ordinary methods of computation. Yet in the sixty years which intervened between the occupation of Rome and the conclusion of the Lateran Treaties, there were recurring moments, not a few, when the stability of the edifice which those men had built seemed to be seriously menaced, when the best friends of Italy in this and other countries were assailed by doubts as to the permanence, perhaps even the value, of the work the building embodied. These doubts have been happily dispelled. Englishmen who love Italy, next only to their own country, may regret that necessity has dictated the suspension of certain liberties which, in their insular and parental pride, they are wont to label 'constitutional'. Nevertheless, they can feel unfeigned satisfaction that Italy has been rescued, by the strong hand of a benevolent dictatorship, from the menace of anarchy and dissolution. Mrs. Browning, ardent lover of Italy as she was, had doubts as to the permanence of the work of the *Risorgimento*:

> But Italy, my Italy,
>   Can it last this gleam?
> Can she live and be strong?
>   Or is it another dream
> Like the rest we have dreamed so long?

It is no dream. The doubt is at long last dissipated. Italy will live and be strong.

SHORT LIST OF AUTHORITIES

For full bibliographies see: Bolton King, *History of Italian Unity*; Mr. G. M. Trevelyan's four books (below), and *Cambridge Modern History*. The following is only a short working list of books, mainly for English readers.

SHORTER TEXT-BOOKS:

J. W. Probyn: *Italy, 1815–1890*. 1891.

Countess E. Martinengo-Cesaresco: *The Liberation of Italy, 1815–1870*. 1895.

W. J. Stillman: *The Union of Italy, 1815–1895*. 1898.

L. Villari: *Italy*. 1929.

B. Croce: *Italy, 1871–1915*. (E. T. Ady.) 1929.

LARGER OR MORE SPECIAL BOOKS:

E. Driault: *Napoléon en Italie*. 1906.

R. M. Johnston: *Napoleonic Empire in South Italy*. 1904.

—— *Roman Theocracy and Republic, 1846–9*. 1901.

W. R. Thayer: *Dawn of Italian Independence*. 2 vols. N.Y., 1893.

—— *Life and Times of Cavour*, 2 vols. N.Y., 1912.

Bolton King: *History of Italian Unity*. 2 vols. 1899 (and later editions).

—— *Mazzini* (with bibliography of Mazzini's writings). 1902.

—— (ed.) *Mazzini's Essays*. 1894.

—— *Life and Writings of Joseph Mazzini* (E.T.). 6 vols. 1870.

J. Mazzini: *The Duties of Man*. (Trs. E. A. Venturi.) 1877.

Countess E. Martinengo-Cesaresco: *Cavour*. 1895.

—— *Italian Characters*. 1890.

A. J. Whyte: *Early Life and Letters of Cavour*. 1925.

—— *Political Life and Letters of Cavour*. 1930.

G. M. Trevelyan: *Manin and the Venetian Revolution of 1848*. 1923.

—— *Garibaldi's Defence of the Roman Republic*. 1907.

—— *Garibaldi and the Thousand*. 1909.

—— *Garibaldi and the Making of Italy*. 1911.

J. T. Bent: *Giuseppe Garibaldi*. 1882.

A. Werner and J. W. Mario (ed.): *Garibaldi's Autobiography* (E.T.). 3 vols. 1889.

G. S. Godkin: *Victor Emmanuel II*. 1880.

F. Nielsen: *History of Papacy in Nineteenth Century*. 1906.

E. Bourgeois and E. Clermont: *Rome et Napoléon III*. Paris, 1907.

A. Débidour: *L'Église Cath. et l'état sous la trois. répub*. Paris, 1906–9.

R. de Cesare: *Roma e lo stato del papa dal ritorno di Pio IX*. 2 vols. Rome, 1907 (abridged American translation *Last Days of Papal Rome*. Boston, 1909).

E. A. R. Cecil: *A Dreamer in Christendom* (Pius X). 1925.
C. Gallet: *Le Pape Benôit XV et la Guerre*. 1921.
Dom Cuthbert Butler: *The Vatical Council*. 2 vols. 1930.
J. B. Bury: *History of the Papacy, 1864–1878*. 1930.
C. Rinaudo: *Il Risorgimento Italiano*. Turin, 1910.
N. Bianchi: *Storia documentata Europea in Italia* (1814–61), with many original documents. 8 vols. 1865–72.
M. d'Azeglio: *L'Italie de 1847–1865*. Paris, 1867.
C. P. Castelli: *Carteggio politico*. Turin, 1890.
Farini: *The Roman States* (1814–49). (E. T., W. E. Gladstone.) 1851.
F. Crispi: *Memoirs, 1849–1890*. (E. T.) 2 vols. 1912.
T. Tittoni: *Italy's Foreign and Colonial Policy*. 1912.
—— *Modern Italy*. 1922.
L. Villari: *Expansion of Italy*. 1930.
—— *Fascist Experiment*. 1925.
—— *The Awakening of Italy*. 1924.
H. W. Schneider: *Making the Fascist State*. N.Y., 1912, 1928.
I. Bonomi: *From Socialism to Fascism*. 1924.
M. Sarfatti: *Life of Mussolini*. (E.T.) 1925.
Severino (ed.): *Speeches of Mussolini*.
Tomaso Sillani (ed.): *What is Fascism and Why?* (E.T.) 1931.
Lives of Napoleon I by Holland Rose, Sir J. R. Seely, and A. Fournier; of Napoleon III by P. Guedalla and F. A. Simpson.
See also General Histories of Europe in the Nineteenth Century by C. A. Fyffe, Alison Phillips, R. B. Mowat, J. A. R. Marriott (Methuen, 1931), and others, and General Bibliography *ap.* Marriott.

G. F. H. Berkeley: *Italy in the Making, 1815–46*. 1932.
G. F. H. & J. Berkeley: *Italy in the Making, 1846–8*. 1936.
Benito Mussolini, Scritti e discorsi (edizione definitiva). 1934–7.
Hancock, W. K.: *Ricasoli and the Risorgimento in Tuscany*. 1926.
Petrie, C.: *Mussolini*. 1931.
Barnes, J. S.: *Fascism*. 1931.
Einzig, P.: *Economic Foundations of Fascism*. 1933.

INDEX OF PROPER NAMES

(For subject-index see analytical Table of Contents)